MUSIC
of the
PEOPLES
of the World

William Alves

Harvey Mudd College

THOMSON

SCHIRMER

Australia • Canada • Mexico • Singapore • Spain
United Kingdom • United States

THOMSON

---✦---™

SCHIRMER

Music of the Peoples of the World
William Alves

Music Editor: Clark Baxter
Development Editor: Beth Hoeppner
Senior Assistant Editor: Julie Yardley
Editorial Assistant: Emily Perkins
Technology Project Manager: Matt Dorsey
Executive Marketing Manager: Diane Wenckebach
Marketing Assistant: Rachel Bairstow
Marketing Communications Manager: Patrick Rooney
Project Manager, Editorial Production: Emily Smith
Art Director: Maria Epes
Print Buyer: Doreen Suruki

Permissions Editor: Joohee Lee
Production Service: Greg Hubit Bookworks
Text Designer: Lisa Delgado, delgadoandcompanyinc.
Photo Researcher: Linda Rill
Copy Editor: Richard Wingell
Compositor: G&S Book Services
Cover Designer: Stuart D. Paterson
Cover Images: Globes: Brand X Pictures;
   Instrument Illustration: Kris Granmoe
Text and Cover Printer: Transcontinental Printing/
   Interglobe

Printed in Canada
1 2 3 4 5 6 7 09 08 07 06 05

For more information about our products, contact us at:
Thomson Learning Academic Resource Center
1-800-423-0563
For permission to use material from this text or product, submit a request online at
http://www.thomsonrights.com.
Any additional questions about permissions can be submitted by email to **thomsonrights@thomson.com.**

Library of Congress Control Number: 2005930366

ISBN 0-534-59230-9

Thomson Higher Education
10 Davis Drive
Belmont, CA 94002-3098
USA

Asia (including India)
Thomson Learning
5 Shenton Way
#01-01 UIC Building
Singapore 068808

Australia/New Zealand
Thomson Learning Australia
102 Dodds Street
Southbank, Victoria 3006
Australia

Canada
Thomson Nelson
1120 Birchmount Road
Toronto, Ontario M1K 5G4
Canada

UK/Europe/Middle East/Africa
Thomson Learning
High Holborn House
50–51 Bedford Row
London WC1R 4LR
United Kingdom

Latin America
Thomson Learning
Seneca, 53
Colonia Polanco
11560 Mexico
D.F. Mexico

Spain (including Portugal)
Thomson Paraninfo
Calle Magallanes, 25
28015 Madrid, Spain

I dedicate this book to

LOU HARRISON

and

GILBERT BLOUNT

CONTENTS IN BRIEF

CONTENTS

PREFACE

In 1934, the American composer Henry Cowell began teaching his ground-breaking course, Music of the Peoples of the World. At the time, the class was a great rarity. Today, seemingly every imaginable type of music is just a few mouse clicks away, but Cowell's call for a deep and sensitive understanding of the music and its place in culture to guide our open-minded listening remain just as important. This book emphasizes the necessity of this understanding to truly appreciate the profoundly beautiful worlds of music available to us, drawing upon diverse perspectives to guide the student, including music theory (the analysis of music and musical systems), musicology (the history of music), and ethnomusicology (the study of music in culture).

To help us accomplish this goal, *Music of the Peoples of the World* offers distinctive and unique features.

CULTURAL IMMERSION

■ The many full-color photographs in the book illustrate the amazing variety of every culture's instruments, the people who make music with these instruments, and the kinds of venues in which these people play.

■ Elements of Music opens the text and introduces the basic terms and listening skills that we will use throughout our survey. This section allows students with no background in music theory to appreciate, interpret, and discuss knowledgeably the music we survey. This section makes every effort to avoid presenting these principles from a particular cultural perspective, although nothing in this approach should prevent instructors from describing music in whatever way makes it clearest to their students. The Schirmer Audio Dictionary of Music, a dictionary of music complete with sound clips, is available free through the Schirmer home page (*www.Wadsworth.com/music*).

ORGANIZATION AND CONTENT

■ Each of the nine musical cultures in the book is the subject of a Part that encompasses the music of a specific region. Within each Part, several chapters discuss that region's history and musical life and examine individual works that represent the variety of the music of that culture. This format should make it easy for instructors to focus on, and students to review, the aspects of any musical culture that deserve special attention.

Parts are also organized so that instructors can rearrange the order of presentation.

■ *First Listen* opens every Part and introduces the music we will discuss in each region. *First Listen* is further evidence of the emphasis we will place on listening to music in its cultural context.

■ Boldface terms and their italicized definitions help the student review unfamiliar material.

■ Listening Guides keyed to the audio selections and displaying thumbnail photographs of the performing instruments lead the student from the initiate's first listen through a thoughtful discussion of representative works. Schematic diagrams often visually represent the contours of a musical idea or characteristic.

ANCILLARIES

■ **CDs**. A two-CD set of the audio selections we examine in each Part is available for purchase with the text.

■ **Active Listening Tools**. Full-color modules on each representative culture include an animated listening guide for each audio selection, instruments seen and heard in isolation, and video clips of diverse performances. These modules are available on the Schirmer Thomson website at *http://music.wadsworth.com/alves* Intended especially for the student unfamiliar with music theory, each illuminates the music on the 2-CD set.

■ **For Instructors**. An online eBank database supplies a test bank and additional materials for the instructor.

MUSIC NOTATION AND REPRESENTATION

Representing music visually, as we will do in this text, is a tricky business. Notation inevitably involves simplifications and choices about what to emphasize about the sound and how to depict it. Such decisions can introduce cultural bias, a problem which can be especially acute when adapting a notational scheme developed for one kind of music to represent another very different tradition. Western notation, for example, is useful for showing diatonic melodies, but when pressed into service to represent music of very different scales and tuning systems, it becomes potentially confusing or misleading.

Yet visual representation of music can be a very powerful tool for understanding what is otherwise a time-based art that disappears as we experience it. Even professional musicians with highly trained ears often rely on some kind of notation to analyze the frequently complex listening experience at a glance.

This text adopts certain conventions of displaying music schematically (sounds shown as lines with pitch down to up, time left to right). Like all such schemes, this one involves simplifications and other assumptions, but its easily understood principles allow us to visually analyze some aspects of many different types of music with consistent conventions. For those who prefer Western notation even as they understand its potential shortcomings, we have made available Western notation of many of the examples in the text on the Schirmer Thomson website at *http://music.wadsworth.com/alves*

LANGUAGES AND ORTHOGRAPHY

The multiplicity of foreign terms from many languages creates many challenges for a text such as this. Sometimes competing transliteration or spelling standards may create unavoidable inconsistencies between different publications. At other times the same musical term may exist in related languages with different spellings. I have endeavored to be as clear and consistent as possible in my choices.

A particular problem involves the use of plurals. Plurals are handled very differently in various languages, sometimes creating words quite dissimilar from the singular versions. Other languages handle plurals by context or reduplication. Meticulously following this multiplicity of rules potentially means that the number of foreign terms the student faces effectively doubles. Therefore, I have adopted the expedient convention of using the singular form of the word for both the singular and plural (with a few exceptions, notably terms that have become English words). While this convention risks confusing native speakers of those languages, I believe it is a reasonable approach for the large majority of students.

THE WHOLE ROUND WORLD OF MUSIC

Henry Cowell's approach strongly influenced his student, my dear friend and inspiration, Lou Harrison. Before his death in 2003, Lou, who had gone on to teach his own course on Music of the Peoples of the World, enthusiastically supported my first drafts of this project. He expressed to me a belief that dedication to arts from around the world can be a pacifying force in an otherwise troubled planet. Echoing a well-known saying of Cowell's, Harrison wrote, "When you grow up and leave home, there is a wonderful Whole Round World of Music."[1] It is my hope that you, the student, will come to share this sense of exhilaration from the exploration of music around the world.

---

[1] Lou Harrison. *Lou Harrison's Music Primer*. New York: Peters, 1971, 47.

ACKNOWLEDGMENTS

Cowell's own like-minded teacher, Charles Seeger, together with Mantle Hood, influenced another crucial teacher, mentor, and friend, Gilbert Blount. Gil helped shape my ears and mind and introduced me to many of these wonderful worlds of human expression.

As a generalist, I am greatly indebted to the many intrepid specialists who defined their fields and upon whose work mine depends. I would especially like to thank those who generously provided direct help with *Music of the Peoples of the World*, including Lydia Ayers, Robert Brown, Lina Doo, Janet Farrar-Royce, John Gilbert, David Hagedorn, Katherine Hagedorn, Yao Hong, Margaret Hontos, Maria Johnson, Katalin Kovalcsik, Alfred Ladzekpo, Danlee Mitchell, N. Muralikrishnan, Kathleen Noss, Leonard Pronko, Jihad Racy, George Ruckert, Melinda Russell, David Schmalenberger, Scott Warfield, Albi Wethli, and particularly Bill Shozan Schultz.

I would also like to thank my own teachers in the performance areas covered in this book; they include Kobla Ladzekpo, Philip Schmidt, David Trashoff, Trustho, Wayne Vitale, and I Nyoman Wenten. Among the many people who supported the writing of this book, I would especially like to acknowledge the efforts of Brett Campbell. I also thank Clark Baxter, my publisher at Schirmer Thomson. And I thank the students at Harvey Mudd College, Claremont Graduate University, and the Massachusetts Institute of Technology who provided early and valuable feedback on this text.

I extend special thanks to my wife, Lynn Burrows, in part for her remarkable forebearance during this project, and to my family as well as to all those students, fellow performers, and colleagues who continue to inspire me.

MUSIC
of the
PEOPLES
of the World

Elements of Music

INTRODUCTION

1

THE ROUND CONTINUUM OF MUSIC

In 1987 a group of independent record label owners met in a pub in Islington, England, to discuss the increasing number of albums that did not fit into established record store categories. The beats and singing styles of these CDs—specifically those in languages other than English—struck many listeners as novel, even exotic. For years, the few such recordings to appear in record stores were either lost in the sea of general pop albums or dumped behind an "International" bin divider alongside collections of the world's national anthems and field recordings of Pygmy chants.

Art rock icon Peter Gabriel had been among the first in his field to explore this music beyond early experiments with psychedelic sitar tracks. In 1982, the former Genesis singer and songwriter had begun the World of Music, Arts, and Dance (WOMAD) Festival as a way to bring together great bands from around the world. But despite an enthusiastic reception, the bands still found distribution of their CDs in the Euro-American market difficult. As a solution the independent labels proposed a publicity campaign to popularize a new category—their choice for its name was "World Music."

The label "world music" had popped up frequently before, sometimes to describe New Age and jazz groups that drew inspiration and techniques from Indian or African music. But during the 1970s a growing access to audio technology (first radio, then cassettes) in developing countries had produced the inevitable cross-influences that led to an internationalization of the music business—and made it increasingly clear that musical appeal was not limited to North American and European music. Rhythms from Africa and South America soon found their way into popular music (Peter Gabriel's own songs among them) and, increasingly, musicians

FIGURE **1.1**
Peter Gabriel performing at the World of Music, Arts, and Dance Festival.

© Reuters/CORBIS

looked to the world's traditional and classical musics that lay at the root of these pop hits. This text is an introduction to many of those traditions.

The *Graceland* Controversy

The "World Music" label began popping up in record store bins in 1987, the same year that the most influential album to spotlight international musics appeared—Paul Simon's *Graceland*. Like Gabriel, Simon was open to diverse sources and musical collaborations. In 1984 he first heard *mbaqanga* music from South Africa, also known as "township jive." This music, bubbling with the fizz of early rock and roll, featured characteristically African elements that we will hear in a later chapter.

Simon was intrigued enough to explore other South African styles, including the choral style known as *iscathamiya* and the energetic dances of mine workers called *gumboot*. These and other influences came together in the immensely successful *Graceland* album. Intended as a tribute to the musicians and musical styles of the black South African culture then suffering under apartheid, the album soon became a center of controversy—precisely because of those very goals.

At the time, the United Nations had enacted a cultural boycott to exert economic pressure on South Africa's minority white regime. Some thought Simon had broken that boycott. Furthermore, they considered foreign white liberals condescendingly presumptive, even exploitative, in their borrowing from black South Africa's repressed culture. The debate boiled over at a talk Simon gave at the predominantly black Howard University in Washington DC. There a student asked, "How can you justify taking over this music? For too long artists have stolen African music. It happened with jazz. You're telling me the Gershwin story of Africa." (*Jet* 1987) [George Gershwin, 1898–1937, was a hugely successful white songwriter whose compositions frequently drew upon his experience of African-American jazz.]

Like other pop musicians, Simon had assimilated South African musical influences in the same way that he had absorbed the music of American blues, R&B, and Doo Wop artists. "I went as a musician, and I interacted with other musicians," Simon responded.

By emphasizing the essential unity of musical cultures over geopolitical boundaries, Simon was echoing a tradition of twentieth-century classical composers. One of the first composers to advocate non-Western music as a source of enrichment rather than novelty was the American composer Henry Cowell (1897–1965). He applied his careful study of the music of India, Java, and other regions to his own modern compositions in the same way that he learned lessons from Bach and Beethoven.

His student Lou Harrison, whose cross-cultural explorations we will visit in Chapter 50, commented on Cowell's approach:

> During a conference in Tokyo in 1961, Henry Cowell made a plea on behalf of hybrid musics, pointing out that combinations of the kind have often proved new and stimulating. Out of my respect for him I took his remarks

at face value (and "on faith" as it were) until a little while later when I realized that the full idea was: "don't underrate hybrid musics BECAUSE THAT'S ALL THERE IS." It is as though the world is a round continuum of music. Perhaps here a particular kind of expression is at its most intense and perfect. Then by gradual and geographic degrees we move to some other center with a special expression. Anywhere on the planet we may do this—always by insensible degrees the music changes, and always the music is a compound, a hybrid of collected virtues. (Harrison 1971)

Against a history of colonialist exploitation, it is perhaps not surprising that some might view these universalist sentiments with some suspicion. To incorporate another culture's music in one's own, Western music was to threaten the authenticity of the other culture's music in order to benefit one's own. As Paul Simon himself said, the Howard University students saw the music of *Graceland* as "neither Zulu, Xhosa, Shangaan, or American [but as] . . . a dilution of cultures" (Simon 1998).

Music and Culture

"I *hate* world music," wrote rock star David Byrne, a stunning statement from someone who is known as a pioneer in that very category.

In my experience, the use of the term *world music* is a way of dismissing artists or their music as irrelevant to one's own life. It's a way of relegating this 'thing' into the realm of something exotic and therefore cute, weird but safe, because exotica is beautiful but irrelevant; they are, by definition, not like us. . . . It's a none too subtle way of reasserting the hegemony of Western pop culture. It ghettoizes most of the world's music. A bold and audacious move, White Man! (Byrne 1999)

From nineteenth-century operas to contemporary techno tracks, Euro-American music has a history of adopting the sounds of other cultures for the sake of simple novelty or **exoticism**. While everyone always has his or her own cultural perspective, reducing music to an exotic status can be **ethnocentrism**, that is, *judging music by its relationship to our own cultural experience*.

In this text we will endeavor to understand music cultures on their own terms. To achieve a deeper understanding of music, musicians use a variety of disciplines that overlap considerably. **Musicologists** study the history of music; **music theorists** analyze composition and musical systems; and **ethnomusicologists** study music as a part of people's way of life. New listening experiences can challenge and enrich the perspectives we've grown up with.

SOUND AND CULTURAL CONVENTIONS

The mind has a remarkable facility for categorizing new experiences into learned patterns. It is a process that reduces the new to the conventional and allows us to make sense of the new sounds and images we encounter every day. No matter how musically open-minded we try to be, our experiences can lead us to expect music to exhibit certain common elements in certain contexts.

For example, a person growing up in the United States is inclined to expect harmony as a standard musical trait. **Harmony**, *several notes occurring at the same time to form a chord*, is found in virtually everything we hear on the radio, in music videos, film scores, classical music concerts, church choirs. But this musical element, at least in the familiar chords of the West, is a European invention. And while we may find music without harmony strangely thin, listening for what's not there instead of what is can make us deaf to other dimensions of sound—nuances of melodic variation and pitch, for example.

Furthermore, sound is not the only dimension that shapes our musical expectations. We also understand musical experiences through their place in our social lives, their context. Much of the music-making that we hear in Western culture comes from professionals who are paid to entertain. At a party, few of us nonprofessionals would feel comfortable singing a song for others. But in many areas of traditional Africa, where not singing is like not talking, everybody sings as a natural social function.

The Functions of Music

Think for a moment about the contexts in which you hear music—on headphones, at parties and concerts, in films, and on TV. Music as entertainment is so pervasive a function in the West, and in popular music around the world, that we might consider it a standard function of music in all society, but that is not always the case.

Certainly we can think of other functions of music—to inspire religious dedication, to express political protest, to coordinate work, to lull one's baby to sleep, and so on. In these examples, participation in the music is at least as important as its sound. Through such functions, music can reinforce family ties or strengthen communities; it can provide a path to meditation, exhibit devotion, or act as an inseparable component of rituals. And it may not be directed to human listeners at all. In some cultures music is performed as entertainment for, or communication with, the divine.

In these cases the conventional tripartite division of musical participants into composer/performer/listener may not be the most helpful model for understanding the musical process. In the case of improvisation, for example, the composer may be one and the same with the performer, and the composition may be a communal effort. The composer of folk music may be a skilled artisan rather than a tortured songwriter, but he or she challenges the conventional dismissal of folk music as lacking an individual composer. This example brings up a conventional classification of traditions as **folk music**, **art music**, and **popular music**. Folk music is *created by amateurs for their own community's enjoyment*. Popular music, on the other hand, is *created by professionals for mass audiences*, usually with the intention of selling it as a commodity. Art music or classical music *is also created* *by professionals, but selling it to large audiences is less important than depth of expression*, which can be very complex and sophisticated. While these categories are useful in some cultures, they can also be problematic: popular and folk music can be very sophisticated, sometimes in ways different from art music; folk songs can be performed by professionals, and so on. Nevertheless, we will frequently find it useful to refer to this general division.

Listening

The focus of this text is on listening. In addition to the cultural and historical backgrounds in each unit, listening guides closely examine the recordings on the CD set. Your investment in careful listening will not only open worlds of deep enjoyment and appreciation but also offer a listening approach that you can apply to your future CD purchases. The next chapters on the essential elements of music will give us a basic vocabulary to discuss the music we hear.

But if cultural and social context are crucial to a real understanding of non-Western music, a novice might despair of ever fully appreciating it. True, you may never understand the music of the Ashanti people of West Africa the way Ashantis do, but as long as you make the effort to listen with open mind and ears, you will be able to enjoy the music as music. And just as important, you may see your own culture and music from a new and deeper perspective.

PITCH IN MUSIC

2

WHAT IS PITCH?

Musicians describe **pitch** as *the quality of a note that distinguishes a high note from a low one*. So commonly do we speak of "high" versus "low" notes that we sometimes forget that these terms are metaphors. Other cultures may use a different metaphor, such as a "big" versus "small" pitch (reflecting the size of a xylophone bar), or a culture might reverse "high" and "low" to reflect the hand position on a string instrument. This text will indicate pitch schematically by showing high pitches toward the top of the page and low ones toward the bottom, although this convention is arbitrary.

Pitch relates closely to the physical property that scientists call **frequency**—that is, the number of sound waves per second. This measurement is called **hertz**, after a nineteenth-century physicist, and abbreviated hz. For example, the frequency of 261.6 hz (261.6 sound waves per second) corresponds to the pitch known as "middle C" in the West. This correspondence has varied somewhat over time, but modern pitch has been standardized in popular music and Western classical music.

Pitch is one of the most important elements in music all over the world. Variation in pitch (along with rhythm) gives us **melody**, and playing different pitches simultaneously creates **harmony**. As it is a natural part of the human voice, pitch is found in all musical systems the world over.

This is not to say that all instruments have definite pitch. Many drums can be tuned to a pitch, but it is often difficult to hear a pitch from a drum. Instead we hear a "thump" that, while we may be able to describe it as relatively low or high, lacks the specific pitch of, say, a string instrument. Likewise a cymbal does not seem to have any pitch at all. Bells and triangles have pitches, but they are sometimes difficult to hear precisely (Figure 2.2). They are on the borderline of what we would call the **definability of pitch**.

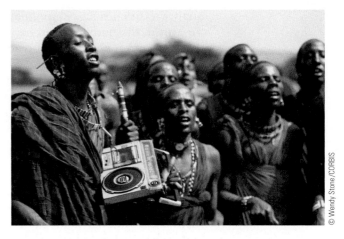

FIGURE **2.1**
The human experience of pitch and its place in musical systems is universal, probably because pitch is a natural part of the human voice and we all share the experience of singing. Here a group of Masai people from Kenya sing along with a cassette machine.

The Octave   An **interval** is *the distance in pitch between any two notes*, and the octave is the most fundamental interval in music. It is one of the few musical elements found in virtually all cultures in the world. A possible reason for its fundamental nature is that, apart from a unison, the **octave** is defined by *the simplest possible ratio between two different frequencies, 2:1*. While a ratio like this may seem a mathematical abstraction, there is a distinctive

FIGURE **2.2**
Musical instruments may have varying degrees of definability of pitch. While it is usually easy to hear the pitch of a string or wind instrument, bells such as this Japanese *densho* temple bell seem to have a less defined pitch or perhaps several perceptible pitches at once.

quality to pitches an octave apart. The fact that in musical systems around the world, the names of pitches an octave apart are often the same reflects this perception of octave equivalence.

Two pitches an octave apart sound so much alike that sometimes we hardly recognize them as distinct. When men and women sing together, for example, they are actually singing melodies an octave apart from each other, but because the notes an octave apart blend so well, we scarcely consider it any different from singing in unison (that is, all on the same pitch). *Two otherwise identical melodies sung simultaneously an octave apart* are said to be in **parallel octaves**.

Introduction to Tuning Systems

All musical systems include octaves; the next question is which other pitches and intervals should be included. A **tuning system** is *the method by which a musician decides what frequencies will be represented on instruments or in a musical system*. The tuning system now standardized in the Americas and Europe, as well as in virtually all music derived from those cultures, is called **12-tone equal temperament** (Figure 2.3). This standardization of tuning enables Western musicians to notate music and easily recombine their instruments into different ensembles.

Some cultures have multiple or flexible tuning systems because the instruments may be more flexible and more easily tuned than, for example, the piano. With such instruments the fine points of a tuning system can largely be left up to the players on a particular occasion. For example, in India,

FIGURE **2.3**
Twelve-tone equal temperament, the tuning system developed in the West, is reflected in the configuration of a piano keyboard. Each octave of the keyboard repeats the same pattern of twelve keys, seven white and five black.

William Alves

FIGURE 2.4
Each Balinese orchestra, such as this ceremonial *gamelan selonding*, is tuned to its own tuning system, although they share general characteristics. Therefore, each orchestra has its own distinctive sound.

while some theorists recognize a tuning system of twenty-two pitches per octave, in practice a solo *sitar* player may decide the precise tuning system; if other musicians are present, they tune their instruments to match the sitar. This process is relatively easy with instruments that take the performer just minutes to tune, as opposed to instruments such as the piano which may take a specialist much longer to tune.

The musical cultures of the islands of Java and Bali often use orchestras of bronze instruments that can take hours to tune. For this reason, a tuning system is fixed, usually when the instruments are built. However, because a particular group of instruments is built to be played only with each other, the tuning system for one orchestra may not match that of the orchestra in the next village. In the classical European orchestra, the players own their instruments and may play in several ensemble groups. This is not the case in Bali, where a school, club, or village often collectively owns an orchestra of instruments (Figure 2.4). The idea of removing one instrument from the orchestra and taking it to play with another group is unthinkable.

Tonality In many melodies, one pitch within the octave has a special significance—it functions as a gravitational center that the melody always comes back to at the end or other points of rest. Try singing a familiar melody leaving out the last note. The feeling of dissatisfaction comes not just because the lyrics may be interrupted, but because the truncation leaves the melody sounding almost unbearably unfinished.

This "home base" pitch, no matter its octave, is called the **tonic** or sometimes the **tonal center** or **key center**. This isn't to say that the tonic is the

FIGURE **2.5**
The tuning system of classical Thai ensembles divides the octave into seven roughly equal parts, making identification of a tonal center sometimes difficult.

most common or even the most important pitch. Much of the interest and even drama in many types of music results from the artful play of tension between withholding and resolving into this central pitch. The feeling that a melody revolves around this pitch is called **tonality**, and we call music that uses tonality **tonal**.

In this very general sense, the phenomenon of tonality is found in virtually every musical culture on earth. However, not *every piece* is necessarily tonal. Some Western classical composers have sought ways to evade a sense of tonality, creating so-called **atonal** music. There are many pieces around the world which may also seem to have ambiguous or nonexistent tonal centers. Some of the music of Thailand, for example, may seem to defy the identification of a tonal center (Figure 2.5). Whether one should call these pieces "atonal" is perhaps debatable (the term "nontonal" is sometimes preferred), but often the feeling of tonality is highly subjective and learned within a culture.

Modes   Not every piece of music uses all the pitches available within the tuning system at all times. Pieces very often use only a select subset of pitches in the tuning system. Western classical and popular music usually uses only seven of the available twelve pitches at a time. This particular subset, represented in one form by the white keys of the piano keyboard, is called the **diatonic** set. One Javanese tuning system has seven tones, but typically only five are used at a time.

Once we have identified one of these pitches as a tonic, we have the basic material that defines a **mode**. Modes with five, six, or seven pitches are known as **pentatonic**, **hexatonic**, and **heptatonic**, respectively. If we arrange the pitches of the mode in one octave to start on the tonic and end on tonic in the next octave, we have defined a **scale**. A scale is therefore *a convenient construction for illustrating the tonic and pitch set used in a piece of music.*

Chinese theorists identify a tuning system of twelve pitches per octave, but traditional music generally uses only five of those pitches at a time. Any of those pitches in the subset may serve as the tonic, meaning that there are then five possible pentatonic modes. Each of the scales of the five modes has its own characteristic sequence of intervals, and melodies in each of the different modes therefore have their own distinctive characteristics.

Because of these differences, many cultures consider that different modes impart distinct emotional or expressive characteristics to melodies. Whereas many listeners in the West associate the major mode with happy melodies and the minor with sad, elsewhere these associations may be much more complex and powerful. The ancient Greek philosopher Plato proposed that the government should ban modes believed to make people prone to drunkenness and licentiousness. Classical musicians from India, who have dozens of modes to choose from, associate very specific emotions, as well as times of day, with different modes (Figure 2.6).

While a subset of the pitches of a tuning system and a tonic within that subset are the two most basic necessities for the definition of a mode, many other musical qualities may distinguish modes in some cultures. For example, certain melodic practices may be appropriate to one mode but not to other modes, even though they may share the same scale. A certain **motive** or *melodic fragment* may be characteristic of a certain mode but not others. Specific ornaments or embellishments might occur on some notes in one mode but elsewhere in others. One pitch may be used in ascending passages but a different one when the melody is descending. Sometimes the range of a melody may be a part of a mode's defining characteristics. In India, the melodic implications of different modes are immensely complex, and

British Library

FIGURE 2.6
In North India modes known as *ragas* have such specific associations that painters and poets can depict these modes according to certain conventions. In this raga, a girl worships Brahma, who sits between two fires on a terrace.

students spend years learning them. It would be quite inadequate to represent such modes with a simple scale.

Definition of a Mode   Depending on the culture, therefore, the definition of a mode may include any of the following criteria:

■ the pattern of intervals in the octave scale, that is, the subset of tones from the tuning system used

■ the tonic or starting point within the pattern

■ certain motives, ornaments, or other melodic practices

■ melodic range

Through all of these characteristics, the mode becomes the basis for melody, often with specific emotional associations. Modes can help us to characterize and categorize melodies in a particular culture.

Keys and the Relativity of Pitch Perception   One of the fundamental principles of our musical hearing is that we recognize melodies not by the absolute pitch or frequency of each note, but by the relative relationship of one pitch to another—that is, the intervals between successive notes in the melody. We can easily recognize a familiar tune no matter what pitch it starts on. The song "Happy Birthday" is "Happy Birthday" no matter if it starts on the frequency 260 or 320 or 440 hertz. Intervals and relative pitches define melodies, not a sequence of absolute pitches.

A mode in music is also defined relatively—by its tonic within the tuning system. We can derive a minor scale starting on any pitch in the tuning system and using the set of intervals that define the minor mode. All of these scales will sound "minor," and we would recognize a minor mode melody in any one. We distinguish these different minor scales—that is, the minor that starts on one pitch from the minor that starts on another pitch—as different **keys**. We said above that Chinese theorists recognize a tuning system of twelve pitches per octave and five possible pentatonic modes. This means that there are twelve possible keys for each mode, for a total of sixty possible pentatonic keys.

MELODY

3

Many people think of melody, a sequence of pitches in rhythm, as the most important element of music. It's what you whistle after hearing a piece that has made an impression on you. Virtually all cultures have melodic music of some kind, perhaps because of the ubiquity of singing. However, melody may not be important or even present in some types of music. Also, the concept of what makes a beautiful melody differs considerably from culture to culture, and, of course, from person to person.

What makes a melody distinctive and memorable is far more than a particular sequence of pitches. Rhythm or other elements may contribute to making a melody memorable because all dimensions of a piece of music work together toward a single effect on the listener.

CHARACTERISTICS OF MELODIES

Melodic Contour and Motion   If we adopt the conventions of showing pitch relative to height on the page and time moving from left to right across the page, then we can graph a melody such as the one here, an excerpt from the Balinese version of the composition *Gambang Suling* by Gandera (Graphic 3.1). Although such a representation cannot clearly show all important characteristics of melody, we will show many examples in this text this way.

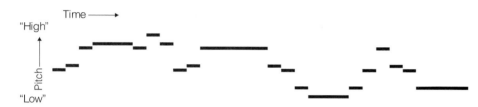

It is easy, then, to abstract a *general direction or shape of a melody over time*, a characteristic called the **contour**. Despite momentary changes in direction, we can hear the melody of Graphic 3.1 as having the general contour shown in Graphic 3.2. In many melodies contours may be more complex, and they are often exploited for expressive purposes. For example, the peak of a contour is often the most important point in a song.

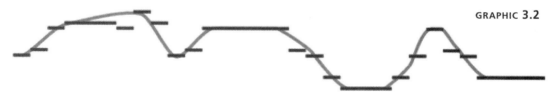

A related musical characteristic is called melodic motion. The sizes of the intervals between adjacent notes in the melody define the steepness of the curves of the contour. The motion of melodies with relatively small intervals between adjacent notes is called **conjunct** motion, while the motion of melodies with relatively large intervals between adjacent notes is called **disjunct** motion. Conjunct motion is by far the most common type of motion throughout the world, although most melodies are an artful mixture of both.

Melodic Range and Tessitura   Where a melody lies in relation to the absolute pitch system is described by two characteristics: range and tessitura. **Range** refers to *the difference between the highest and lowest notes of a melody* and can be relatively wide or narrow. Most folk songs have relatively narrow ranges, often less than an octave. Other songs may have a range of two or more octaves, as in European opera or Mongolian long songs.

The **tessitura** of a melody is *where the melody lies in relation to the possible range of the singer or instrument.* For example, Tibetan ritual melodies are known for lying at the very bottom of the singer's range, that is, having a low tessitura. Some roles in Chinese opera are sung in a very high tessitura.

Cadences and Phrases   It is common for melodies to have points of "rest" where the music momentarily pauses or gives the feeling of having momentarily "arrived." When speaking, most people take breaths at logical stopping points, such as the ends of sentences or clauses. Singers and players of melodies must take breaths as well, both literally (with wind instruments) and figuratively. Such *points of momentary rest or arrival* are called **cadences**. Cadences of melodies are often on the tonal center or another important pitch. Cadences of some kind are found in almost all melodies. *The section of the melody from one cadence to another* is called a **phrase**. The obvious analogy is language, in which natural pauses also occur to set off sections of speech.

Cadences and phrases are found throughout the world. In many songs, the cadence serves as a literal breathing point for the voice, and in fact, some phrase lengths seem to be determined by the natural length of time that one can sing in a single breath. However, the rhythm does not always have to come to a momentary halt for us to feel the cadence. Other elements of the music, including relative importance of pitches, the contour, the harmony, and so on, can influence our sense of rest or arrival. A recurring melodic fragment, called a **cadential motive**, may also signal cadences.

ORNAMENTATION

One very common cadential motive in eighteenth-century European music includes a rapid alternation between two notes a step apart, called a *trill*. The duration and even number of notes in this alternation may vary according to the wishes of the performer, although the performer does not have this latitude to vary the other notes of the melody. That is, one performer may sing or play more and faster notes in the trill than another performer, and yet they would both be correct.

To indicate this freedom, the Western composer does not write down each separate note in a trill, but instead indicates this ornament with this special symbol consisting of the letters *tr* followed by a wavy line above the affected note.

Another reason for this shorthand notation is that in a trill we don't really perceive a melody with many notes as much as we perceive a single note (the one written) with a kind of flourish added to it, in this case to draw the listener through to the cadence.

The trill is an example of a musical device called an **ornament**—added notes or other small changes in pitch or loudness that don't change the overall character of the melody as much as they enhance or ornament it. The composer may compose only the bare unornamented melody, leaving the inclusion and execution of ornaments up to the performer, or as in the example above, notate obligatory ornaments with special symbols.

Although the name "ornament" connotes an unessential decoration, certain ornaments are expected or even required, given a certain style, mode, or melodic situation. Very strict rules often govern when a certain ornament is or is not appropriate. A performer on the Chinese *guqin* zither, for example, will bend the pitch only on certain tones and never on the cadence note. Folk singers in regions of Romania and Bulgaria have a distinctive ornament of a sudden leap up in pitch, but it occurs only at cadences in certain types of songs.

In general, music of the West—at least that of the last two centuries—is relatively bare of ornamentation when compared to some of the rich melodic traditions elsewhere in the world, especially in Asia and the Middle East.

MOTIVES AND THEMES

One of the most important ways of unifying a melody is through repetition. The recognition of previous musical materials serves to form a structure, a coherent whole, in the mind of the listener. Repetition often occurs on many levels in a melody, from just a few notes to repetitions of whole sections several minutes long.

A short melodic fragment that is repeated at certain points is called a **motive**. A motive is usually only a handful of notes and is often used as a "cell" or "building block" from which composers can construct larger melodies. We have already seen how musicians often use motives to indicate important cadences.

A **theme** is *an entire melody recognizable as a discrete entity* and may stretch from one phrase to over a minute in length. The recognition by the listener of these repeated melodies is one of the most important ways by which performers and composers structure a piece of music.

STRUCTURE

Structure or **form** is the name given to the very largest levels of musical architecture. Structure is what guides our listening experience—the expectations and surprises that come from following repetitions and contrasts, sectional changes, and variations. If we don't perceive the structure of a piece of music, it will soon become boring, like reading a book of unrelated pages. However, if we are aware of the immense drama being worked out in an intricate and artful performance, we will often be entranced.

What exactly is it that tells our mind that one section is ending and another beginning or how one section is related to another? There are many methods to articulate these important sign posts. At the low level, there is the cadence, or resting point in a melody.

At higher levels, there are contrasts—in loudness, harmony, tempo, the instruments playing, and so on. In Japanese *gagaku* music and Javanese *gamelan* music, certain instruments periodically punctuate the musical texture, creating clear delineations.

Phrases and Hierarchical Structures   At the lower level of structural building blocks are melodic phrases. The resoluteness or finality associated with a cadence may vary. There are some cadences that create a resting point in relation to what immediately precedes, but could not be used to end the piece. Sometimes these cadences are called **half-cadences** or **semi-cadences**. In Javanese music, composers put together phrases with cadences of varying levels of finality into large-scale hierarchical structures, so that the most final cadence comes at the end of the section or piece, the next most final often at the halfway point, and so on.

To extend the metaphor of a melodic phrase, phrases may join together to form the "sentences" or "paragraphs" of a large musical composition. Using this analogy, we can relate a chapter to the musical term **movement**. Movements are set apart by actually stopping the music between each one, but still they are large sections within a single composition.

Another metaphor which comes to mind is musical structure as architecture. As in architecture, pieces of music have small parts that add up to larger and larger parts, structures within structures, eventually resulting in a large building. While hierarchical structures such as this are common, in some types of music phrases may simply be strung together one after another with no implication of a higher grouping level.

Repeating Structures   Repetition as an important structural element exists not only in the recurrence of melodic motives and themes, but on many different levels. In writing about these structures, it is sometimes convenient to use letters to represent the different melodic phrases: *A* the first phrase, *B* the next unique phrase, *C* the third, and so on. Repetition in simple songs creates forms we diagram as *AAB*, *AABC*, or *AABA*, for example.

Letters can be used at levels higher than the phrase as well. Each letter may stand for a group of phrases (sentence or paragraph). A song that repeats a group of melodic phrases over and over but with different words is called **strophic**. Each repetition is called a verse, a stanza, or a strophe. Modern Christian hymns are often strophic, as are many folk songs. The form of the music of such a hymn would be simply *AAAA*. Sometimes, if the music is varied slightly from one repetition to another, prime marks are added to distinguish the different versions: *A*, *A'*, *A''*, *A'''*, and so on, pronounced *A*, *A prime*, *A double prime*, and so on.

An even more common variation of this form is to repeat a section with the same words, called a **refrain**, after every strophe. Such a form, nearly ubiquitous in modern popular songs, is called **verse–refrain** or stanza–refrain form. In this form, the stanza may be constructed so that the verse does not end on a final cadence, thus helping to propel us into the refrain.

Variation In some musical contexts, repetition by itself is perceived as dull. Therefore composers or performers introduce variation to increase interest while maintaining elements of repetition. One of the most fundamental ways in which a melody can be varied is by playing it at a different pitch level, that is, by **transposition**. Hungarian folk songs often repeat a phrase but start it at a different pitch. If we perceive the tonic to have temporarily changed to this new pitch, or, to put it another way, the melody to have changed key, then the melody is said to have **modulated**. Modulation can also mean temporarily changing modes, even if the tonic does not change.

There are innumerable ways to vary a repetition, but some common ones include:

■ transposition
■ increased or different ornamentation
■ different mode
■ different tonal center
■ different tempo or rhythmic density (number of notes per beat)
■ different instruments used
■ different texture (see Chapter 5)

In fact, the possibilities are so numerous that many composers have written pieces that are artful studies of these possibilities called **theme and variations form**. This form is common in the West, in China, in Africa, and elsewhere. In this structure, a melody (theme) or sometimes a characteristic chord progression will be introduced at the beginning. It is then played many times in different variations. These variations are often arranged so as to articulate a larger form with a beginning, middle, and end, with rising tension in one variation giving rise to resolution in another and final resolution at the end, and so on.

RHYTHM

4

Rhythm is the term that describes *how music is organized in time*. It may seem difficult to conceptualize, but different people and different cultures perceive time itself in very different ways. In these cases it is important to make a distinction between **psychological time** and **clock time**.

Our psychological-time perception of the organization of events in music may vary considerably over the course of a piece or different performances. For example, we might estimate that a particularly boring piece of music lasted twice as long in clock time than it actually did. But once we learn how to discern events in the music to which we were not formerly attuned, suddenly our interest grows and the sense of time changes remarkably.

Cultures may profoundly influence perceptions and thought processes that affect the ways in which people organize sound in music and the ways that they perceive sound in time. For example, psychologists have found evidence that time sense in highly goal-oriented societies tends towards shorter and shorter intervals.

Organizing Time   If we were to look at a graph of a piece of, say, piano music that showed loudness versus time, we would see not only the gradual rise and fall of overall volume, but on a smaller scale, a series of sudden jumps corresponding to the beginning of each note. Here, we show an actual amplitude (loudness) plot of a melody played in the introduction to a Javanese *gamelan* orchestra composition. The beginnings of each of the notes are clear from the sudden jumps in loudness.

GRAPHIC **4.1**

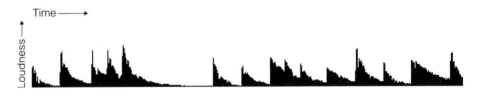

To a brain trying to make sense of this information, there are certain obvious ways to divide the time of this music into discrete events. In particular, at certain places the loudness changes suddenly—so does the pitch, if we were to look at that dimension. We call these discrete events notes, and they are so clearly delineated by our listening process that we hardly even think about it. To see how these notes are categorized by time, let's look at the pattern formed by their beginnings—that is, the sudden changes in loudness (Graphic 4.2). If we mark the times each note begins in Graphic 4.1, it is apparent that many of the note durations are the same or nearly the same, and others are two or three (or some other whole number) times the shortest of the durations.

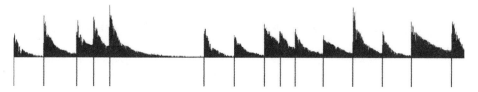

GRAPHIC **4.2**

One remarkable thing about this analysis that the brain (the greatest of pattern-finders) would notice is that many of these lengths of time are the same. Not only that, but the longer lengths are pretty consistently two or three times the smaller lengths. This suggests that the whole piece could be put on a fairly consistent time grid (Graphic 4.3). Every note now begins on one of these lines marking a constant interval of time. Our brain interprets the passage of time in music this way when it is able to find such a pattern.

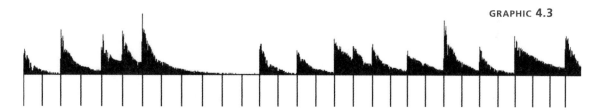

GRAPHIC **4.3**

Even though the spacing isn't always exactly even, the brain forgives slight deviations and interprets others as speeding up or slowing down. Most music can easily fit into such a grid, so that all of its notes fall on one of these equally spaced periods of time or even divisions of it. This is such a natural part of our listening process that we don't need any training to find this grid—even in relatively complicated pieces of music we often find our feet tapping out these regular pulses. This *regular division of time* is called the **beat**.

The Beat   Most of us know intuitively what a beat is—we find ourselves tapping our feet, clapping, or otherwise moving our bodies along with music. But does all music have a beat? If the timing of notes cannot be interpreted as falling into a periodic pattern or if the music defies our ear's attempt to find events that can be identified as "notes" at all, then we may not be able to clap along. Such music is called **non-pulsatile**. Still other music we might call **quasi-pulsatile**, that is, notes of more or less the same length follow one another, but the rhythm is so free that it is hard to pin down a constant pulse.

Non-pulsatile music is sometimes called **non-metric** music, but it is *not* correct to say that it "has no rhythm." Because all music somehow organizes time, all music has some kind of rhythm. What people probably mean by such a statement is that familiar landmarks to time organization, such as a steady beat, are missing. Such music still organizes the notes in time—which is rhythm—and this organization may, in fact, be very complex.

Tempo In a pulsatile piece, the rate at which the beat passes is called the **tempo**. In order to specify an absolute tempo, musicians indicate the number of beats per minute. For example, a tempo of 120 beats per minute means that every beat lasts exactly one-half second. Most popular music has a tempo of between about 90 and 140 beats per minute, while the tempos of Western classical music can vary widely, from about 50 to 180 beats per minute. Some Japanese traditional music may unfold very slowly, sometimes as slowly as 30 beats per minute; at this tempo unaccustomed ears might not at first detect a beat.

Since our impression of the passage of time is based on a variety of psychological factors, specifying tempos relative to absolute clock time has limited usefulness. Often musicians express tempos with more subjective terms and may vary tempos according to the circumstances of a particular performance. Of course tempo may change over the course of a piece. A tempo may change suddenly or gradually. A gradual speed up of tempo is called an **accelerando** and a gradual slowing down is a **ritardando** or **rallentando**.

Meter In the graphic showing the beginnings of notes, it is clear that there does not need to be a note on every pulse for the beat to be perceived. As long as the notes that are there fit into the steady grid of time divisions, our brain can still find the beat, even though some notes are two or three beats long. Sometimes notes may last less than a beat in time, but in those cases, the note is often either one-half or one-third of a beat. The ways in which the beat can be divided into smaller periods or grouped into larger ones tends to be consistent through a piece of music. The ways in which beats are organized in a piece of music is called the **meter**.

Meter is *an organization of beats, divisions of beats, and groupings of beats into distinct levels of the passage of time*. If you ask someone to clap along with a piece with a tempo of 120 beats per minute, chances are they hear that beat and clap every half second. However, some people might clap along at half that rate—that is, at a tempo of 60 or one beat per second. Both are correct—they just demonstrate different perspectives. One person hears the beats at 120 and faster notes as divisions of beats. The other hears notes faster than 60 as divisions of the beat. In fact, it may also be possible to identify a plausible pulse at 240 beats per minute or even other speeds. The beginnings of notes nearly always coincide with one of these divisions (Graphic 4.4). The same rhythm outlined in Graphic 4.2 here is shown not only against a grid of short durations extending in time left to right, as in Graphic 4.3, but also as a hierarchy of groupings of those pulses. When you tap your foot to a song, you are unconsciously identifying one of these levels in the hierarchy as the beat.

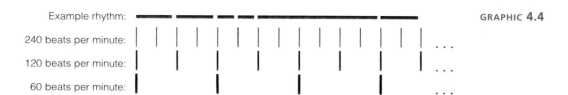

GRAPHIC **4.4**

Because in this example each division or grouping of pulses is by twos, one might write the relative hierarchy from long to short as 2:2, that is, one of the longest pulses (60 bpm) equals 2 beats, each of which equal 2 divisions of beats. One should keep in mind, however, that in a metrical system such as this, one could mark any number of levels of subdivisions or groupings, but in a practical sense, we are mainly concerned with the groupings and divisions of the beat.

A meter with hierarchies of two such as this is very common in music around the world, but beats may be grouped and divided in different ways. In Graphic 4.4 they are grouped into twos. The most common grouping other than two is three. In Graphic 4.5, beats are grouped in threes. In this example, the beat is grouped into threes but divided into twos. This meter is called simple triple and is well known as the meter for the European waltz.

GRAPHIC **4.5**

Subdivisions of the beat:

The beat:

Groupings of beats:

In this case the hierarchy is 3:2—that is, the beats are grouped in threes, but still divided by two. A meter in which the beats are grouped in threes is called a **triple** meter, while a meter in which beats are grouped in twos is called a **duple** meter. The beat itself may also be divided into three (Graphic 4.6).

GRAPHIC **4.6**

Subdivisions of the beat:

The beat:

Groupings of beats:

A meter in which the beat is divided into three is called a **compound** meter, while a meter in which the beat is divided into two is called a **simple** meter. Graphic 4.6 shows a compound duple meter—that is, beat groupings in twos and divisions in threes. Graphic 4.7 shows a compound triple meter in which the beat is both divided by and grouped into threes. While uncommon, this is the meter of the Irish dance called a slip jig.

GRAPHIC **4.7**

Subdivisions of the beat: | | | | | | | | | | | | | | | | | | | | | | | | . . .

The beat: | | | | | | | . . .

Groupings of beats: | | | | . . .

How does this grid of beats and beat groupings relate to rhythm? Very simply, a rhythm that exists in a certain meter nearly always has notes that begin on a beat or its subdivision, although they may last any number of beats.

The hierarchy of beat levels can be extended in both directions—that is, the beats may be grouped into larger segments and the divisions of beats may themselves be subdivided. In cultures such as India or Java, large-scale groupings of beats may grow to very large structures of 256 or more beats. Following such an expansive meter can take intense concentration.

Metrical Stress and Syncopation   Musicians often speak of the point in time that coincides with the beginning of a whole group of beats, such as the lines in the highest levels of Graphics 4.4 through 4.8, as "stressed" beats. This term does not mean that notes on those beats are necessarily played more loudly, nor that they are somehow more important. All beats, groupings, and subdivisions are important because they represent the organization of time in a pulsatile piece of music.

Rather, the amount of stress associated with a beat refers to a sense of expectation, of a new beginning, which that level of organization can articulate. In some pieces of music, such a beat might be emphasized or associated with a hearty stamp in a dance, but sometimes such emphasis may be deliberately withheld in order to give the music a floating quality or a sense of surprise.

Syncopation is a term for *rhythm in which the metrical stress of a note is displaced in the meter so that the emphasis occurs on normally unstressed beats*. This type of rhythm is especially characteristic of ragtime, jazz, and some Latin American dances.

The shifting of stress normally occurs one of two ways. The first and most common is for a note which begins on a normally unstressed beat to extend through the next stressed beat (Graphic 4.8). In this example showing the simple duple meter from Graphic 4.4 with the rhythm of a Brazilian *maxixe*, a note starting on an unstressed division (a point with only one vertical bar below it) extends through a following stressed beat (a point with more than one vertical bars aligned). The note seems to get more stress than it otherwise would, because the rhythm temporarily shifts metrical stress and creates a syncopation. Notes that begin on an unstressed division but do not extend through the following stressed beat do not have the same sense of shifting stress and are therefore not syncopated (such as the fourth and fifth notes in this example).

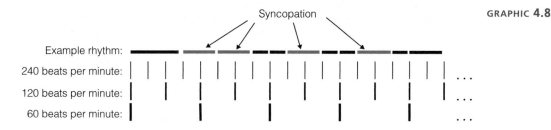

GRAPHIC **4.8**

The other way that a composer or performer can shift stress is to emphasize notes on normally unstressed beats by playing them more loudly or giving them a harder attack. Such an emphasis given to a single note is called an **accent**.

TIMBRE AND TEXTURE

5

TIMBRE

Timbre (pronounced TAM-ber) is a French word that means "tone color"—that is, *the quality of an instrument's sound that distinguishes an oboe from a flute or a voice or a trumpet*. Musicians have a poor vocabulary for describing the differences between timbres, using such general metaphors as "bright" or "dark." Typically, musicians describe the timbre of one instrument by comparing it to the timbre of another. One should take care in making comparisons this way, because it may reinforce an attitude that the instruments of a particular culture form the standard to which all other music is compared.

In most music, timbre is controlled through instrumentation and orchestration. **Instrumentation** refers to the choice of *instruments that play a certain piece*. **Orchestration** is *the art of combining the instruments in different ways for musical effect*. The term orchestration, by the way, does not necessarily mean that it applies only to the orchestra; it can just as well apply to any combination of instruments. A good orchestrator knows, for example, that certain instruments make a good musical "foreground" for solos when combined with certain other instruments that serve as "background."

Ensembles may have **heterogeneous** (all different) or **homogeneous** (all similar) instrumentation. The *gagaku* orchestra of Japan, for example, has a well-balanced heterogeneous instrumentation consisting of plucked

FIGURE **5.1**
Ensō Quartet at the
Banff Eighth Annual
International String
Quartet Competition.

Ensō String Quartet photo by Donald Lee. Reprinted by permission and by courtesy of Concert Artists Guild.

strings, flutes, double-reed aerophones, metal idiophones, and drums. The *sho* mouth organs form a constant background against which the solo double reeds and flutes are easily heard. The nonsustaining string and percussion timbres fill in the slow melody with occasional punctuations.

The Western string quartet is an example of a homogeneous ensemble (Figure 5.1). It is made up of two violins, a viola, and a cello, all string instruments of the violin family. This choice of instruments enables them to achieve great variety of sound and yet blend beautifully when necessary.

TEXTURE

When two or more instruments or singers play together, they often have different roles. For example, a guitar may play a supporting role to a singer who sings the main melody. We call the guitarist's part the accompaniment. When a choir sings, they may all sing a single melody, they may sing in harmony, or they may sing accompaniment to a single singer (the soloist). These are all examples of different **textures**.

Texture is *the musical characteristic that describes the relative importance and distribution of the various instrumental or vocal parts*. Each single melody is called a line, a part, or a voice (even when it's played by an instrument). Just as in the cloth metaphor from which the term "texture" comes, these lines can be woven like threads loosely, tightly, and in many other different ways. Texture is an important musical characteristic in ensemble music, in which changes in texture over the course of a piece often articulate important sectional divisions and make them obvious to the ear.

Musicologists generally divide textures into four large categories, but there is a great amount of overlap, and many textures may not seem to fit neatly into any of the categories.

Monophony   The first type of texture is **monophony**, meaning *one sound*. It is simply that—a single melody (Graphic 5.1). When an instrument plays only one note at a time or a singer sings a melody, that is monophony. Even when a number of voices or instruments are playing, if they are all playing the same melody, it is still monophony. Monophony is extremely common throughout the world, much more than those who are used to harmony accompanying melodies might think. Here is a graph of a monophonic texture, this one a song from Lebanon.

Time ⟶

Pitch ↑

GRAPHIC **5.1**

While the definition and identification of monophony may seem fairly straightforward, many situations blur the distinction between monophony and other textures. For example, when men and women sing together, they do so in **parallel octaves** (Graphic 5.2). Even though strictly speaking there are two different melodies, they are not really distinct to the ear. Singing in parallel octaves sounds virtually the same as a single melody to us; therefore we still call it monophony.

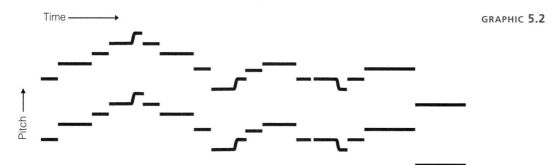

Time ⟶

Pitch ↑

GRAPHIC **5.2**

When other types of music have melodies in parallel but separated by intervals other than the octave, our ear in those cases more readily discerns separate melodies. Such textures begin to blur the line between our impression of monophony (one melody) and polyphony (more than one independent simultaneous melody).

Homophony *A single melody accompanied by supporting harmony* is called **homophony**. Virtually all popular music and much Western classical music has a homophonic texture, also known as melody and accompaniment. Sometimes homophony is described as a melody accompanied by other tones of lesser importance, but perhaps "focus" is the better word. None of the parts can be omitted without harming the music, although our attention is focused on the melody in the spotlight, so to speak. In this graph of a homophonic texture, from a Mexican folksong, the melody the voice sings is the principal melody we associate with the song. The parts played by the guitar and bass accompany it.

GRAPHIC **5.3**

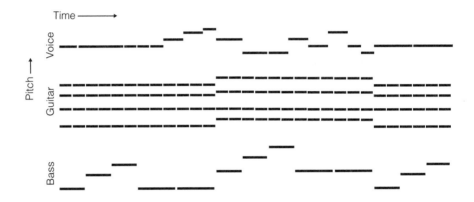

While most of the accompaniment in much popular music consists of strummed guitar chords, accompaniment may also consist of several melodies combined into harmony, as is often the case when a choir sings. Each section of singers has its own melody, but only one of those melodies (generally the highest) has the focus in a homophonic texture. While elements such as drums and drones are also accompaniment in a sense, they are not usually perceived as separate melodies and so are treated differently, as we will explain shortly.

Polyphony While it is common for one melody to dominate our attention in a texture with multiple melodies (homophony), sometimes a texture divides our focus between several simultaneous melodies. When there are *several melodies of more or less equal focus at the same time*, the texture is called **polyphony**. In this graph of a polyphonic texture, from a piece for choir by the medieval English composer John Dunstable, there are three different melodies (indicated by the different colors), no one of which always has the focus.

Time ——→

GRAPHIC **5.4**

Pitch ↑

One of the most familiar forms of polyphony in the West is the **round** or **canon**, such as "Row, Row, Row Your Boat," in which singers sing the same melody at staggered time intervals. Even though there is just one melody, because we perceive two different things happening at the same time, it is polyphony. More specifically, it is an example of **imitative polyphony** in which *one line imitates the melody in another line*. No one line can be said to be any more important than another in the way the melody in homophony is more important than the accompaniment.

Imitative polyphony is found in Western classical music, Indian vocal music (in which an instrumentalist sometimes imitates the singer), and elsewhere. However, non-imitative polyphony is more common elsewhere, as in the intricate textures of Javanese *gamelan* orchestras, West African ensembles, or traditional Thai ensembles. In these cases, many different melodies, guided by common structural principles, weave around each other.

Heterophony   In some cultures, musicians playing together would consider it dull to play the same melody in exactly the same way. Instead, each musician enriches the texture by adding his own ornamentation and variations to the melody. Although we would perceive a single basic melody, the texture is not monophony, because each rendition is somewhat different. At the same time, it cannot be polyphony because there is only one basic melody. This texture of simultaneous variations is therefore classified as a separate category known as **heterophony**. Heterophony is common in many cultures around the world, though not in the West. This graph of a heterophonic texture shows the performances by a south Indian singer (blue lines) and violinist (red lines). Although they sing and play the same basic melodies, their slight differences in notes and ornamentation create simultaneous variations.

Time ——→

GRAPHIC **5.5**

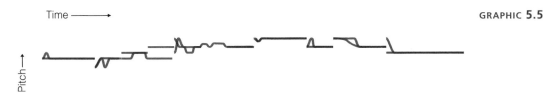

Pitch ↑

Other Textures   Many textures are hybrids. One example of a hybrid texture is a homophonic piece in which the melody is played heterophonically by two instruments or singers. This texture would not fit easily into either the homophonic or heterophonic categories; therefore, it would be best simply to describe it as what it is.

The Drone   A **drone** is *a long, constant pitch played throughout all or part of a composition*. The ear does not recognize a drone as an independent melody, but as kind of a background scrim of sound which, in the case of Indian classical music, for example, serves as a foundation and point of reference over which the soloist improvises. While the drone in such a texture in one sense is an accompaniment, it makes more sense to describe this texture as monophony with a drone rather than homophony, since the drone is not a melodic or harmonic accompaniment.

Drums   Drums are very important to texture in some musical cultures, such as those of Africa, the Middle East, India, Japan, Korea, and Western popular music. At some point in an Indian classical performance, the drone and melody are joined by a drummer, but drums and other nonpitched percussion instruments do not fit neatly into the general classification scheme. While it is possible for drums to be tuned to give an impression of pitch, so that a set of such drums could play a melody, a drum more often provides rhythmic punctuation to the melody.

The Indian texture is best described as a melody and drone with drum accompaniment. Because the accompaniment isn't harmony, it would be stretching the definition to call this texture homophony. Besides, sometimes the drummer takes the leading role and the melodic soloist the subordinate role.

The great drum ensembles of West Africa often have only a single sung melody, or sometimes no melody at all. Instead, most of the focus is on the complicated polyrhythmic drum lines. It would not be out of place to compare these performances with polyphony, because each individual drum has a line all its own, but the "melodies" of the drums are very limited, if they can be called melodies at all. This type of texture has been called **drum polyphony**, which is as good a name as any. With a single sung melody the texture might be described as "a melody with polyphonic drum accompaniment."

LOUDNESS IN MUSIC

Although **loudness** is an important part of much music, it is usually treated with much less precision in theory and notation than pitch or rhythm. *The use of loudness as a musical element* is called **dynamics**. *Gradually getting louder* is called a **crescendo** and *gradually softer* a **decrescendo**.

While composers of Western classical music frequently notate such changes in dynamics or levels of relative loudness, the performers, together with choices of instrumentation, control loudness as an expressive element in most cultures. The lack of notation or even a precise language to indicate dynamics does not mean that the music does not change in loudness nor that those changes are unimportant, just that the musician does not need the aid of notation or precise terminology.

As one might expect, loud dynamics are often used to correspond to sections of music that are highly dramatic, joyful, celebratory, or in some way climactic. However, sometimes very soft sections can portray just as much drama and intensity. It is more often the artful contrasts of loud and soft that make for effective musical expression.

6 MUSICAL INSTRUMENTS

6 Musical instruments are important to people not just for the sounds that they make, but often for the ways in which they reflect a musician's personality, expression, and culture. They can be rudimentary or extremely expensive, simple or technologically sophisticated, mass produced to a standard or unique. The fact that some musicians give names to their instruments reflects the bond they feel with them, for an instrument can become a direct extension of a musician's expressive thought. In some cultures, musicians may personify their instruments in other ways or consider them spiritually charged. The respect that they give them goes far beyond their monetary value.

Resonance   Instrument makers can change an instrument's tone quality and loudness by building in hollow chambers or solid pieces called resonators, which work by filtering and amplifying the sound waves in specific ways. Not only are sound waves caused by moving objects, but sound waves themselves can cause other objects to move. For example, plucking a string on a *sitar*, an Indian string instrument, can cause another nearby string tuned to the same pitch to vibrate softly even though the second string was untouched. If you put your ear next to this string, you hear its "ghost" sound, as if it were played very softly, because of a phenomenon called **sympathetic vibration**. The air is being pushed and pulled by the first string, and the air slightly pushes and pulls the second string.

However, only the string tuned to the same note vibrates; the others are silent because they are not designed to move at that frequency. Each string has its own vibrating frequency that depends on the string's length and tension. This frequency is called the resonant frequency of that string. All physical things have at least one resonant frequency and sometimes a range of frequencies. When a wave in the air around them matches this frequency, the object vibrates in sympathy, making the original sound seem louder.

FIGURE 6.1
The Balinese *gendér wayang* has a separate bamboo tube resonator for each bar. The inside of each tube is stopped at different points (marked by the hearts on the tubes) to tune them to the correct resonant frequency.

For example, a violin maker constructs the body of the instrument to have roughly equal resonant frequencies throughout the violin's range. However, certain frequencies resonate better than others, and the precise loudness of these frequencies is largely responsible for the violin's distinctive sound.

A resonator may be a solid board, such as the sound board of a piano, an open box, or some other open or closed cavity. Some instruments have a resonator for each pitch, such as the marimba or the Indonesian *gendér* (Figure 6.1).

Classification

Musical instruments around the world come in an astounding variety, and there are equally various ways of classifying them. Instruments are classified by their musical function, their range, their construction, their method of producing a sound, and so on.

One common method of classification organizes instruments into three categories: string instruments (instruments whose strings are the sounding body), wind instruments (instruments that are blown through), and percussion instruments (instruments that are struck). Like any classification scheme, there are problems with this one. Strings and winds are classified by what makes the sound, whereas percussion instruments are classified by how a sound is made. The piano, for example, is an instrument whose strings are struck. Is it a string instrument or a percussion instrument? It has been classified both ways. While this classification works well for Western orchestras, for which it was developed, it is not as useful for other types of ensembles. In Korea, instruments are classified by the principal material of their construction—wood, metal, stone, skin, and so on—but, again, this scheme is less useful outside a Korean orchestra.

Two early researchers of musical instruments from around the world, Erich von Hornbostel and Curt Sachs, drew up a similar but more consistent classification scheme that ethnomusicologists commonly adopt today. At the highest level, they arrange the instruments by precisely what makes the sound:

1. **chordophones** (string instruments): a vibrating string, whether plucked, bowed, or struck, makes the sound.

2. **aerophones** (wind instruments): a column of air within the instrument makes the sound.

3. **membranophones** (drums): a membrane (skin) stretched over a resonator or frame makes the sound.

4. **idiophones**: the entire instrument vibrates to make the sound.

5. **electrophones**: the instrument makes sound through a loudspeaker.

Note that this classification scheme is very similar to the strings/winds/percussion organization scheme, except that it divides conventional percussion instruments into two groups. Not only does this division make the method more consistent, but it is also less ethnocentric, because in many cultures, percussion instruments are the majority, not the minority. Because of this consistency, the piano is now more clearly classified as a chordophone. There are still gray areas and hybrids, of course, though not as many.

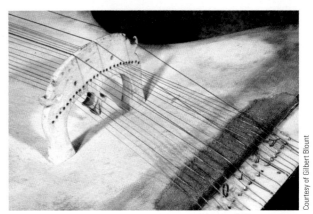

FIGURE **6.2**
A string instrument bridge lifts the string above the instrument and forms an edge for the vibration of the string. This bridge on a *dilruba* from India has a main set of strings which cross over its top and another set of strings that are threaded through holes in the middle.

Chordophones

Chordophones share many general characteristics. First, the strings have to be stretched somehow. They must be secured at both ends but allowed to move freely in between. Usually a construction known as a **bridge** is used to lift the string up over the body of the instrument so that it vibrates freely (Figure 6.2). A string instrument often has two bridges, one at each end, although one may be higher than the other. In the case of such instruments as the violin or guitar, the higher piece is usually called the bridge. A single bridge may serve for several strings or each string may have its own bridges. The Hungarian *cimbalom* and Iranian *santur* often have a bridge in the middle of each string, so that it is possible to play different pitches on each side of a center bridge.

There are several methods for obtaining different pitches on a string instrument. First, one may have a different string for each pitch, as in a piano. On other chordophones the pitch of a string may be varied by pressing the string down at a certain point and therefore shortening its vibrating length. In this case, the finger itself can determine the vibrating length, or the finger can push the string down so that it is stopped by an intermediate bridge, called a **fret** (Figure 6.3). Guitars and mandolins are examples of string instruments with frets, while violins and *sarods* are examples of instruments without frets.

FIGURE **6.3**
Frets on a *ty ba*, a lute-type chordophone from Vietnam. Pressing down behind the fret stops the string at that point.

FIGURE 6.4
When playing the Korean *kayagum* curved board zither, the player plucks with the right hand and then presses down behind the bridge with the left hand to bend the pitch.

There are several reasons to use frets: they make the task of finding the pitch easier and thus make it more practical to finger several strings simultaneously, as is common on the guitar. Because the fret creates a sharp, hard point, the string vibrates longer and more loudly than it does when stopped by the flesh of the finger. But frets lock the player into a certain tuning and generally make it impossible to change pitch by sliding the finger along the string. However, blues guitarists in the United States began to use the tops of soft drink bottles to obtain **glissando** (sliding pitch) effects in the 1930s. This technique evolved into the slide guitar, which is an example of a movable bridge.

Adjusting the tension of the string can also vary its pitch, and in this way players of fretted instruments can create small changes in pitch like a vibrato, a continuous wavering of pitch often used on the classical guitar or the Indian sitar. On zithers such as the Chinese *zheng* or Japanese *koto*, the player may press down on the string behind a tall bridge to create pitch slides or vibrato (Figure 6.4). The **whammy bar** is a modern innovation used on electric guitars to slide the pitch up and down by varying string tension.

Some kinds of chordophones may have more than one string tuned to a certain pitch. For example, some guitars have two adjacent strings per pitch in the configuration known as a twelve string guitar. *The collection of adjacent strings associated with a particular pitch* is called a **course**; when there are two strings in a course it is a double course, three strings a triple course and so on (Figure 6.5). There may be several reasons for having multiple courses, but the most common is that they provide extra volume. When describing a chordophone, it is common to refer to it as a "six-course" rather than a "six-string" instrument, for example.

FIGURE 6.5
The Iranian *santur* uses multiple courses for each pitch to increase volume. This *santur* uses quadruple courses (four strings for each pitch).

Let's look at some ways in which chordophones are divided even further:

Zithers   Chordophones in which the strings are parallel to a resonator that extends their entire length.

■ stick zithers—those in which the sounding board is relatively narrow and round, like a stick. The similar bar zither has a string attached to a curved stick (see Figure 9.6, p. 55).

■ tube and curved zithers—strings attached around the outside of a tube that serves as a resonator (Figure 6.6). When a part of the tube is cut away to form a surface for the instrument, it is known as a half-tube or curved-board zither.

■ raft zithers—those with a flat sounding board parallel to the strings (see Figure 9.8 right, p. 56).

■ flat box zithers—those with a hollow box resonator (Figure 6.7).

■ trough zithers—those in whose sounding board has been carved a trough for resonance (see Figure 9.8 left, p. 56).

Lutes   Chordophones in which the strings are parallel to the body that holds them, with a resonator at one end.

■ spike lute—mostly bowed and hence also known as "spike fiddle." The neck is a round stick which extends through the resonator and forms the spike (Figure 6.8).

■ fingerboard lute—the neck is a flat surface that the fingers press the strings down to.

■ without frets (Figure 6.9).

■ with frets (Figure 6.10).

FIGURE **6.6**
The *valiha* from Madagascar is an example of a tube zither.

FIGURE **6.7**
The *kecapi* from West Java, Indonesia, is a zither with a box resonator.

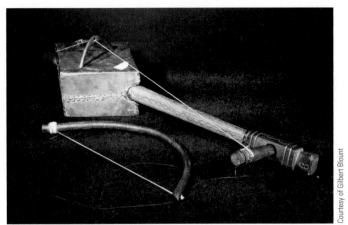

Courtesy of Gilbert Blount

FIGURE 6.8
The *masingo* is a spike lute chordophone from Ethiopia. Also
known as a spike fiddle, the string is supported on a single stick
which extends through a resonator at the bottom end.

William Alves

FIGURE 6.9
The European cello or violoncello is a lute
instrument with a flat neck but no frets.

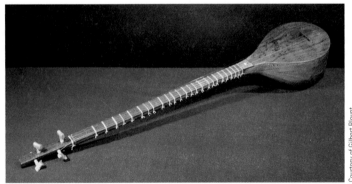

Courtesy of Gilbert Blount

FIGURE 6.10
The Iranian *sehtar*, an example of a fretted lute chordophone.

Lyres Sometimes considered a form of lute, but in these chordophones the strings are attached to a crossbar held up by two posts with a resonator at the bottom (Figure 6.11).

Harps Chordophones in which the strings are perpendicular to a resonator.

■ angle harps—the strings are stretched between two pieces of wood joined at an angle (Figure 6.12).

■ bow harps—the strings are stretched between the sides of a single piece of wood shaped like a curved bow (Figure 9.7).

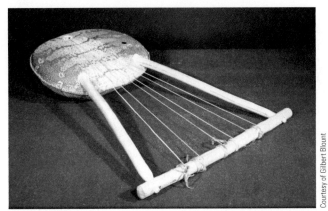

Courtesy of Gilbert Blount

FIGURE 6.11
The *seron* is a lyre from Uganda.

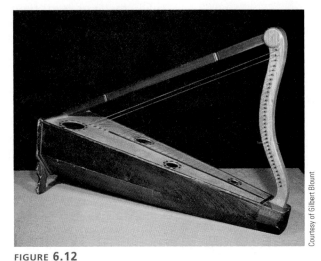

Courtesy of Gilbert Blount

FIGURE 6.12
A harp, like this one from Jalisco, Mexico, has strings attached more or less perpendicularly to the resonator rather than parallel to it. In this photograph the resonator is on the bottom, though in performance it would lean against the player's shoulder. In an angle harp, like this one, the other end of the string is attached to a bar (on the right in this picture) attached at an angle to the resonator.

Aerophones

In aerophones it is not the physical instrument or string that vibrates, but the air itself, inside a vessel such as a tube. This air is called an **air column** even though the tube it is in may be wrapped around many times, as in a trumpet. Just as a string vibrates only at certain frequencies when stopped at a certain length and tension, air inside a tube vibrates only at certain frequencies.

Courtesy of Gilbert Blount

FIGURE **6.14**
A single reed, like
this one attached to
the mouthpiece of a
saxophone from the
United States, is a
flat piece of wood or
some similar material
that vibrates on top
of the end of the
tube when blown.

William Alves

These frequencies correspond to the **harmonic series**. The player can make the instrument vibrate in different frequencies in this series by increasing the air pressure, a technique called **overblowing**. For the pitches in between the notes of the harmonic series, the player varies the length of the tubing through the use of **valves** (European trumpets), holes (*zurna*, clarinet), or **slides** (trombone).

The aerophone player may set the air into motion in a number of different ways. In flutes, the player blows over a sharp opening or notch. When the angle is just right, the stream of air oscillates over and under the opening, causing the air inside to vibrate. In double reed instruments, the player ties two flat pieces of wood, plant, or plastic (the **reed**, often actually made of reed) tightly together and fixes them in the end of the tube (Figure 6.13).

When under air pressure, the reeds quickly open and close, creating the vibration of the air column. In single reed instruments, the reed is attached tightly to the end of the instrument itself (Figure 6.14).

The aerophone player may also buzz his or her lips into the end of the tube. In the West, such instruments are called brass instruments because of the material of their construction, but buzzed-lip aerophones elsewhere are frequently made of wood or other materials.

The tone may be varied also by the shape of the tubing, called the **bore**. For example, the European trumpet's tubing varies very little in diameter over the vast majority of its length. Only the bell at the end is flared. Thus we say that overall it has a **cylindrical bore**. However, the bore of the French horn gets gradually larger over its length; thus we say that it has a **conical bore**.

The ways in which the air column is set into motion have been briefly categorized, but let's break it down even further:

Flutes Aerophones in which a stream of air is focused on a sharp edge.

■ endblown notch flute—the player holds the tube straight away from the mouth, but blows over the rim of the hole of the tube (Figure 6.15).

■ transverse or sideblown flute—the player holds the tube perpendicular to his head and blows over an open hole (Figure 6.16).

■ duct flute—the player blows directly into a hole (the duct) which directs the air stream to another hole with a sharp ramp, called a *fipple* (Figure 6.17).

■ globular—the sound body is a roughly spherical chamber rather than a tube (Figure 6.18).

Double Reed   Aerophones in which two pieces of reed or other material are tied tightly together at the end of a tube, and when put under enough air pressure, begin to vibrate against each other:

■ cylindrical bore.

■ conical bore (Figure 6.19).

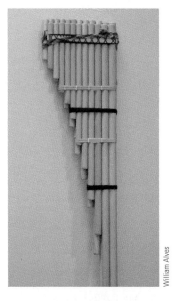

FIGURE **6.15**
Panpipes, such as this *zampoña* from Bolivia, are collections of end-blown flutes. The player blows over the edge of each pipe to create the vibration.

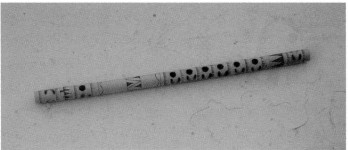

FIGURE **6.16**
A transverse flute, like this *bansi* transverse flute from Sulawesi, Indonesia, is held out perpendicular to the player's head. The player focuses a stream of air over the hole on the left.

FIGURE **6.17**
A duct flute, like this *suling* from Indonesia, directs an airstream over a sharp notch in an opening. In this case, there is a small opening between the ring around the top of the instrument and the stopped end of the tube. When the player blows into this opening, the air stream is automatically directed over the notch in the opening below.

FIGURE **6.18**
An ocarina globular flute from Mexico.

FIGURE **6.19**
Here are two slightly different sizes of *shahnai*, a double-reed instrument from India.

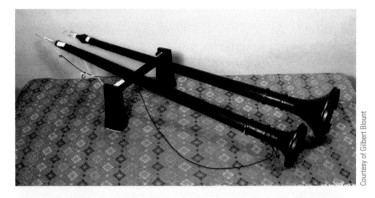

FIGURE **6.20**
The *duzele* is a single reed instrument from Azerbaijan and related regions. This one is actually two single-reed instruments bound together so that the same player can play two tones at once.

FIGURE **6.21**
Despite its name, the *gong bambu* of the Banyumas region of Indonesia is really a buzzed-lip aerophone. Its deep tones are used to imitate the tolling of large gongs.

Single Reed Aerophones in which a flat piece of wood is tied to the mouthpiece of a tube and blown over, causing it to vibrate.

■ cylindrical bore (Figure 6.20).
■ conical bore.

Buzzed-Lip Instruments (also known as **brass**) Aerophones in which the player buzzes his or her lips into the end of a tube.

■ cylindrical bore (Figure 6.21).
■ conical bore.

Membranophones

Membranophones, or drums, have some kind of skin or thin plastic stretched tightly over a frame or resonator. The side with the skin is called the **head** and may be played with the hands or with sticks. There are several

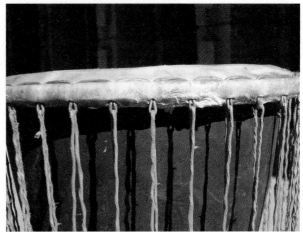

FIGURE 6.22
The skin of the *bedug* drum from Java, Indonesia is attached with rivets around the edges of each head.

FIGURE 6.23
In this *donno* drum from West Africa the head is kept at tension with string threaded through the edges of the drum head.

methods for stretching the head tightly over the resonator. It may be attached with rivets (Figure 6.22), with strings threaded through its edges and tied to the drum (Figure 6.23), with a hoop tightly pressed on top of the head and over the drum resonator (Figure 6.24), or with glue or other methods.

Resonators come in a variety of shapes for a variety of different types of sound. They form the basis for the most basic classification of most membranophones:

■ **bowl-shaped** (Figure 6.25)
■ **cylindrical** (Figure 6.26)
■ **barrel or waisted** (Figure 6.27)
■ **hourglass** (Figure 6.28)
■ **conical** (Figure 6.29)
■ **goblet shape** (Figure 6.30)
■ **frame drum** (Figure 6.31)

FIGURE 6.24
In this head of a *doumbak* drum from North Africa, the skin is kept taught under a hoop which is fastened onto the drum body with bolts.

Drums are sometimes provided with rattles or other secondary sources that vibrate sympathetically with the drum. The tambourine, for example, has jingles inserted in its frame, and the snare drum is named for small wires that rattle inside the drum. Such instruments are actually combination membranophones and idiophones.

FIGURE **6.25**
Drums with bowl-shaped resonators are found in Europe, the Middle East, and South Asia, such as these *dukar-tikar* drums from Jammu and Kashmir, India. (Two musicians are playing *shahnai* double reeds at the left.)

FIGURE **6.26**
The *tupan* bass drum from Bulgaria has a cylindrical resonator.

FIGURE **6.27**
Many drums have a barrel-shaped resonator, that is, one that bulges outward in the middle. This *petia* drum of the Ashanti people of West Africa is covered in leopard skin.

FIGURE **6.28**
The *donno* drum
from Ghana has
an hourglass-
shaped
resonator.

William Alves

FIGURE **6.29**
The *mpuunyi* drum
from Uganda has a
conical resonator.

© CORBIS

FIGURE **6.30**
The *zarb* or *tombak*
is a goblet-shaped
drum from Iran.

Courtesy of Gilbert Blount /CORBIS

FIGURE **6.31**
Frame drums are simply skins stretched over hoops or frames so shallow that there is effectively no resonator. Frame drums are common in the Middle East as well as among people of the Arctic, such as these Koryak people from Ossora, Russia.

© Kevin Schafer/CORBIS

Idiophones

Idiophones are instruments in which the entire body of the instrument vibrates when struck or (more rarely) rubbed or otherwise set in motion. They include all sorts of bells, cymbals, wood blocks, gongs and so on. Almost anything can be made an idiophone if you hit it. Because of this variety, idiophones classification can be difficult. For the purposes of this book, we will classify idiophones not by their construction, but by the identifiability of their pitch, even though that characteristic can be a spectrum more than definite categories:

- **instruments of definite pitch** (Figure 6.32)
- **instruments of semi-definite pitch** (Figure 6.33)
- **instruments of no definite pitch** (Figure 6.34)

The choices a culture makes in its construction and selection of musical instruments contribute to that culture's expression of **musical style**—*the complex and fluid combinations of all the elements we've discussed in this section that help us to generalize about related musical compositions and performances.* In Part 1 of this book we have looked at many ways we can describe and analyze the sound of a piece of music and how that sound is created. However, we should never lose sight of the fact that musical style cannot exist independently of the culture and society which produce it. In the following parts we will focus on paths toward understanding musical style within its social context and enriching the listening experience.

REFERENCES

Byrne, David. "Crossing Music's Borders in Search of Identity." *The New York Times*, Section 2, page 1, October 3, 1999.

Harrison, Lou. *Lou Harrison's Music Primer.* New York: C. F. Peters, 1971.

Simon, Paul. "Highbrows and Hits: A Fertile Compound." *The New York Times*, Section 2, page 1, August 30, 1998.

"Singer Paul Simon Strikes Sour Chord . . ." *Jet* 71 (Feb. 2, 1987):59.

FIGURE **6.32**
Idiophones of definite pitch are often collected into sets played with mallets, such as this marimba from Mexico.

Courtesy of Gilbert Blount

FIGURE **6.33**
Gongs, such as this *gong cina* from Java, Indonesia, often have a semi-definite pitch.

William Alves

FIGURE **6.34**
Unpitched idiophones include rattles, such as these seed rattles from Africa.

Courtesy of Gilbert Blount

Notice not only the contemporary political boundaries but the geographical divisions that we use in this unit: West Africa, East Africa, Central Africa, and Southern Africa. (We cover North Africa in Part 3.)

c. 3500–2000 BCE

Agriculture begins in upper Nile, Ethiopia, and West Africa, eventually helping to create the first large kingdoms in sub-Saharan Africa.

c. 400 BCE

Iron forging begins in the Sudan, creating new weapons and musical instruments.

c. 100 BCE

Trade with Arabia, India, and Indonesia brings important high-yield crops to East Africa, which were eventually traded into West Africa. Some musicologists argue that Asian musical influences followed these routes as well.[1]

[1] A. M. Jones, *Africa and Indonesia: The Evidence of the Xylophone and Other Musical and Cultural Factors* (Leiden: E. J. Brill, 1964).

c. 0 CE–1000 CE

These crops and other trade enable the Bantu-speaking cultures of West and Central Africa to sustain much more dense populations and migrate south. As they eventually occupy most of Central and Southern Africa, they displace the indigenous Central African Pygmy and South African Khoikhoin and San ("Bushmen") populations.

PART 2

Sub-Saharan Africa

c. 400–1076

Kingdom of Ghana, one of the first of the powerful West African kingdoms which became rich largely through trans-Sahara trade in gold. Royal retinues have a long history of patronizing sophisticated drumming orchestras in West Africa as well as praise-singers, reciters, and musical storytellers. Later kingdoms would include those of Mali, Benin, and Songhai.

c. 1000

Islam comes to the area immediately south of the Sahara. Kingdoms that depend on the trans-Saharan or east African coastal trade adopt Islam and many Arabic musical instruments, such as the *rabab* fiddle. The wealth of key trade centers, such as Timbuktu and Gao, also brought Islamic scholarship to the mosques there.

1456

The Portuguese establish the first regular slave trade.

1652

The Dutch settle Capetown, South Africa. The British take over the colony during the Napoleonic wars. For the most part, disease and African armies prevent the Europeans from colonizing elsewhere until the nineteenth century.

▶

INTRODUCTION TO THE REGION

7

FIRST LISTEN
CD 1:1
Atsia Suite

Listening to this first recording, you may find the intensity of the many drums exciting, even overwhelming. You may find yourself moving with the music, perhaps tapping your foot. Certainly you would find many onlookers in a Ghanaian village dancing and clapping when this drumming orchestra played. Still, as engaging as this sound is, the real story lies below the surface in a nuanced web of relationships such as community and family, the most basic social structures in Africa.

1960–1980
African countries gain independence. Governmental support for traditional art forms has sometimes accompanied the growth of African nationalism. For example, in 1978 L'Orchestre National of Cameroon was founded, consisting of thirty-four musicians playing adaptations of traditional works on combinations of European and indigenous instruments. In addition, African popular music has become widespread and influential both within and outside of the continent.

1880–1900
Advanced firearms as well as the depopulation and interethnic warfare caused by the slave trade enable the Europeans to claim vast territories as colonies, often with artificial borders that ignore traditional ethnic boundaries. These political expedients led to significant interethnic strife within modern African nations.

1760–1810
Height of slave trade, depopulating large areas of West Africa and disrupting nations and cultures. Millions of Africans were taken to the Americas, bringing with them their music and other aspects of their cultures.

1993
Apartheid ended in South Africa

FIGURE 7.1
Togbui Adeladza II, Paramount Chief of the Anlo-Ewe, and his entourage enter the Durbar grounds of Hogbetsotso festival at Anloga, Ghana. The drum orchestras (just visible on the left) that accompany them reflect the hierarchy and interconnectedness of society symbolized in such ceremonies.

Many Africans reckon the bonds of family not only laterally, that is, as a relationship between siblings, cousins, and so on, but linearly back in time, sometimes far back. Thus an entire village may trace their genealogy back to a common ancestor. In some cultures, one of which we meet in Chapter 11, it is the job of a professional caste of musicians to memorize these genealogies and recite them in song.

Scholar and musician C. K. Ladzekpo quotes the African proverb "A dead animal cries louder than a live one," meaning that an ancestral spirit may have more influence dead than alive. The dead animal skin of the drum cries out when it is played, representing that spiritual influence through its powerful sound. Many Africans consider each musical instrument to have a spirit of its own that musicians must respect.

The Ewe drumming ensemble that we hear in the first recording reflects the structure of the family. The lead drum is the metaphorical father of the ensemble, guiding the other drums by means of musical signals—when to start, stop, move to the next section, and so on. Likewise, mother and brother drums engage in a musical conversation, often in an almost literal way. Because certain syllables represent different drum strokes, each drumming pattern is not only a rhythm, but also a melody and a linguistic phrase. The lead drum and a timekeeper instrument, an iron bell in this case, unify the many layers of sound. They keep the lively and complex conversation from dissolving into an un-African chaos that would represent the dissolution of the order of the family and the forces of nature.

Yet this tight cooperation still allows for individuality, for different points of view, through the most distinctive of traditional African musical characteristics—polyrhythm. **Polyrhythm** means *different meters or metrical starting points going on at once*. Like the disparate dynamic forces of the spiritual world that ideally find equilibrium, so the polyphony and polyrhythm of the drums are tied together in an exhilarating affirmation of life.

CHARACTERISTICS OF TRADITIONAL AFRICAN MUSIC

8

The many languages and distinct cultures of the huge area of sub-Saharan Africa clearly demonstrate its diversity. In addition to industrial economies in the growing urban areas, many traditional ways of life are still vital: farming, nomadic herding, hunting, and gathering. Despite the difficulties of generalizations, several musical characteristics are common throughout sub-Saharan Africa. For the most part these characteristics apply to the music of traditional cultures, although their influence is felt even in popular music.

■ **Polyrhythm** Referring to *rhythms that occur simultaneously in two different meters, or with different starting points*, polyrhythm is found only occasionally elsewhere in the world. Polyrhythm can be very difficult and, in traditional African music, extremely complex.

■ **Responsorial Forms** These forms feature *an exchange between a single performer's vocal or instrumental* call *and a group* response. Often simply called call-and-response, this practice is very common in African music, sometimes in very subtle ways.

■ **Ostinato** *A short pattern that repeats over and over;* **ostinato** most often refers to a repeating melody, but can also refer to a repeating rhythm. In Africa, *ostinatos* often form foundations for improvisation, variation, or the addition of other patterns.

■ **Use of Percussion** This characteristic reflects the Sub-Saharan emphasis on making music with drums, rattles, bells, xylophones, and *mbiras*. (We will discuss these instruments later.) Some orchestras include only percussion instruments, and non-percussion instruments are sometimes played in a percussive manner. Nevertheless, such instruments as harps, lyres, horns, and flutes are equally important in many areas.

■ **Background Shimmer** African musicians often attach beads, coins, or other small objects to their instruments to create a constant buzzing or rattling sound in the background of a performance.

■ **Close Connection between Music and Language** Drums executing a combination of rhythm and pitch that represent spoken syllables and form a kind of speech illustrate the close association between music and words. Nearly all traditional African music involves song. Even purely instrumental pieces are considered songs without words—that is, pieces in which melody and rhythm imply words.

■ **The Participatory Nature of the Arts**   Most traditional cultures in Sub-Saharan Africa share the expectation that music is something everyone does. While many societies have professional musicians and some musicians are recognized as having more talent than others, no Western-style gulf separates musician from audience.

■ **A Close Connection between the Performing Arts**   Many African languages have no separate word for "music," and while a word for "song" often exists, it may also imply poetry and dance. Thus most African cultures share the expectation that a musical performance will involve singing and dancing. Music without dance is rare. Even in solo performance, the musician may also dance or move while he plays, remembering the physicality of the performance as much its sound.

POLYRHYTHM

Despite its literal translation, "many rhythms," polyrhythm more specifically means two distinct rhythmic patterns in different meters or with different starting points superimposed on one another. While many pieces may have different rhythms in different simultaneous parts, they are rarely polyrhythmic because they all align to the same meter. One of the simplest examples of polyrhythm is mixing a meter that is two groups of three pulses (compound duple) with a meter that is three groups of two pulses (simple triple). Both meters take the same amount of time—they are just different groupings of the same six pulses.

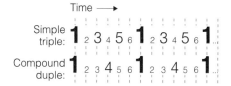

GRAPHIC **8.1**

While the superimposition of different meters in this example is very common in traditional African music, displacement of one of these layers can also create polyrhythm. In this case, two or more parts may have different **downbeats** (*the stressed beginning of the metrical cycle*). Sometimes these two effects are combined. Here we see polyrhythm formed by combining simple triple with compound duple, but offset by two pulses.

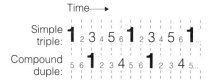

GRAPHIC **8.2**

♫ MUSIC AND LANGUAGE

Many languages of sub-Saharan Africa are **tonal**, that is, words may have different meanings depending on their **inflection**, *the relative pitch at which they are spoken*. While inflection may carry meaning in European languages as well, a word in tonal languages may have three or more different meanings depending on its being spoken at a high, medium, or low pitch. In addition, accent or emphasis on a word or syllable is indicated more by long or short duration than a louder sound. Thus many African languages have a very musical quality to them.

More than other cultures with tonal languages (such as those of China and Southeast Asia), many African cultures have connected the tonal nature of their language to their music. An example is the so-called **talking drum**— *a drum that can imitate the rhythm and most common pitch levels of speech*. A skilled player of such a drum can imitate speech so well that listeners can understand what is being said.

Because the sounds of drums can carry over long distances, this ability has been used as a signaling device. While some drums or idiophones are built especially for this purpose, *all* drums can "talk." A player in an African drumming orchestra is always thinking of the words or special drum syllables that he will make the drum "say." The carefully controlled pitches of the different strokes are as important as the rhythm, and drum parts are literally melodies—melodies of just a few pitches, but melodies nevertheless. We hear these qualities in the drumming orchestra performance on our first African recording (CD 1:1). Below is a graphic of musical instrument language transcribed from a portion of a recording of the Ndokpa people in the Central African Republic.[1] The graphic demonstrates how a xylophone (black rectangles) can imitate the rhythm (shown left to right) and three pitch levels of speech so that listeners can understand what is being said without spoken words. The sentence here means, "It rained just now; it will be fine tomorrow."

GRAPHIC **8.3**

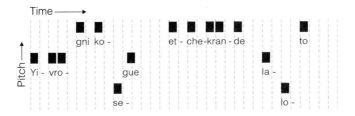

---

[1] Recorded by Charles Duvelle on *Musique centrafricaine.*

TRADITIONAL AFRICAN INSTRUMENTS

9

In addition to drums, African musicians play a wide variety of traditional instruments including lyres, harps, zithers, lutes, flutes, and trumpets. The linguistic diversity of Africa compounds the difficulty of cataloguing the many instrument types. A single instrument type may have dozens of different names across the continent. Therefore this section gives only representative names or general descriptions.

Rough-hewn construction from readily available materials characterizes many of Africa's instruments. While professional instrument makers produce beautiful instruments, almost anyone can make various types of African instruments, a feature that facilitates the general population's participation in music.

Membranophones

Drums are, of course, the most famous instruments of Africa, and they come in a staggering variety of forms—cylindrical, conical, goblet-shaped, hourglass-shaped, or barrel-shaped. Hemispherical drums (such as the European timpani) are not as common, and the shallow frame drum is mostly associated with Islamic areas where it has been introduced from the Middle East.

Drummers use either their hands or sticks (sometimes one of each) to hit the drum head. One distinctively African stick is the **elbow stick** (Figure 9.1). Made of two sticks attached at an angle or carved from a single piece of wood, the elbow stick allows the player to stand behind the drum and strike the head with a solid, straight impact.

Idiophones

Prominent in Africa, idiophones sounded by shaking, hitting, or rubbing the entire instrument range from a dancer's tiny jingles to large multi-player xylophones. Some instruments known as "drums" are actually idiophones, such as log drums, slit drums, and pottery drums. The slit drum consists of a box or hollowed-out log resonator with slits cut in the surface to form wooden tines of different pitches.

A xylophone may be very large or small enough to suspend from the neck and carry in procession. It consists of wooden keys suspended over tuned resonator boxes, gourds, or a simple pit in the ground (Figure 9.2) and played with mallets. Occasionally played as a solo instrument, more often the xylophone is an ensemble instrument with several instruments playing at once or multiple players on a single instrument. As with drums, xylophones can imitate speech and are sometimes used in narrative musical forms.

Courtesy of Danlee Mitchell

FIGURE **9.1**
African drums may be closed at the bottom or open for greater resonance. If open, the drum may be held at an angle between the legs to allow the sound to escape, or, if the drum is too large, it may be mounted at an angle on a frame (above) or (right) constructed on feet that raise the bottom and allow the sound to escape. The image above shows a group of drummers from Ghana, West Africa. Notice that their sticks are L-shaped, a shape that allows the performers to stand behind the drums and hit the heads with a perpendicular impact. The image on the right shows royal drummers playing footed drums in Ho, Ghana. Notice the laces and pegs on the sides of the drums. The laces attach the edges of the hide to the drum heads and tighten around pegs hammered diagonally into the drum's body. The drummer may periodically hammer at these pegs to keep the skin taut and the drum in tune.

Courtesy of Danlee Mitchell

FIGURE **9.2**
The **balafon** or **bala**, an instrument common to the *jalolu* (see Chapter 11) of West Africa, is a wooden xylophone with gourd resonators under each rough-hewn bar. Sometimes pebbles are placed inside the gourds to add a rattle to the sound.

Courtesy of David Schmalenberger

African slaves brought the xylophone to the Americas, where one variety has retained its African name—the marimba. "Marimba" is a variant of *mbira*, a term in southern Africa for an instrument that consists of metal tines fixed to a resonator and plucked with the player's thumbs. Variations of this instrument, a kind of personal xylophone, are common throughout central and southern Africa under a variety of names. We discuss the *mbira* in detail in Chapter 12.

Rattles can be made of baskets, gourds, seed pods, or other materials, and their beads may be contained inside or wrapped around the outside in a net. Bells, jingles, and other idiophones made from forged iron are common, although cymbals of the type found in the Middle East are not.

Aerophones

As in most cultures, the human voice is a fundamental musical instrument, and its use in Africa is as diverse as the region's cultures. Open-throated sounds distinguish much of sub-Saharan singing from the more "husky" or nasal tones preferred in many Islamic cultures of the North. Other distinctive kinds of African singing include **whisper singing**, a soft, breathy, almost growling tone, and **yodeling**, well known among the Pygmies of Central Africa.

While reed instruments are generally found only in areas with Arabic influence, flutes occur in virtually every form on the African continent: vertical and horizontal, with and without notches, with a wide or limited range, and so on (Figure 9.3).

© CORBIS

FIGURE 9.3
The *endere*, an end-blown flute from Uganda, appears in a historical photograph, which, according to ethnomusicologist Peter Cooke, represents the royal flute ensemble in use among the Kiganda people in the early twentieth century.

Courtesy of Danlee Mitchell

FIGURE 9.4
A group of horn trumpet players in Ho, Ghana. Generally, mouth holes are bored on the side of the horn, making these instruments transverse trumpets.

Buzzed-lip or trumpet-type instruments are widespread and often made from animal horns into which a hole has been bored at the small end (Figure 9.4). In some cases trumpets have large gourds attached to one end for greater resonance.

Although trumpets and flutes may have a limited range, even just a single note, a large group can create a melody by dividing the notes up among the different players, a practice called **alternation playing**. Thus one player plays the first note, another the second, another the third, and so on. The alternating parts may also be polyrhythmic ostinatos, becoming rather like pitched versions of drumming ensembles.

Chordophones

String instruments are popular in Africa often because a single player can create polyrhythmic ostinatos by plucking in different patterns. The simplest type of chordophone is the **musical bow** (Figure 9.5), which consists of a single string attached to two ends of a curved stick, like the bow archers use. As in other African chordophones, the string may be vegetable matter (such as a vine), animal gut, or (more recently) nylon cord which is plucked or struck with a stick. The instrument frequently has a half-gourd in the middle of the bow that serves as a resonator or may be placed next to the player's mouth for resonance, like a jaw's harp. Even though the musical bow usually produces only a single pitch, the player can resonate various harmonics in his mouth, in effect creating a second melody above the monotone sound of the bow string.

Harps and lyres are common in many parts of Africa, especially in Central Africa, where they are thought to have come from ancient Egypt via the upper Nile. The lyre consists of a symmetrical frame with several strings in the middle and often a resonator at the bottom. The strings may go over a bridge set on the resonator or may be attached directly to the resonator or the bottom of the frame (Figure 9.6).

The most common type of harp in Sub-Saharan Africa is the **bow harp** (Figure 9.7), which is similar to the musical bow, except that it has several strings instead of just one strung across a curved stick.

The **triangular harp** consists of a wooden frame of two or three parts with strings strung between them. This type of harp is more commonly found in North Africa, although one particularly African variant is the bridged harp or harp-lute, a hybrid of the two forms. We will discuss the *kora* harp-lute in Chapter 11.

Zithers come in many different forms as well (Figure 9.8), including tube zithers, bar zithers, raft zithers, trough zithers, and box zithers. Lutes are not as common in sub-Saharan Africa as in North Africa and the Middle East. Except for the harp-lute, most instruments of the lute type in sub-Saharan Africa appear in Islamic areas where the influence from the Middle East is the strongest.

FIGURE 9.5
By resonating different harmonics, the player of the musical bow can create a melody, rather like a jaw's harp.

FIGURE 9.6
The *endongo* is a bridged lyre of Uganda, where there is an especially large variety of harps and lyres. The strings are made of ox tendons attached to metal rings that can be slid along the crossbar for fine tuning.

FIGURE **9.7**
The *akadinda* bow harp from Uganda is played by Bukenya Richard, Zaake Nathan, and Ntambi Abbey of the Ensemble Akadinda.

Courtesy of Face Music

Courtesy of Face Music

Courtesy of Gilbert Blount

FIGURE **9.8**
The *inanga* from Uganda (left) is called a trough zither because of the carved wooden trough over which the strings are strung, thus eliminating the need for separate bridges. Alternatively, the *totombito* from the Congo (above) has a bridge and is called a raft zither because its simple flat sound board acts as a resonator.

DRUMMING IN WEST AFRICA

10

In the cold pre-dawn hours on the outskirts of a village of the Ewe people of southeastern Ghana (see map), a music and dance club of costumed young men and women have gathered under a large tree.[1] Several months earlier they paid a local composer to create a new piece for them, and their leader has also taught the group related compositions that they have been practicing at night, after work, ever since. Today they have assembled early to surprise the town with their inaugural performance.

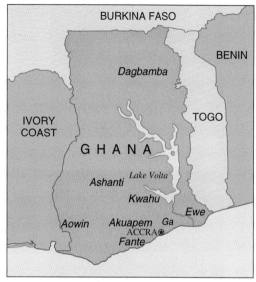

Map of Ghana. Notice the locations of the Ewe and other ethnic groups.

The leader pours a libation on the ground and intones an invocation to ancestors for a successful performance. After one last dress rehearsal, the group assembles in a parade and enters the town's main street, playing the drums, rattles, and bell and dancing as the sun rises. Most people who hear the music rush out and follow, clapping along and moving to the music. The parade may stop at the house of a mayor or other town official to encourage celebrity participation. The group comes to a halt in the community's outdoor dance arena and the large crowd of onlookers, though they are participants as well, form a semi-circle around the troupe (Figure 10.1).

After another libation and prayer, the singers begin their signature song. The bell player accompanies in a characteristic rhythm and the lead drummer plays a loud signal to bring in the rest of the ensemble and dancers. Throughout the performance, the lead drummer not only sets the tempo, but also directs the other drums and the

Kobla Ladzekpo

FIGURE **10.1**
A traditional music and dance ensemble performs in an Ewe village.

---

[1] Much of the following description is adapted from Kobla Ladzekpo, "The Social Mechanics of Good Music: A Description of Dance Clubs among the Anlo Ewe-Speaking People of Ghana," *African Music Society Journal* 5/1 (1971): 6–21; and A. M. Jones, *Studies in African Music* (New York: Oxford University Press, 1959).

THE INSTRUMENTS THAT WE HEAR IN THE *ATSIA* SUITE, CD 1:1

FIGURE 10.2
The *atoke* is a small circular piece of iron folded in half, thus resembling a boat or (to some) a banana. It is held loosely on the palm and hit with a small metal stick.

FIGURE 10.3
The *gankogui* double iron bell is the indispensable timekeeper of the group. The two bells welded together give two different pitches. Similar instruments are common throughout West Africa and as far away as Brazil, where the *agogo* performs a comparable function in the African-derived samba.

FIGURE 10.4
Instead of having beads or pebbles inside the gourd, as in most rattles (like maracas), the *axatse* has a loose net of beads woven together around its outside. The player can shake the *axatse*, lightly hit it against a palm or leg, or twist it to give a swishing sound. On our recording, the performer alternately brings the rattle upward to the other hand and downward to the knee. Similar rattles are common throughout West Africa, and, depending on the variety of gourds grown in the area, can be quite large.

dancers. By playing certain audible patterns, the lead drummer signals the others to start, stop, or go on to the next section. These same patterns also signal the dancers to change their steps. Unlike a performance of European orchestral music in which a conductor gives visual cues, here the cues are built into the music. This performance will continue for some hours as the club plays the different pieces in their repertory. At times they will play a *hatsiatsia*, or bell piece, during which the dancers rest.

These West African forests and grasslands were the home of powerful ancient kingdoms made wealthy largely through the lucrative trans-Sahara trade, the same trade that brought the influences of Islam and Christianity to this region. The kings and other feudal lords often kept retinues of drum-

William Alves

FIGURE 10.5
In performance, the ***atsimewu***, shown here with Ewe drummer Alfred Ladzekpo, is the so-called master or lead drum, played by the leader of the orchestra with a combination of sticks and hands. It is a large, long drum, usually about five feet tall and roughly cylindrical, but thicker in the middle and smaller on bottom than on top. The bottom is open, and the drum skin is attached to the top by a series of straps attached to pegs, which are hammered into the side of the drum at an angle. (All the Ewe drums have similar heads.) Because of its height, the *astimewu* is supported on a stand at an incline.

Danlee Mitchell

FIGURE 10.6
This photo shows an Ewe drumming ensemble in Kpata, Ghana, similar to the one heard in our *Atsia* recording. From left to right in the front row, the drums are *kaganu, kidi, sogo*, and *boba* (a cylindrical drum not heard in *Atsia*). The lead drummer stands behind them. The *kaganu* player holds the drum between his knees and plays with long sticks. The *kidi* drum is slightly larger and rests on the ground. The *sogo* is larger yet and is played with either hands or sticks. In smaller ensembles it can function as the lead drum.

ming orchestras and other musicians. Drumming ensembles were and still are crucial components in religious societies, in which particular deities and rituals have specific, often secret repertories of music. Similar musical religious practices are also found among African cultures in the Caribbean and South America. Although this chapter focuses on the specific practices of drumming among the Ewe people, traditional drumming orchestras are common throughout this region.

Although today the modern nation-state has replaced the political power of the kings, and people today drum as much for recreation as for ritual, orchestras such as this still represent the interconnected bonds of the family that is this community.

Listening Guide

CD 1:1. *Atsia* Suite

Hatsiatsia—played entirely on iron bells

0:00	A single *atoke* (bell) sounds the timekeeping pattern.

GRAPHIC 10.1
Basic timekeeping cyclic pattern of 12 pulses.

Pulse:	1	2	3	4	5	6	7	8	9	10	11	12	1...
Atoke 1:	X		X		X	X		X		X		X	X
	long		long		short	long		long		long		short	long

The long notes are twice the length of the short notes, leading to a characteristic rhythm in a metrical cycle of twelve pulses. Many Ewe pieces use this standard pattern, and its asymmetrical rhythm helps orient the other players.

0:02	The second *atoke*, and two *gankogui* enter, creating an intricate polyrhythmic web.

Any latitude in these parts would ruin the carefully crafted conversation; therefore the players do not improvise. Each *gankogui* has two different pitches that players refer to by syllables. The precise pitches of these instruments are not as important as the overall texture of interrelated, polyrhythmic bell sounds. Notice that the second *gankogui* part has the same rhythm as the second *atoke* part, but offset in time.

GRAPHIC 10.2
Polyrhythmic layers.

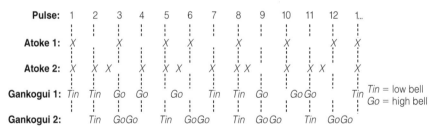

Pulse:	1	2	3	4	5	6	7	8	9	10	11	12	1...	
Atoke 1:	X		X		X	X		X		X		X	X	
Atoke 2:	X	X X		X	X X		X	X X		X	X X		X	
Gankogui 1:	Tin	Tin	Go	Go		Go		Tin	Tin	Go		Go Go		Tin	Tin = low bell
Gankogui 2:		Tin	GoGo		Tin	GoGo		Tin	Go Go		Tin	GoGo		Go = high bell

First Song—call-and-response between the lead singer (usually the lead drummer) and the chorus (who may be the dancers, other drummers, or even onlookers)

Second Piece —"Circle" *Atsia*, a round dance

1:53	One *gankogui* player takes over the timekeeping pattern, playing the first note on the lower bell and the other notes on the higher bell.

The *axatse* rattle enters with a standard *axatse* pattern that is a simple variation of the *gankogui* pattern and links the two instruments in texture.

Lead singer begins the next song.

1:59	Chorus answers the lead singer.
	The lead drummer on the *atsimewu* (Figure 10.6) mirrors the timekeeping melody by striking the side of his drum with a stick.

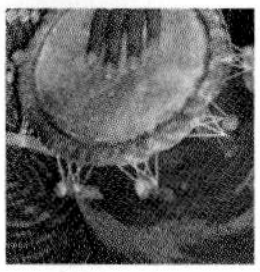

2:04	The *atsimewu* drummer sounds a distinctive call, a signaling pattern to the drums and dancers, who respond by whirling around and moving on to a new repetitive movement pattern.
	Whenever this signaling pattern comes from the lead drum, the dancers

GRAPHIC 10.3
Signaling pattern.

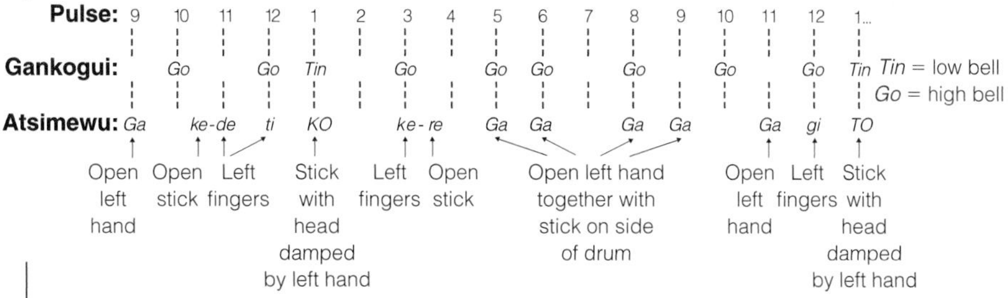

Pulse:	9	10	11	12	1	2	3	4	5	6	7	8	9	10	11	12	1...
Gankogui:		Go		Go	Tin		Go		Go	Go		Go		Go		Go	Tin

Tin = low bell
Go = high bell

Atsimewu: Ga   ke-de   ti   KO   ke-re   Ga   Ga   Ga   Ga   Ga   gi   TO

Open left hand / Open stick / Left fingers / Stick with head damped by left hand / Left fingers / Open stick / Open left hand together with stick on side of drum / Open left hand / Left fingers / Stick with head damped by left hand

respond. The lead drummer therefore acts as a conductor for the performance, giving cues in his drumming patterns. There are many different call patterns for a particular piece, each signaling a different change in the choreography. The syllables that guide the drummer are a kind of drumming language known as *wu-gbe*. Different syllables are associated with different types of strokes, although they may also vary according to the context of the pattern.

2:08	The *kaganu*, *sogo*, and *kidi* drums respond to the lead drummer's *atsimewu* pattern and begin the first section of the circle dance.
	The timeline that follows shows the ostinato patterns from the circle dance section *Atsia*. As each drummer plays, he thinks of certain syllables, each of which corresponds to a particular stroke and therefore often a different pitch. Players repeat these patterns (only the *kidi* and *sogo* may introduce slight variations) until the lead drum signals a move to the next section. (The *atsimewu* is not in this timeline because it does not play a constant ostinato pattern.)
	These patterns overlap different meters. The *gankogui* bell and *axatse* rattle repeat an asymmetrical pattern of long and short beats, while the claps and the low-pitched *sogo* divide the cycle into four groups of three. (The second and

(*continued*)

fourth beats are played damped with the open hand rather than a stick. The hand comes down on the head of the drum, but presses there rather than bouncing up; it thus damps the vibration, giving the note a higher pitch and a dryer sound.) The high-pitched *kaganu* plays a pattern of short-long four times in the span of the *gankogui* cycle, but offset in relation to the *sogo*. The *kidi* drum plays two sets of six notes, each set arranged in patterns of four plus two. (The group of four notes is distinguished from the other two because they are played as damped strokes.) The *kidi*'s pattern thus forms an almost literal dialogue with the *sogo*. Many Ewe compositions contain such interplay between the parts. This diagram does not show the dancer's movements, which add another layer of rhythm to this polyrhythmic web.

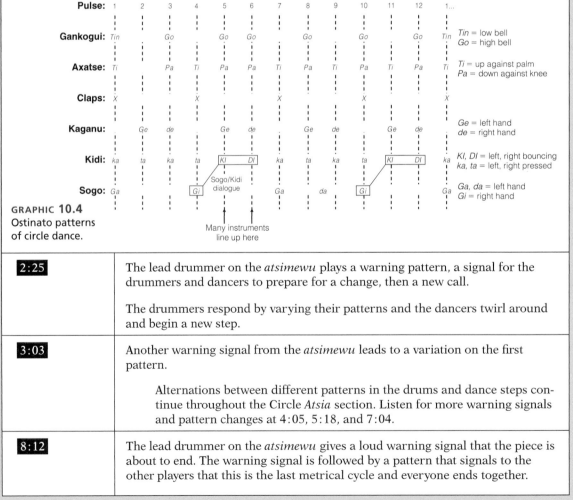

GRAPHIC 10.4
Ostinato patterns of circle dance.

2:25	The lead drummer on the *atsimewu* plays a warning pattern, a signal for the drummers and dancers to prepare for a change, then a new call.
	The drummers respond by varying their patterns and the dancers twirl around and begin a new step.
3:03	Another warning signal from the *atsimewu* leads to a variation on the first pattern.
	Alternations between different patterns in the drums and dance steps continue throughout the Circle *Atsia* section. Listen for more warning signals and pattern changes at 4:05, 5:18, and 7:04.
8:12	The lead drummer on the *atsimewu* gives a loud warning signal that the piece is about to end. The warning signal is followed by a pattern that signals to the other players that this is the last metrical cycle and everyone ends together.

 CD1, Track 2 Hatsiatsia examples, Track 3 Circle Atsia examples, Track 4 Atsimewu part

A Drumming Orchestra Performance

Some Ewe music clubs specialize in the drumming orchestra piece *Atsia*, which is several hundred years old, according to the Ewe. Like most traditional Ewe pieces, new song melodies may be added to the core rhythms, and the drumming itself may vary according to the tastes of the performers. Thus, while some characteristics always identify what an *Atsia* club plays as *Atsia*, the piece may vary considerably from one club to the next. Thus *Atsia* itself is somewhere between an individual work and a genre. A full performance, which could last for several hours, is a suite of different songs and dances, all related versions of *Atsia*.

The name *Atsia* means simply "display" or "style," referring to the musicians and dancers showing off their performance. The song lyrics speak directly of the music itself and the club, sometimes bragging about the performance. This suite begins with a bell song, a *hatsiatsia*, accompanied in a beautiful polyrhythm by two types of iron idiophones: the **atoke**, a folded piece of iron (Figure 10.2), and **gankogui**, a clapperless double iron bell (Figure 10.3). In this *hatsiatsia* two performers play each instrument.

Like many *Atsia* songs, the lyric simply refers to the piece itself. Here is a paraphrased translation of the lyrics.[2] Dzokoto is a revered historical figure to the Ewe, so the lyric "Dzokoto's music" is intended to indicate how great the music is. "Coming outside" means that the club is coming out to start the piece.

LEADER:	*Atsia dogbe loo*	Atsia is speaking!
	Mekawoe nye huna miya yawoda	Go and get the drummers.
CHORUS:	*Atsia dogbe loo*	Atsia is speaking!
	Mekawoe nye huna miya yawoda	Go and get the drummers.
	(Leader and chorus repeat.)	
LEADER:	*Dzokotovua digo*	Dzokoto's music is coming outside.
CHORUS:	*Todeme ha*	In our community circle,
	Dzokotovua digo	Dzokoto's music is coming outside.
	Mile wage	We will perform it.
	(Leader and chorus repeat.)	
CHORUS:	*Atsia dogbe loo...*	Atsia is speaking! ...

---

[2] These lyrics are adapted from the translation and explanation in Dan Gorlin, *Songs of West Africa* (Forest Knolls, CA: Alokli West African Dance, 2000). © 2000 Dan Gorlin, alokli.com, reprinted by permission.

MUSIC OF THE *JALOLU*

11

The function of musicians in the kingdoms of ancient West Africa was only partly entertainment. In societies without a written language, the history of a people and the stories of their ancestors must be committed to memory. In West Africa, musicians often specialized in these mnemonic feats, and, because their languages have an inherent musical quality, it is a small step to make words into songs. Just as blacksmiths of this period achieved powerful status as the artisans of weapons, these musicians were the "artisans of the word"[1]—keepers of a people's history, of legendary stories, of royal genealogies, and singers of praise songs of kings, religious leaders, and patrons.

One of the most important traditions in West Africa is the specialized caste of musicians the French called *griots*, who have different names in each of the languages of the region. Among the Mande people of Gambia, Senegal, and Mali, these musicians are known as **jalolu** (plural of **jali**, also known as **jeli**). Not anyone can become a *jali*—normally one must be born into the profession, and many of these musicians trace their musical lineage back to a time when their ancestors were important members of the royal retinues of West Africa's historical kingdoms. Today, however, a *jali* is more likely to find patronage singing at a market, at a festival, or, increasingly, as a part of a popular music band.

The principal instrument of the *jalolu* is the **kora**, a large chordophone that has been described as a hybrid harp-lute (Figures 11.1, 11.2). Because its twenty-one strings are stretched on two sides of the bridge, the performer's left hand plays the eleven strings on the left side of the bridge and the right hand plays the ten strings on the right side. Such an arrangement, common among African chordophones, makes possible intricate polyrhythmic patterns between the hands.

Kora pieces are based mostly on standard ostinato patterns called *kumbengo*. A characteristic sequence of core tones defines *kumbengo*, but musicians weave many elaborate variations of these basic outlines. Contrasting embellishments called *birimintingo* periodically interrupt the constant cycle of kumbengo. While *kora* pieces may be entirely instrumental, more commonly the performer, either the *kora* player himself or another *jali*, sings a song on top of the set of variations.

Singers may also polyrhythmically clap, snap their fingers, tap on the *kora* resonator, or play small iron bells. Songs are commonly praise songs for ancestors, patrons, or Islamic leaders but may also be historical stories, mythic tales, or improvised verse. While *kora* players are traditionally men, both men and women sing.

---

[1] This description is from Eric Charry's *Mande Music* (Chicago: University of Chicago Press, 2000), an excellent survey of the music and musicians of this region.

Another instrument of the jalolu is the **balafon** or *bala*, a wooden xylophone with gourd resonators under each rough-hewn bar (Figure 9.2). Both the *balafon* and the *kora* are heptatonic (seven tones per octave), although the intervals of the *kora* may vary considerably depending on the player and the song. The *kora* player may tune to the *balafon* so that the two may be played together, an especially popular ensemble today.

Some *jalolu* also rely on popular concerts and recordings as a new source of patronage. Several, including Mory Kanté from Senegal, have produced rock-fusion albums. One of the most famous in this popular style is Foday Musa Suso, who moved to the United States and founded the Mandingo Griot Society in America in 1978. Since then he has produced his own albums and collaborated with American composers Herbie Hancock and Philip Glass.

Youri Lenquette

FIGURE 11.1
Musician and singer Mory Kanté plays the *kora*, a hybrid lute-harp from West Africa. The resonator of the *kora* is a very large hemispherical gourd covered with antelope or other animal hide. The long neck extends up vertically from the gourd and opposite the player. A small, flat piece of metal is loosely attached to the bridge and serves as a jingle that provides the background buzz so common in this region. Traditionally the twenty-one strings were made of leather, but today nylon is more common.

Courtesy of Gilbert Blount

FIGURE 11.2
In a close-up of the *kora* bridge, notice that the strings stretch over the sides of the bridge, not the top, so that the fingers of each hand can reach half the strings. The sticks parallel to and below the strings stretched under the resonator cover are hand posts used to hold the instrument while playing.

12

Along the dirt roads of southern Africa, it is not uncommon to hear buzzing, metallic sounds ringing from within a large hollow gourd held by a dusty traveler. Inside is an instrument consisting of rows of metal tines stretched over a series of bars so that the ends can be plucked with the player's thumbs. The gourd serves as a resonator and may also have shells or bottle caps attached to it to create the buzzing background players consider indispensable. Known as the **mbira** to the Shona people of Zimbabwe, this instrument has a number of names for its many variations across the continent. It is often a traveler's personal pastime instrument (Figure 12.1).

The instrument also has a deep spiritual significance among the Shona, for it has the crucial function of calling to the ancestors in a ritual called the *bira*. As Paul Berliner described in his landmark 1978 study *The Soul of Mbira*, at all-night ceremonies people call upon the spirits to answer crucial questions; the constant variations in the *mbira* performance aid the participants in going into a trance in which spirits take over the participant's body. While the *mbira* has become an important national symbol and even taken over the function of the guitar in so-called "mbira pop" bands of the region, the Shona never forget these spiritual connections.

Despite the instrument's popularity as a personal recreational instrument, the Shona usually consider a solo performance incomplete. There must be at least one other *mbira* to form the community of the ensemble—that is, to play interlocking polyrhythms with the first player. A kind of rattle called a *hosho* and sometimes a small drum called a *ngoma* are also common additions to the ensemble, and of course singing and dancing are often just as important.

A Shona *mbira* piece is really a framework for a short ostinato melody. However, the flexibility of this framework allows for nearly endless variations on the basic melody and can continue for hours. On top of these complex yet infectious intertwining parts, the *mbira* player sings, at times in a near-whisper, at other times with emotional cries. These songs may be composed or improvised, but always draw their melody out of the fabric of the gently cycling *mbira* parts.

FIGURE **12.1**
The large traditional *mbira* of the Shona is the *mbira dzavadzimu*. It consists of twenty-two metal tines arranged in three rows. When the player plucks the keys with his or her thumbs and right index finger, the bottle caps lightly attached to the metal plate on the bottom provide a constant background buzz. The player usually puts the instrument inside a large hollow gourd (not shown here) for further resonance.

William Alves

An *Mbira* Performance

The Shona consider *Nyamaropa* to be among the oldest and most representative traditional pieces in the standard repertoire. It can be played for rituals as well as for entertainment.

The *mbira* part consists of a basic melody repeated over and over with variations. The basic melody, which lasts forty-eight pulses, goes by quickly—about every eight seconds for each repetition in this recording. The following graphic shows a representation of the notes as small rectangles arranged so that time is represented horizontally and pitch vertically.

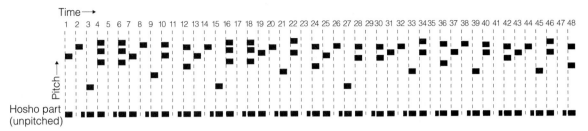

GRAPHIC 12.1

The basic *mbira* part for *Nyamaropa* (after Berliner 1978).

While such a graph may be helpful, the notes are as yet undifferentiated. The experience of listening to the piece is much different, sounding to the ear like multiple melodies—as indeed there are. In fact, a single musician is playing three distinct melodies *polyrhythmically*. Graphic 12.2 shows the same graph, but now with the notes of the three melodies distinguished by color. Though unified by the forty-eight-pulse cycle, each melody exists in its own meter, made clear when they are separated in Graphic 12.3.

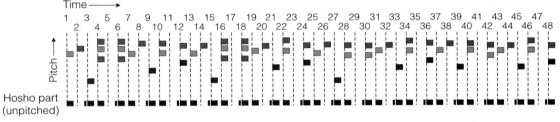

GRAPHIC 12.2

Here, the three melodies that make up the *mbira* part are colored red for the high melody, green for the middle melody, and blue for the low melody, demonstrating the different layers that the *mbira* player creates.

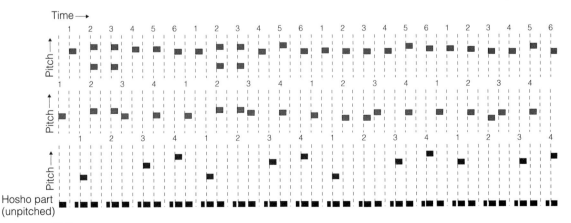

GRAPHIC 12.3

Each of the different layers has its own meter and start time. Here the three melodies are separated and their pulses numbered to show the metrical cycle for each one.

In the recording, we hear two *mbira* performers. Neither performer plays the above basic melody all the time. Each plays a separate variation of the melody, interlocking in such a way as to create yet another polyrhythmic level in the piece. In all the repetitions on this recording, the players create variations that diverge significantly from the bare version yet remain true to the structure that makes this piece recognizable as *Nyamaropa*. This structure is crucial to understanding this music.

Shona *mbira* pieces use only a certain subset of pitches at a given time during the basic melody. This rhythmic progression of pitch sets is as much a defining feature of a particular piece of music as its melodies, because while the melodic contours and rhythmic interactions may change considerably throughout all the variations in a performance, the sequence of available pitches remains the same. They create a sense of gentle back-and-forth motion, rocking with the participants of the *bira*.

What most distinguishes *Nyamaropa* from other *mbira* pieces is not the melodies themselves, but the sequence of available pitches during the cycle. For example, as we see in Graphic 12.4 below, for the first four pulses (counting from the point shown), only the tonic (pitch 1) and the fifth note of the scale (shown above as 5) are allowed. In the next three pulses, only pitches 3 and 7 are allowed, and so on.

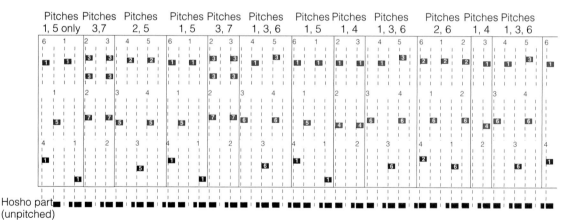

GRAPHIC **12.4**

This structure gives *Nyamaropa* a certain distinctive sequence of pitches similar to Western harmonic progressions but without Western chords. The number of pulses for each of the pitch sets is also important since it adds a characteristically asymmetrical harmonic rhythm—4+3+5 pulses for the first three quarters with a contrasting 5+2+5 phrase at the end.

The *mbira* part is only part of the performance. At least as important is the vocal part, which is usually sung by the lead *mbira* player in different singing styles appropriate for the words. Pieces may include a precomposed song with poetic lyrics, perhaps a short allegorical poem or a longer epic narrative. The singer may improvise poetry about the specific occasion, people in the audience, politics, and so on, or may use syllables without

Listening Guide

CD 1:5. *Nyamaropa* (excerpt), Hakurotwi Mude, voice and *mbira*; Cosmas Magaya, *mbira*; Ephraim Mutemasango, *hosho*.	
0:00	Listen to the low tones of the *mbira* to orient yourself to the basic melody cycle.
0:10	Singer enters in the *huro* style, loud cries improvised at the top of the singer's range, frequently ornamented with glissandi (sliding pitches) and yodeling (quick jumps between vibrational modes in the vocal cords).
0:31	Singer makes a sliding transition into the *mahon'era* style, a soft breathy voice at the bottom of the singer's range, also improvised with vocables. The singer spontaneously creates the melody by picking out notes in the *mbira* part.
0:54	Singer returns to the *huro* style.

CD1, Track 6 Nyamaropa examples (basic ostinato, high melody, middle melody, low melody)

specific meanings. On our listening selection we hear alternating *huro* and *mahon'era* singing styles—sung on **vocables**, syllables chosen for their expressive qualities but without any other meaning. This recording is excerpted from a long performance.

AFRICAN POPULAR MUSIC

13

In the mid-1970s, entering the famous club Afrika Shrine in Lagos, Nigeria was like opening the doors to a blast furnace of sound. A half-dozen percussionists, three or four trumpet and saxophone players, several guitarists, and six or seven singers fed a dense wall of rhythm with an ostinato-based groove that could go on for more than half an hour on a single song. Alternately playing saxophone and keyboards or singing was the lean, shirtless, face-painted leader of this band, a madman or hero, depending on your perspective, named Fela Kuti.

Fela (as millions familiarly called him) was the son of a pastor father who was also a musician and a mother who was a pioneering activist for social justice and women's rights. He built his own career in equal measure around music and social justice. As a youth, jazz, traditional African music, and the urban popular music styles known as highlife and juju formed his musical world. When given support by his parents to study medicine, he went to London but enrolled in a music school instead. Returning to a newly independent Nigeria in 1963, he started his own highlife band with a unique blend of European jazz, African beats, and American rhythm and blues.

FIGURE **13.1**
Fela Kuti performs at the Afrika Shrine.

A tour to the United States in 1969 brought a life-changing exposure to the African-American militancy of Malcolm X and the Black Panthers. Fela's music became a forum for protests against Africa's military dictatorships, the oppression of the poor, Western imperialism, and corruption. To reflect the pan-African identity he sought in his music as well as his politics, he dubbed his unique sound "Afro-Beat" and sang in pidgin English (a hybridized language spoken in much of West Africa) rather than his native Yoruba.

The successive military governments of Nigeria took notice, and at various times Fela was beaten and imprisoned, his residence burned to the ground. Soldiers even threw his then eighty-two-year-old mother out a second-story window. Such incidents only seemed to make his songs and the legendary harangues against political evils that he delivered between sets during his four-hour concerts all the more caustic. For his willingness to stand up for these principles, he became a hero to millions of Nigerians and a powerful symbol of popular music as a social force in modern Africa.

Popular music in Africa has often reflected the continent's uneasy struggle with issues of identity and nationalism, tradition and modernity. Even while adopting Western harmonies, instruments, and song forms, Fela and others also enriched it, self-consciously or not, with ostinatos, emphasis on percussion, responsorial forms, and layered textures (though not, in general, polyrhythm), all derived from their traditional African heritage. Still other influences, while ostensibly American, originated in or were influenced by the African diaspora (the scattering of Africans throughout the Americas because of slavery)—the horn sections from swing bands and rhythm and blues; the rhythms of Caribbean dances, especially the Cuban rumba; American funk and soul, especially that of James Brown; and reggae, to name a few.

When Fela died in 1997 from AIDS-related illness, more than a million people attended his funeral procession down the streets of Lagos. His son Femi Kuti is a very popular performer in his own right who carries on the Afro-Beat legacy at the Afrika Shrine and through tours and recordings.

Popular Forms in West Africa

Fela's Afro-Beat had its roots in the coastal and urban areas of West Africa, where there is a long history of Africans adapting European popular forms and instruments to their own expression. Originally known as palm-wine music, after the favorite beverage drunk where these entertainers played, this lively guitar music was by the 1920s known as **highlife**. Popular dance bands in the 1950s known for their large horn sections took over the name and style. **Juju** was a similar popular band music in Nigeria. Beginning in 1966, civil war and political instability in Ghana and Nigeria led to the dispersion of these styles, spreading them to other African countries and also to Europe.

Some highlife and juju artists, such as "King" Sunny Ade, became multi-millionaire pop stars and attained success in Europe and the United States. The same Africanist impulses that influenced Fela around the 1970s also fed into a new Nigerian style known as **fuji**. Drawing from a tradition of Islamic praise songs, traditional talking-drum music called *apala*, and popular dance music, fuji featured huge percussion sections but no guitars. The style known as **mbalax** in Senegal also popularized innovative connections to traditional instruments, styles, and forms.

Sometimes the most impressive characteristic of bands in each of these styles is their sheer size, often numbering over two dozen performers, all contributing to a powerful groove. Despite the lack of polyrhythms, this multilayered groove is the amplified version of the traditional ostinato, and the bands still reflect the African sense of community.

Popular Forms in Southern Africa

The ethnic diversity of South Africa, combined with its economic development and creative responses to apartheid, make it arguably the most creatively active country on the continent in the area of popular music. An early example is **gumboot** music or *isicathulo*, a style of dance performed by workers at the diamond mines, who wear long waterproof boots. To the accompaniment of a guitar they clap and slap their boots, creating their own percussion.

In the 1920s and 30s, tightly improvised folk harmonies (developed from the Western chords introduced in missionary schools and the polyphony found in traditional African music) sung by a cappella groups (consisting entirely of singers without instrumental accompaniment) became very popular in Zulu areas. One of these groups, the Original Evening Birds, in 1939 recorded chorus leader's Solomon Linda's "The Lion" ("Mbube") which became such a hit that the style itself became known as *mbube*. After this song found its way across the Atlantic, it eventually became the 1961 doo-wop hit "The Lion Sleeps Tonight," although at first Linda was not credited.

Although American jazz influenced many South African bands, most disbanded following the forced removal of black South Africans to townships and "tribal homelands" in the 1950s. An exception were the homemade bands of cheap pennywhistles and one-string basses who played music known as **pennywhistle jive** or *kwela*, which was also related to British "skiffle" music. From such humble groups larger and very popular bands developed in the 1950s.

By the 1960s saxophones and electric guitars replaced the pennywhistles and acoustic strings. Together with the influence of American rhythm and blues, traditional ostinatos, and gumboot music, these bands originated a style known as **sax jive** or *mbaqanga*. They soon added female choruses reminiscent of mbube's tight harmonies, though often with a contrasting male "groaner" voice. A cappella music, often now called *iscathamiya*, continued to be popular although white authorities frequently banned many of these groups.

FIGURE **13.2**
Ladysmith Black
Mambazo in concert.

Sax jive and iscathamiya eventually caught the attention of American pop composer Paul Simon. Simon collaborated with some township jive musicians and the a cappella group Ladysmith Black Mambazo in his African-influenced album *Graceland* of 1986. The album was a huge hit, and exposed Ladysmith Black Mambazo and others to a wide international audience (Figure 13.2).

REFERENCES

Discography

Drumming from West Africa

Various artists. *Ghana: Ancient Ceremonies, Songs, and Dance Music*. New York/Los Angeles: Elektra/Nonesuch 9 72082-2, 1979/1991.

Various artists. *Rhythms of Life, Songs of Wisdom: Akan Music from Ghana, West Africa*. Smithsonian Folkways SFCD40463, 1996.

Music of the Jalolu

Kanté, Mory. *Sabou*. London: Riverboat Records/World Music Network TUGCD1034, 2004.

Konte, Dembo, Kausu Kuyateh and Mawdo Suso. *Jaliology*. Danbury, CT: Green Linnet Records XEN 4036, 1995.

Mandingo Griot Society. *Mandingo Griot Society*. Chicago: Flying Fish FF70076, 1979/1992.

Various Artists. *Mali: Cordes Anciennes*. Paris: Buda Records 1977822, 2001.

Mbira Music

Various artists. *Zimbabwe: The Soul of Mbira*. New York/Los Angeles: Elektra/Nonesuch 9 72054-2, 1973/1995.

Other Traditional Music

Adzido Pan-African Dance Ensemble. *Traditional Songs and Dances from Africa*. East Grinstead, UK: ARC Music EUCD 1590, 2000.

Various artists. *Africa—Drum Chant & Instrumental Music*. New York: Elektra/Nonesuch, 9 72073-2, 1976/1988.

Various artists. *African Tribal Music and Dances*. Beverly Hills, CA: Legacy International CD 328; also Santa Monica, CA: Laserlight/Tradition Records 12 179, 1993.

Various artists. *Echoes of the Forest: Music of the Central African Pygmies*. Roslyn, NY: Ellipsis Arts 4020, 1995.

Various artists. *Kenya and Tanzania: Witchcraft and Ritual Music*. New York/Los Angeles: Elektra/Nonesuch 9 72066-2, 1975/1991.

Various artists. *Musique centrafricaine*. France: Ocora OCR 43, 1962, 1983; re-released on *Musique banda*, France: Prophet 22 CD 468448-2, 2004.

Various artists. *Sierra Leone: Musiques traditionnelles*. Paris: Ocora C 580036, 1992.

Popular Music

Ade, King Sunny. *Juju Music*. New York: Mango CCD 9712, 1982. (Juju)

Ayinde, Sikiru "Barrister." *New Fuji Garbage*. London: Ace Records/Globe Style CDORBD 067. (Fuji)

Kuti, Fela. *The Best of Fela Kuti*. Universal City, CA: MCA Records 314 543 197-2, 2000. (Afro-Beat)

Ladysmith Black Mambazo. *Shaka Zulu*. Los Angeles: Warner Bros. 25582-2, 1987. (Iscathamiya)

Maal, Baaba. *Djam Leelii*. London: Rogue Records: FMSD 5014, 1989. (Mbalax)

Mapfumo, Thomas. *The Best of Thomas Mapfumo*. Culver City, CA: Hemisphere 7243 8 35582 2, 1995.

Touré, Ali Farka. *Niafunké*. Salem, MA: Hannibal HNCD 1443, 1999.

Various artists. *The Rough Guide to the Music of South Africa*. London: World Music Network RGNET 1020, 1998.

Bibliography

Arom, Simha. *African Polyphony and Polyrhythm: Musical Structure and Methodology*, trans. Martin Thom, Barbara Tuckett, and Raymond Boyd. Cambridge: Cambridge University Press, 1991.

Barz, Gregory. *Music in East Africa*. Oxford: Oxford University Press, 2004.

Bebey, Francis. *African Music: A People's Art*. New York: L. Hill, 1975.

Berliner, Paul. *The Soul of Mbira: Music and Traditions of the Shona People of Zimbabwe*. Berkeley: University of California Press, 1978.

Charry, Eric. Mande Music: *Traditional and Modern Music of the Maninka and Mandinka of Western Africa*. Chicago: University of Chicago Press, 2000.

Chernoff, John Miller. *African Rhythm and African Sensibility: Aesthetics and Social Action in African Musical Idioms*. Chicago: University of Chicago Press, 1979.

Floyd, Malcolm, ed. *Composing the Music of Africa: Composition, Interpretation, and Realisation*. Brookfield, VT: Ashgate, 1999.

Graham, Ronnie. *The Da Capo Guide to Contemporary African Music*. New York: Da Capo Press, 1988.

Jones, A. M. *Studies in African Music*. London: Oxford University Press, 1959.

Merriam, Alan P. *African Music in Perspective*. New York: Garland, 1982.

Nketia, J. H. Kwabena. *The Music of Africa*. New York: W. W. Norton, 1974.

Stone, Ruth. *Music in West Africa*. Oxford: Oxford University Press, 2004.

Europeans originally used the term *Middle East* to loosely define the area between the Near East (modern Turkey, near Europe) and the Far East (China and Japan, far from Europe). Modern journalism is responsible for broadly defining the Middle East as the Islamic crescent stretching from North Africa to Iran, including the Jewish state of Israel. In addition, the term Middle East is sometimes stretched to include Turkey, Armenia, Azerbaijan, and Pakistan. Although many ethnic groups in this area have an ancient history, this chapter will concentrate on three of the most prominent ethnic-linguistic categories: the Arabs, the Iranians, and the Jews. We will not have space to discuss the Turks separately, nor other important and distinct groups.

559–330 BCE

Achaemenid dynasty in Iran conquers Babylon, Assyria, Egypt. Musical influences possibly travel between India, Persia, and Greece. Western influences are strong when Alexander conquers the Achaemenids and extends a Greek empire all the way to India. Greek music theory includes a complex scale theory and an association of arithmetic and numerology with musical scales.

c. 1000 BCE

Rise of ancient monotheistic Hebrew civilization in Palestine. A hereditary caste of musicians known as the Levites direct sacred music.

c. 3000–2000 BCE

Sumerian civilization includes harps and tuning by fifths.

c. 3000–1080 BCE

Ancient Egyptian music also emphasizes harps and flutes.

PART 3

The Middle East and North Africa

395–1453
Byzantine empire with capital at Constantinople (Istanbul). Byzantine music was based on modes called *echoi*, which implied not only a particular scale, but also appropriate melodic patterns for each. Names of what seem to be modes are also recorded in early Iranian music, possibly the early basis for the modal systems of *dastgah* (Iranian) and *maqam* (Arabic).

70 CE
Romans destroy Jewish Temple in Jerusalem. Musical practice of the Levites is ultimately lost and replaced by regional practices in synagogues led by cantors. In the centuries after the destruction of the Temple, many Jewish people leave Palestine to settle in North Africa, Europe, and elsewhere.

c. 4 BCE–28 CE
Lifetime of Jesus. Early Christian chant is apparently based on Jewish models.

64–30 BCE
Middle East and Egypt come under Roman rule.

INTRODUCTION TO THE REGION

14

**FIRST LISTEN
CD 1:8**
Dastgah Mahur.
Hussein Ali Zodeh,
tar.

As you enter the cool marble monument surrounding the tomb of Hafiz (c.1325–c.1389), one of Iran's most famous poets, your gaze is drawn not down onto the tomb itself, but upwards toward a beautiful example of pattern in Islamic art (Figure 14.1). Every space in the swirling design is filled with intricate figures and lines that weave elaborate paths.

These visual patterns find a counterpart in the ornate melodic paths of classical Iranian solo improvisation, where every space also seems to overflow with gracefully fluid ornamentation. Classical improvisation in

---

632–736
Period of Islamic conquest, spreading Islam from Spain through North Africa, the Middle East, Armenia, Iran, and India. Arabic musical influences and instruments follow through these areas, also into much of Europe. Arabic language and scholarship becomes a unifying element throughout Islamic areas. The establishment of affluent courts forms the basis for the secular patronage of art music.

9th–13th C
Golden age of Islamic scholarship at Baghdad. Many works of ancient Greece, including works of music theory, are translated. Period of the great Islamic music theorists: al-Kindi, al-Farabi, Ibn Sina, and Safi al-Din.

c. 570–632
Lifetime of Muhammad, founder of Islam.

1096–1187
European crusaders invade, occupy Palestine, including Jerusalem.

Iran is based on linear melodies assembled, like mosaic tiles, one after the other and decorated with tiny motives and ornaments.

In mosques and other holy places, visual patterns draw one into contemplation, perhaps of the **Qur'an**, *the holy book of Islam*. Its eternal message is reflected in the ever-repeating and circular patterns found in mosaics, carpets, calligraphy, and architecture in the Middle East. Just as the radial symmetry of the Hafiz tomb mosaic draws the eye ever inward, so does the elaborate music of Iranian improvisation invite thoughtful reflection. Still, this introspection can find surprisingly passionate, emotional expression as well, a feeling of transcendence that is at once deeply spiritual and profoundly human, as expressed in this poem by Hafiz himself:

> O keep squeezing drops of the Sun
> From your prayers and work and music
> And from your companions' beautiful laughter
>
> And from the most insignificant movements
> Of your own holy body.
>
> Now, sweet one,
> Be wise.
> Cast all your votes for Dancing!

—From "Cast All Your Votes for Dancing!"
by Hafiz of Shiraz[1]

[1] From *I Heard the God Laughing*, by Daniel Ladinsky. Copyright © 1996 by Daniel Ladinsky. Reprinted by permission of the author.

© CORBIS

FIGURE 14.1
The ceiling of the tomb of Hafiz (c. 1320–c. 1389) at Shiraz, Iran, shows elaborate mosaic patterns. These patterns reflect the intricacy also found in Islamic art music as well as its preoccupation with mathematics in music theory.

1483–1918
Period of the Turkish Ottoman Empire, which eventually includes much of Eastern Europe, Syria, Armenia, Egypt, and Mesopotamia.

1798–1918
Napoleon's entry into Egypt begins the period of European colonization of North Africa and the Middle East. Cultural influences come from Europe, sometimes prompting a backlash. Western-style pedagogy has been adopted in many national universities and music schools, and the use of Western harmony is common, especially in popular and light classical music.

1948
Israel is established as an independent Jewish state.

1949–1962
North African states become independent. In some countries nationalism has produced a revival of indigenous art music, often government-sponsored, as well as distinctive popular music.

1979
Iran becomes fundamentalist Islamic state, restricts the practice of some music.

ELEMENTS OF MIDDLE EASTERN MUSIC

15

As one would expect from an expansive geography and diverse traditions, generalizations are difficult. Nevertheless, here are some of the most distinctive qualities characteristic of much of the music of this region.

■ **Elaborate Melodies and Melismas** Middle-Eastern melodies are often ornate and filled with intricate figurations. Elaborate **melismas**, *sung melodies with many notes to a syllable*, are common.

■ **Improvisation Based on Basic Tones or Melodies** In the Middle East improvisations are based either on elaborations around the traversal of a series of core pitches, or, as in Iran, more explicit melodies.

■ **Heterophony** Because Middle Eastern classical music focuses on melody, the melodic instruments in ensemble usually create a characteristic texture of heterophony, the simultaneous performance of different elaborations of the same melody.

■ **Rhythms Based on Beat Patterns** Rhythms are often elaborations of a specific beat pattern or basic rhythm inside the meter.

■ **The Use of Quarter-Tones** Modes in the Middle East have a wide variety of scales, some of which feature intervals that lie almost exactly in the middle between the tones on a Western piano keyboard. These distinctive divisions are called quarter-tones.

The Middle East and Religion

Judaism is one of the oldest continuously practiced religions in the world, and, unlike Islam or Christianity, can imply not only a set of beliefs, but also an ethnic identity. That ethnicity has largely remained through the centuries, in spite of the Jewish **diaspora**, *the scattering of Jews from their ancestral homeland in Palestine* to many areas throughout the world. In the twentieth century, the phenomenon of Zionism has encouraged the return of hundreds of thousands of Jews back to this region, now the nation of Israel. They have brought influences from many different areas around the world but have retained many distinctively Jewish cultural and musical traits, especially in their sacred music. Very old Jewish minorities also exist in areas such as Yemen, Ethiopia, and Morocco. Although the center of Christianity moved from the Middle East to Europe in the early centuries of the modern era, important Christian traditions also remain in countries such as Lebanon, Egypt, and Ethiopia.

Islam is a religion founded by Muhammad (c. 570–632), who, unlike Jesus to the Christians, was a prophet, not a deity. Like Christianity and Judaism, Islam is a monotheistic religion descended from the biblical Abraham/Ibrahim. The Five Pillars of Islamic faith include a confession of faith, prayer five times daily, almsgiving, fasting during the month of Ramadan, and making at least one pilgrimage to Mecca (in Saudi Arabia), the birth-place of Islam. Followers of Islam are also called Muslims.

Islam was founded on the Arabian peninsula, and, after Muhammad's death, spread with amazing swiftness through Arabic military conquest from Spain to Central Asia and eventually India and Indonesia. With the spread of Islam came Arabic culture and language, especially since Muhammad decreed that the *Qur'an* should only be read in Arabic. This rule had the brilliant effect (at least in theory) of binding together all Muslims of the world with a single language and so helped the spread of Arabic music and music theory throughout the Islamic world.

Islam and Music

Even after centuries of debate, the tension between the pious contemplation of the next world idealized by Islam and the celebration of life as found in Hafiz's poetry continues to provide a backdrop of controversy to music and dance in Islamic countries. In Egypt the **ghawazi**, *women who dance for entertainment*, are often in conflict with conservative factions who seek to allow only religious genres of music. According to those conservatives, even classical music, such as the solo improvisation that we will hear, can distract the senses that should be focused on spiritual existence.

There is no such thing as Islamic religious music. The singing, chanting, or instrumental performance that takes place in a religious context is simply not considered music; the Arabic word *musiqa* is never used in a religious context. Certain influential, conservative Islamic scholars have interpreted some Islamic texts as condemning the practice of music, excepting only certain religious non-music, such as the five-times-daily call to prayer, the chanting of *Qur'anic* verses, and some folk songs associated with everyday life. Today Islamic sects differ in what should be allowed.

As a result of this attitude, music never found a patron in religious institutions in the Middle East as it did in Europe. The vast majority of music was and is performed as secular entertainment. Some forms of Islam especially discourage music and dance for entertainment, although this attitude hasn't prevented the development of rich traditions in many Islamic countries.

At certain times and places under especially reactionary Islamic rule, non-religious music has been banned. After the revolution in Iran in 1979, Western music as well as classical Iranian music, if heard at all, was performed only in private homes. However, just before his death in 1989, the supreme Iranian religious leader Ruhollah Khomeini issued an edict that generally accepted music, with some restrictions. More recently, the Taliban government of Afghanistan (1995–2002) banned virtually all non-religious music and punished those caught with cassette tapes, videos, or even musical instruments. While these extremist views are certainly not representative of the majority of Islam, they do highlight the controversy surrounding the legitimacy of certain kinds of music in Islamic history.

One of the most revered forms of Islamic religious music is the *chanting of Qur'an verses*, known as **qira'ah** or **tilawah**. Although very strict rules govern pronunciation, articulation, placement of pauses, and so on, these prescriptions still leave open many possibilities for musical interpretation. Lay chanters learn very simple syllabic settings based on fixed melodic formulas, but in many countries, particularly Egypt, venerated traditions of exceptionally florid *Qur'anic* chant have developed. These artful styles have greatly influenced many secular song styles as well.

The **adhan**, *call to prayer*, is a familiar sound in most Islamic countries. Today, the **mu'adhdhin**, the *singers of the adhan*, chant over loudspeakers placed in the minarets of mosques and often over radio and television as well. These florid two- or three-minute songs float through the streets of most Islamic cities five times a day, and the faithful are expected to pray in response. Allowing for regional variations, *adhan* styles, like *Qur'anic* chanting, are unaccompanied, non-pulsatile, and often include melismas.

Sufism is a mystical form of Islam that is more accepting of music in a religious context than the more orthodox branches of the religion. In the Sufi ceremony known as **dhikr** ("remembrance"), cyclic rhythmic figures accompany repetitive chanting of scriptural text and sometimes dance, eventually inducing a joyful union with God or even an ecstatic trance.

One famous Sufi dance tradition is that of the *Mevlevi* order of Turkey, better known as the **dervishes**, dancers who whirl around and around to achieve this spiritual union. The dervishes are accompanied by a large ensemble of *nay* flutes, *daff* drums, other instruments and a chorus, often singing the words of the thirteenth-century mystical poet Rumi. While the music of these ceremonies has influenced drum patterns and other elements of secular Arabic music, perhaps the most important connection between Sufism and secular Arabic music lies in their shared awareness of music's ability to awaken and express spiritual ecstasy, as described in this medieval Sufi treatise:

> Music is in the coming to rest of all thoughts from the burdens of the human state. It excites the temperament of men. It is the stimulant of divine mysteries. To some, it is a temptation because they are imperfect. For others, it is a sign, for they have reached perfection.
> –Ruzbihan Baqli (d. 1209), *The Treatise on Holiness* [1]

---

[1] Adapted from the translation by Seyyed Hossein Nasr in "Islam and Music: The Views of Ruzbahan Baqli, the Patron Saint of Shiraz," *Studies in Comparative Religion* 10 (1976): 37–41.

16 THE INSTRUMENTS OF THE REGION

Many of the most important musical instruments in the world apparently originated in the Middle East. Countries as far apart as Latin America to the west and China to the east have instruments with a common origin in the Middle East. Very few European instruments are *not* descended, at least indirectly, from Middle Eastern sources.

Plucked chordophones are especially important throughout the region, both in the variety known as the **'ud** and the long-necked variety known generally as the **tanbur**. Both are played monophonically (one note at a time), although drone strings are often intermittently strummed. There are many types of bowed fiddles, and, since the colonial period, the European violin (also known as the **kaman**) has become a popular instrument. Other European instruments commonly used in classical or semi-classical repertories include the clarinet, cello, and double bass. Harps and lyres have an ancient history in the region, although today they are chiefly found in Africa.

Elaborate traditions of singing are common throughout the Middle East. Low, husky tones or rich, reedy timbres are common. Ornamentation is extensive, and vibrato may be wholly absent or present in an exaggerated form as an ornament. Melismas are especially characteristic of Middle Eastern singing. A distinctive folk practice associated with the women of North Africa is the **zagharit**, a *ululation* (*high cry rapidly trilled with the tongue*) that accompanies celebrations. In fast folk dances or other festive pieces, aerophones sometimes imitate the *zagharit*. In order to play long continuous melodies, players of aerophones such as the double-reed zurna practice **circular breathing**—*a difficult technique in which the player blows out while simultaneously breathing in through his nose in order to achieve an uninterrupted air stream.*

INSTRUMENTS OF THE MIDDLE EAST AND NORTH AFRICA

FIGURE **16.1**
Historically, the *'ud*, shown here, is the most important art music instrument of the Islamic region. A fretless, pear-shaped lute with five or six **courses** (*sets of strings*) and a distinctively angled peg box (where the strings are attached to the tuning pegs), it has elaborately carved lattice-work on the sound hole and is traditionally played with an eagle-feather plectrum. While at different times in its history it has had frets, the modern *'ud* has no frets. A highly respected classical instrument, today it is less common than the long-necked lute. After being introduced to Spain, and after the addition of frets, and additional strings, it became the lute (from *al-'ud*) of Renaissance Europe. The *'ud* is found throughout the Arab world and also in Turkey, Iran, Greece, and East Africa, where it is of secondary importance.

FIGURE **16.2**
Long-necked fretted lutes come in many sizes and varieties, sometimes in a single country. Closely related versions of the long-necked lute in this region include the *tanbur* (Arabic countries), the *sehtar* (Iran), *buzuq* (Syria and Iraq), *buzuki* (Greece), and *tambura* (Bulgaria). Here we see the Turkish *saz* or *baglama*. In general, this instrument has a tear-drop-shaped body and three or four strings, the lowest of which may be a drone string. It often uses metal strings and has a much brighter timbre than the *'ud*. Players extend notes by repeatedly strumming them (known as tremolo in the West). In between melody notes, players also often strum drone pitches tuned to the tonic or tonic and the fifth scale degree above.

FIGURE **16.3**
The respected classical plucked lute of Iran, the *tar* is a distinctive variation of the long-necked lute with an hourglass-shaped sound body (resonator) covered in sheepskin.

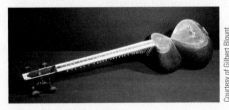

FIGURE **16.4A**
The *rabab*, spike fiddle, is a bowed chordophone with a spike on the bottom. It is held vertically with its spike resting on the ground or ankle. This version has a roughly hemispherical resonator and cylindrical neck but no fingerboard. It may have from one to four strings. Instead of firmly pressing the string down on the neck, the finger stops the string by sliding along it. A common folk instrument with a variety of sizes and types of resonators, the *rabab* is sometimes used as a classical instrument in Morocco and Iraq. Known as the *rabab* in most Arabic countries, the instrument is also known as the *joza* (Iraq), *kamancheh* (Iran), *gijak* (Central Asia), and *k'yamancha* (Armenia), the form shown here.

FIGURE 16.4B

The various forms and names of the *kamanche*—a short-necked fiddle usually with a fingerboard and a pear-shaped body—may overlap with those of the *rabab*. The *kamanche* is known as the *rabab* in North Africa, the *k'aman* in Armenia, the *gadulka* in Bulgaria, and the *kemençe* in Turkey.

© Chris Lisle/CORBIS

FIGURE 16.5

The *santur* is a trapezoidal hammered dulcimer (zither). The strings are stretched over bridges in multiple courses (multiple strings per note) and struck with small wooden mallets. Some varieties are fitted with a damping mechanism. Known as the *santur* in Iran, Iraq, and Turkey, and as the *santuri* in India, the instrument is also found in Europe, China, and Korea.

© Hideo Haga/HAGA/The Image Works

FIGURE 16.6

The *qanun*, here played by Antoíne Harb, is a plucked zither shaped like a rectangle with one corner cut off. It is similar to the European psaltery, but is plucked with ring-plectra attached to the fingers of both hands. A series of levers and intermediate bridges for each string allow quick changes of tunings for different maqam. Elaborate tremolos (repeated notes) and glissandos (scale sweeps) are common. The instrument is also found in Southeast Europe and in Turkey, where it is called the *kanun*.

Sami Asmar, Courtesy of A. J. Racy

FIGURE 16.7

The *nay* is an end-blown notch flute found in Iran, Turkey, and Arabic countries. Note that it is played from the side of the mouth and held at an oblique angle. It is the only aerophone commonly found in classical ensembles.

© Craig Aurness/CORBIS

(continued)

INSTRUMENTS OF THE MIDDLE EAST AND NORTH AFRICA

FIGURE **16.8**

The *zurna* is a loud conical-bore double-reed with a bell flare at the end. There may be a metal disc that the lips rest on. The thick reeds are taken entirely into the mouth, which forms an air chamber in which the reeds vibrate. The *zurna* migrated to medieval Europe, where it became the shawm, ancestor of the modern oboe. Known as the *zurna* in East Arabic countries, Turkey, and the Caucasus, the instrument is also known as the *surnay* (Central Asia), *sornay* (Iran), *gaita* (North Africa), and *mizmar* (Egypt).

FIGURE **16.9**

The Egyptian *arghul* is a single-reed aerophone with two cylindrical pipes tied together and blown at the same time, in effect a double clarinet. One pipe plays the melody and the other is a drone pipe without fingerholes. In another single-reed instrument with double pipes—the *mijwiz* or *zumarrah*—the two pipes are played together but slightly detuned, creating a beating effect. In Mediterranean countries, cow horns may attach to the ends of the pipes. Single-pipe, single-reed instruments came to Europe in the form of the chalumeau, the ancestor of the clarinet. Instruments similar to the *arghul* include the *mizwij* in Iraq, the *jifti* in the Gulf states, the *dozal* among the Kurds, and the *magruna* in North Africa.

FIGURE **16.10**

The *daff* (or *def*) is a shallow frame drum played with hands and fingers. Though used in many ways throughout Islamic areas, it is often associated with religious contexts, such as accompaniment to Islamic chant and Sufi rituals. Small cymbals may be added to the frame to create the familiar form of the tambourine to accompany folk songs and dances. With cymbals, the instrument is known as the *riqq*, *bendir*, or *tar*, depending on the size.

FIGURE **16.11**

Known as the *darabukkah* in most Arabic countries, this instrument is a goblet-shaped drum of various sizes made of ceramic, wood, or metal, and played with the fingers. The bottom is open. Especially popular in North Africa, this instrument is held under the player's arm or on the player's knee. It is also known as the *dumbuk* (Iraq), *zarb* or *tombak* (Iran), and the *darbuka* (Turkey).

ᴬ˙ᵉ ⁿ 🜲 ⓖ ARABIC MUSIC THEORY

17

At a concert of Arabic classical music, one might notice, even more than the music itself, the transported state of the singer, as if expressing the poetry was at once creating a sense of inward ecstasy as well as an outward connection with the audience. This is the feeling of **tarab**, the *transcendent emotional experience* that comes from the combination of highly expressive music and poetry. The importance of the word in Arabic art reflects the importance of the *Qur'an*, which is a single unified work believed to be the literal word of God.

Vocal music, therefore, from art music to folk music is paramount in Arabic musical culture. From pre-Islamic sources we learn of the long tradition of caravan songs, songs of women, entertainers, and other folk songs on the Arabian peninsula. Diverse folk traditions continue to thrive throughout the Arabic world. The traditions of **responsorial** (*alternating leader/ group singing*) and **antiphonal** (*two alternating groups singing*) choral music in Saudi Arabia remind one of the similar poetic forms recorded in the Bible.

Following the expansion of the early Islamic world, a new internationalism brought rich art music traditions from other regions, especially Byzantium (modern Turkey), which had a history of improvisation and composition based on modes known as **echoi**. This tradition, which extended back to the ancient Greeks and probably long before, plus early Greek manuscripts, formed the foundation of a golden age of scholarship centered in Baghdad, where writers such as al-Farabi (d. 950) wrote extensively on the construction of scales and rhythmic modes in music.

Following the fall of Baghdad to the Mongols (1258) and the later rise of the Ottoman empire (especially 1512–1520), however, this sophisticated and unique art music tradition represented by al-Farabi and other Arab theorists, musicians, and poets largely declined. Arabic classical traditions distinct from those of Turkey made a resurgence in the late nineteenth and early twentieth century, when the *modal construct* known as the **maqam** acquired its modern form.

The *Maqam* Scale

Writers usually introduce the *maqam* by its tuning theory, which forms a crucial link not just to the great medieval theorists such as al-Farabi who wrote about it, but also to ancient Greece and Byzantium. Theorists at that time built up scales from *segments of four notes* (**tetrachords**) related to one another by the mathematics of vibrating string ratios. For example, they represented the interval we know as the perfect fifth by the simple ratio 3:2. Successive applications of this ratio created other intervals from which scales derived. This tuning system, known in Europe as "Pythagorean" after its supposed Greek inventor, is also the basis for ancient music theory in China and probably India.

Much more than a mathematical abstraction to the Greeks or to al-Farabi, this process was a way of making perceptible the beautiful mathematical relationships of God's creation, and the mystical importance of numerical ratios is also the basis for the geometrical abstractions of Islamic art. While this tuning system led to the twelve-tone system of Europe, Arabic musicians took it further, creating a theoretical system of twenty-four notes per octave. This tuning system therefore has intervals that are about half the size of the smallest European interval (the semitone) and so are called **quarter-tones**. The question of whether the quarter-tones should be precisely equal, like semitones in modern European tuning, or if they vary slightly to maintain traditional ratios is still controversial. Although fretted chordophones reflect this tuning system, in practice the pitches are varied with subtle inflections to contribute to the ecstatic feeling evoked by the music.

Whatever the details of the tuning system used, each quarter-tone pitch in a two-octave scale has its own name, although many modern writers prefer to use the European alphabetic system, in which the first seven letters of the alphabet represent the basic diatonic pitches, with additional symbols called accidentals. In addition to the sharp (♯) and flat (♭) used in Europe to indicate the displacement of a scale degree by a semitone up or down, respectively, Arabic theorists have added accidentals representing a lowering of a pitch by a quarter-tone (♭) and raising it by a quarter-tone sharp (♯). (Iranians use different symbols.) In this section we will use the letter system.

Like their Greek and Byzantine predecessors, Arabic theorists build up scales from smaller segments, called *jins*, which are usually tetrachords but may also be trichords or pentachords. Some theorists give the scales of *maqam* in versions extending more than an octave and with different pitches ascending and descending. Nevertheless, the central ascending octave of seven pitches is the most characteristic part of this scale, as we see here in one version of the scale *maqam nahawand*. The bold letters indicate the tonic of the scale—G in this case, although it can be transposed to fit any instrument or vocal range. Note that the pitch B exists in two versions: natural when the melodic line is ascending and flat when descending. The brackets show the tetrachords from which this scale is constructed.

GRAPHIC **17.1**

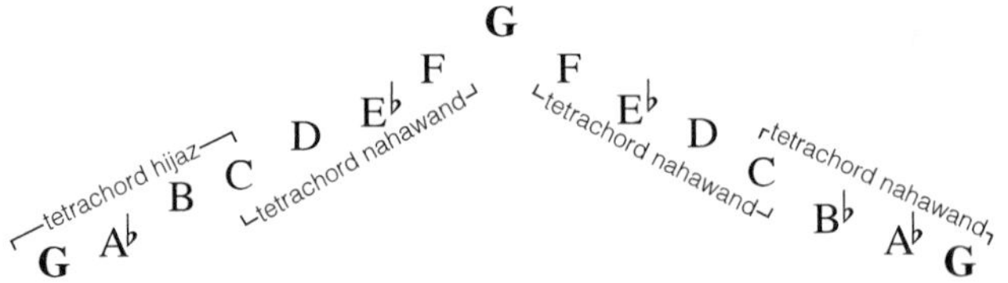

While quarter-tones are not used between adjacent scale steps, steps of ¾ of a tone or 1¼ tone (intervals quite unfamiliar to the Western ear) commonly occur, as we see here in a *maqam huzam*. Here the flat with a slash through it (♭̸) indicates that the note is lowered a quarter-tone. Therefore in this scale, the interval between D and E (♭̸) (E half-flat) is ¾ of a tone, and between E (♭̸) and F is 1¼. Note how this scale indicates that the pitches B and A are sometimes treated differently in ascending and descending versions.

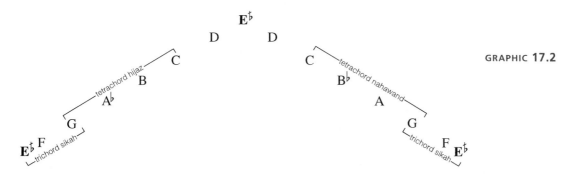

GRAPHIC **17.2**

Other Characteristics of a *Maqam*

The scale is just part of the definition of a *maqam*. Some *maqam* may share the same characteristic scale and yet be treated differently in improvisation, resulting in a distinct emotional experience for each. The *maqam* is therefore represented in its purest form in *non-pulsatile improvisations*, known as **taqsim** if played by a solo instrument. **Layali** is a similar vocal form which use melismas on the syllables *"ya layl, ya 'ayn"* ("oh night, oh eyes") with one or more instrumentalists following the singer's improvisations. Such abstractions, rather like the abstractions of Islamic decorative art, serve as introductions or interludes to extended songs based on classical or colloquial poetry sung by a soloist and accompanied by an ensemble.

The performance of the **taqsim** is *a journey through a sequence of emphasized pitches, the principal tones of the maqam scale*, a form known as the **sayr** (path) of the *maqam*. In this schematic representation from a performance of a *taqsim* in *maqam hijaz* on the *'ud*, Sultan Hamid of Bahrain exposes the nature of the *maqam* by playing around pitches that are temporary focal points. In the first line, his melody undulates around the principal pitch represented by the letter D (indicated by the red dotted line), but by the second line he shifts his attention to the pitch G.

GRAPHIC **17.3**

Each of these pitches will in turn form a point of focus around which the performer weaves supple elaborations of the melodic line. Just as Arabic calligraphy has no sharp corners, the improvisations of the taqsim consists of graceful arabesques connecting one tone to another.

Unlike performances of Indian ragas or other modal types around the world, traditional Arabic performances commonly use **modulation**, *temporary shifts to a related* maqam, and certain modulations are characteristic of different maqam. A tetrachord or other jin which is the same in two maqam scales can serve as a common point to help smooth a modulation from one to the other.

Rhythm in Arabic Music

As one might expect in a tradition so closely bound to the art of the poetic song and the importance of the word, the complex meters of classical Arabic poetry have served as a framework for rhythm in classical music. Known by a variety of names, here as ***iqa'***, these meters are defined not only by durations and accents, but by levels of accents, so that different beats may have characteristic sounds. An *iqa'* is defined more as a characteristic rhythmic pattern than a hierarchy of beat divisions, and different *iqa'* may share the same meter. The *iqa'* rhythmic pattern called ***maqsum***, a simple quadruple pattern, is commonly used in Egyptian folk music, among other repertories. The right hand in the center of the drum makes the low drum stroke "dumm" and the higher tone "takk" is made towards the edge of the drum.

GRAPHIC **17.4**

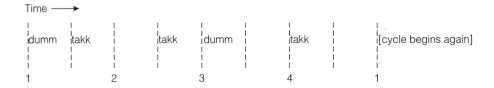

This *iqa'* pattern, called ***wahdah***, while also contained in a simple quadruple meter like *maqsum*, has a very different sound. "Mah" is a low left-hand stroke on the drum.

GRAPHIC **17.5**

The primary carrier of the *iqa'* is often the *riqq* (tambourine) player in the classical ensemble or the *darrabukka* (goblet drum) player in folk and dance ensembles, although they rarely play the *iqa'* pattern in its most basic form. Here is an example of one possible interpretation of the *iqa' maqsum* by a *darrabukha* drummer. *Kah* is a high left hand drum stroke.

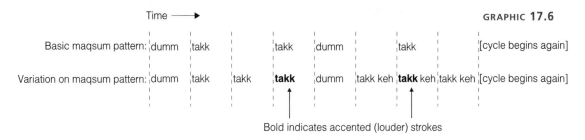

In any case, drummers' mnemonic syllables define the beats of the cycle. For example, the onomatopeic syllable *dumm* refers to the low sound that comes from the middle of the drumhead, while *takk* comes from near the edge of the head.

Iqa' can be considerably more complex than the examples above, especially in the classical tradition. Here is the *iqa' murassa' shami*, which consists of nineteen beats divided into groups of 4+5+4+6. These groups within the cycle are shown by darker dotted lines.

Time ⟶   GRAPHIC **17.7**

| dumm | takk | takk | dumm | dumm | takk | dumm | takk | keh | dumm | takk | takk | takk | takk | [cycle begins again] |

Although surveys differ, some have enumerated 111 different *iqa'* patterns in eastern Arab countries, lasting from just a few to 176 beats, though only a fraction of those are in common use. The very long *iqa'* in particular are attempted only by the most learned and virtuosic musicians.

ARABIC MUSIC PERFORMANCE

18

Music Forms and Practice in Arabic Music

The classic expression of the traditional urban Arabic performance is the **suite**, *a series of songs and instrumental pieces unified by their reference to a single maqam*, despite temporary modulations. These suites artfully contrast metered and unmetered, sung and instrumental, fast and slow genres of songs and instrumental pieces in set formats. These suites have different forms and names in different countries—**nuba** in Morocco, **fasil** in Turkey and Syria, **waslah** in Egypt, **nawbah** in some North African countries, and **maqam** in Iraq—although some are rarely heard today. All these forms share an ability to excite *tarab*, a passionate emotional state, among the connoisseurs who patronize this art.

FIGURE 18.1
The *takht* is the classical Arabic ensemble. The one pictured here is the Ensemble of Classical Arabic Music, with, left to right, violin, singer, *qanun*, singer, *'ud*, and *riqq*. *Takht* also frequently include a *nay*.

The most traditional medium for the Arabic suite is an ensemble of about five musicians called a **takht** (Figure 18.1). A *takht* might include a *qanun* (zither), *'ud* (lute), *nay* (flute), *riqq* (tambourine), violin, a solo singer and perhaps a chorus, or the instrumentalists may act as a chorus. The texture is primarily heterophonic. An Arabic suite often begins with a *taqsim*, an instrumental improvisation to introduce the mood of the *maqam* in its purest form. Some of the other genres that may form movements of the suite or independent forms include the following.

■ **mawwal** a partly improvised song in colloquial (not classical) Arabic that usually follows a *layali* (non-pulsatile vocal introduction).

■ **qasida** a song that sets a poem in classical Arabic language. The singer may render the text melodically in modal improvisation or interpolate improvisatory extensions of a composed setting of the poetic lines. Thus an extended song may result from just a few lines of poetry.

■ **sama'i** an instrumental piece with a refrain that begins in a ten-beat *iqa'*, moves to a lively triple meter, and ends in the original ten-beat pattern.

■ **tahmilah** an instrumental piece in which the various instruments take turns playing solo improvisations, alternating with a refrain, somewhat as in jazz.

In the twentieth century, several important changes occurred in ensembles of the classical tradition. With the growth in popularity of the singers as soloists, shorter forms, such as a *layali-muwwal*, became more popular than extended suites. Under the influence of European orchestras, the *takht* grew into a large ensemble of twenty or more musicians, known as a **firqa** in Egypt, which combined both Arabic and European instruments, including a large section of the violin family.

Because of the size of the ensemble and the popularity of large concert venues, microphones became necessary for singers. Singers such as the Egyptian Umm Kulthum (1904–1975) achieved superstar status through concerts, recordings, radio, and film (Figure 18.2). Composers increasingly adopted European practices such as the use of harmony, use of notation, the avoidance of scales involving quarter-tones, and, by the 1960s, electric instruments. These innovations caused some controversy, especially among the connoisseurs who continue to patronize the now marginalized classical ensemble of the *takht*.

In the 1970s, smaller bands modeled on European and American pop groups began to appear. One distinctive movement has been the working-class and often socially conscious music known as **sha'bi**, which began in Egypt but found a following throughout much of the Arabic world. While such groups adopted European harmonies and instruments for the most part, some also included distinctively Arabic vocal ornamentation, improvisation, and some instruments, such as the *darabukkah* (goblet drum). Modern pop music, known as **al-jil**, is very similar to its Western counterparts, although one genre of songs, known as **nashid**, has explicitly Islamic lyrics.

FIGURE **18.2**
Umm Kulthum.

© Bettman /CORBIS

Waslah in *Maqam Huzam*

A *waslah* is a classical suite of songs and instrumental pieces played by a small ensemble (*takht*) in Egypt. In its original form, the *waslah* died out early in the twentieth century, but in this recording, Nidaa Abou Mrad and the Ensemble of Classical Arab Music have applied this title to a modern suite. In this example the movements are somewhat abbreviated; a full performance could easily last an hour. This excerpt includes four short movements: *bashraf*, *taqsim*, *dulab*, and *muwashshah*. The *maqam* is *huzam* and its distinctive sound comes partly from the fact that the tonic is flattened by a quarter-tone (Graphic 17.2, p. 89). Instead of the fifth scale degree forming a secondary point of stability in the scale, the third scale degree is a point of focus.

This suite begins with a short excerpt from "Qarah Bitaq Sikah" by Khi'dr Agha al-kamani, a piece in the form of a *bashraf*, an instrumental genre adapted from Turkish Sufi music. The *riqq* (tambourine) and the melody articulate the iqa', which is *sama'i thaqil*, a distinctive pattern in a ten-beat meter.

GRAPHIC **18.1**

Time ⟶

| dumm | | | takk | | dumm | dumm | takk | | | [cycle begins again] |

Listening Guide

CD 1:7. *Waslah* (excerpt) in *Maqam Huzam*. Nidaa Abou Mrad (violin), Mohamad Ayache (voice and *'ud*), Maria Makhoul (*qanun*), Ali Wehbé (*riqq*).

The *bashraf*—instrumental form with a refrain (*taslim*) that recurs before and after a series of contrasting phrases (*khana*). Heterophonic.

0:00		*Taslim* (refrain), violin and *'ud*.

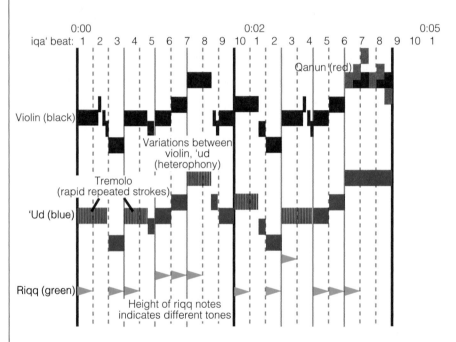

0:14		*Khana* phrase; the *qanun* takes over the melody from the violin.
0:25	*Khana* repeats.	
0:37	*Taslim* repeats.	

The *taqsim*—unmetered interlude that clearly establishes the *maqam* and mood of the following performance. The *sayr*, or path, of central tones creates the melodic structure of the *taqsim*.

0:51	Violin, the leader of this ensemble, goes directly into the *taqsim*'s first phrase.
	Centers on the tonic, though it touches in turn on each of the other important tones. This journey through different focal pitches is an interpretation of the *sayr* of the *maqam*.
	Violin shifts the focus to another pitch.
1:07	*Qanun* (zither) strums a drone, gradually becoming more prominent.
1:16	Pitch focus shifts and the *qanun* part becomes more active and elaborate.
	For variety, the *qanun* often mixes the different pitches that occur in ascending and descending versions of the *huzam* scale even when the contour of the melody is not clear.

Dulab—metered instrumental form—brief heterophonic introduction to the next song.

| 1:48 | Violin leads a new *iqa'* with 16 beats per cycle. |

Muwashshah—"You, with the slender waist"—song form, strophic.

2:10	First verse, sung by the *'ud* player who stops playing.
	Rhythmic cycle returns to *iqa' sama'i thaqil*.
	Dense heterophonic texture.
2:42	Instrumental repeat with variations.
3:14	Second verse.

3:48	The *qanun* leads a non-pulsatile *taqsim*.
	Violin plays a drone.
	Notice the *qanun*'s highly melodic, characteristic techniques: quickly alternating notes between octaves, glissandos (fast strumming up or down several strings), and very fast strums circulating up and down several adjacent strings.

The *muwashah* (at 2:10 in the listening guide) is a song form that developed in the opulent courts of Muslim Spain; thus its text is in classical Arabic and concerns the courtly ideal of a woman's beauty and her love. Like the ornate patterns that cover the walls of the palaces at Alhambra and Granada, this heterophonic texture is so densely ornamented that every crevice is filled in with graceful lines. Although a *muwashshah* typically has an AABA form, this performance leaves out the contrasting section.

MUSIC IN IRAN

19

In Arabic classical music, the intricate interactions of the classical ensemble help to create the distinctive expression of *tarab*, or musical ecstasy. In Iran, solo performances epitomize the classical tradition, and musical expression may be correspondingly introverted and contemplative. This is not to say the music is without the feeling of joy that *tarab* represents, but it is an inward joy, perhaps even expressing the musician's connection with the divine. "We are as the flute," said the famous Iranian poet Rumi (1207–1273), "and the music within us is from thee."[1]

Because Iran sits between India and the Orient on one side and the Middle East and Europe on the other (see map, page 76), opposing influences have operated at different times in its history—as seen in its names. Persia, its early name, came from the name that the Greeks gave it, *Pars*. In 1935, the country's name officially changed from Persia to Iran, a native term derived from Aryan-based languages (such as those in India). Expatriates opposed to the current Iranian government sometimes prefer to call themselves and their music Persian.

Iranian Classical Music

Just as the basis for melodic composition and improvisation in Arabic countries is the *maqam*, in Iran, classical improvisation is based on the **dastgah**. Like the *maqam*, each *dastgah* has a characteristic heptatonic scale, called the **maye**, which may include steps of ¾ of a tone and 1¼ tone.

Unlike the *maqam*, however, a *dastgah* is defined more as a collection or system of many short, related melodies called **gusheh**. The *gusheh* within each *dastgah* are all related by their melodic character, mood, and home scale, although modulation to related scales is common. To construct an improvisation, the performer selects a number of *gusheh* from a single *dastgah* and improvises on them one after another. The *gusheh* is simply a guide to improvisation, the essence behind the player's melody; only a beginning stu-

---

[1] This translation by Reynold A. Nicholson comes from Maulana Jalál al-Dín Rúmí, *The Mathwnawí of Jalálu'ddín Rúmí* (London: Luzac, 1982).

dent would play it in its original form. See the first graphic in the Listening Guide.

Since the number of *dastgah* is limited—there are only twelve—and the number of *gusheh* in each *dastgah* is generally standardized, from ten to thirty per *dastgah*, it should be possible to publish a **radif**—the entire corpus of *gusheh*. In fact, several twentieth-century musicians have done just that, producing large books of several hundred melodies transcribed into Western notation, even though it is difficult to find two musicians who agree on the exact form of any given *gusheh*.

The selection and order of the *gusheh* within a performance is mostly up to the performer, but the performer does not select the *gusheh* randomly. Because they are grouped within the *dastgah* according to their range and the notes that they emphasize, the *gusheh* are generally played in ascending order of pitch so that the excitement within the performance builds.

Like the Arabic *taqsim*, a *dastgah* is played by a single musician on one of a wide variety of instruments, most commonly the *tar* (hourglass lute), the *sehtar* (long-neck lute), the *santur* (dulcimer), the violin, or the voice. Singers' improvisations on the *gusheh* are generally without words, although a verse of a precomposed song often separates each *gusheh*. A performance typically lasts between ten and thirty minutes. A dastgah performance is mostly non-pulsatile but may include contrasting quasi-pulsatile *gusheh* and others, called **chahar mezrab**, which are strongly rhythmic.

While there are other genres of Iranian classical music, these solo improvisations have come to epitomize the mood and essence of the *dastgah*. Nevertheless, through Arabic and European influences, ensemble music has also become important. Genres of ensemble music may be arranged in suites, as in Arabic countries, or interspersed with solo movements, such as a *chehar mezrab* performed independently. Other genres include the following.

■ **pishdaramad** an introductory piece for ensemble in duple or triple meter. Although the piece is mostly precomposed, the texture is heterophonic, with the different instruments offering variations of phrases derived from the *dastgah*.

■ **tasnif** a composed song in a fixed meter accompanied by a soloist or ensemble. While these songs traditionally set words in classical poetic meters, modern ballads, also called *tasnif*, do not.

■ **reng** ensemble music in a dance rhythm. Such music may feature the **tombak** (goblet drum), which is otherwise mainly a folk or light classical instrument.

Musicians known as **motreb** perform light classical, dance, and traditional entertainment music, although restrictions by the Iranian government since the 1979 revolution have made this music rare today. Popular music, and female performers in particular, are also severely restricted, although a thriving music industry exists among expatriate communities in cities such as Los Angeles.

Listening Guide

First *gusheh—daramad*, non-pulsatile

0:00	Relatively slow, gradually revealing the essence of the *dastgah*.
	The main functions of the *daramad*, the few *gusheh* used to open a performance, are to establish the *ist* (tonic), scale, basic mood of *mahur*, and to explore the lower tetrachord (the tonic and the three notes below it).
	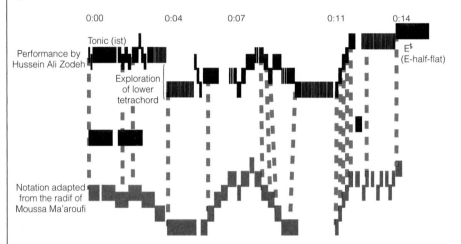
0:14	Sudden introduction of an accidental (note outside the scale).
	Its distinctive sound comes from lowering the third pitch in the scale by a quarter-tone.
	Momentarily back in the home scale.
	Exploration of the lower tetrachord.
	Firm cadence on the tonic closes the *daramad*.

Second *gusheh—kereshmeh* (literally "nod" or "wink"), non-pulsatile.

0:31	Performer moves onto the next *gusheh*.
	Introduction of certain high pitches.
	Distinctive quasi-pulsatile sections.
	Ends with a firm cadence on the tonic.

Third *gusheh*—*chahar mezrab*, pulsatile

1:40	Frequent rhythmic strums on the drone strings establish a compound duple meter.
1:45	The melody enters, but in a simple duple meter, creating a lively polyrhythm with the drone accompaniment.
	The focus in this section is on the dynamic rhythms and patterns; the melodies are fairly simple and are typically developed by means of sequences—that is, the same melodic fragment repeats at successively higher or lower starting points.

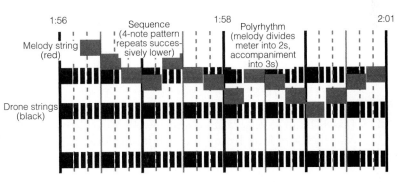

2:55	Comes to an end with a simple phrase that takes us back to the non-pulsatile rhythm and introduces a new pitch, a lowered seventh scale step that will be prominent in the next section.

Third *gusheh*—*shekasteh* (literally "broken" or "doleful")

3:05	Introduces a new scale, creating a sense of modulation, a temporary journey to a different landscape.
	Emotional high point of performance emphasizes the scale's highest pitches.
	New scale includes the lowered seventh step and the third step lowered by a quarter-tone. Centered not on the *ist* but on the fifth scale step, called by some theorists the **shahed** (stressed pitch) in *mahur*.
4:34	A short coda, descending gently from the fifth scale step to the tonic, brings us back home to the *mahur* scale.

A PERFORMANCE OF AN IRANIAN *DASTGAH*

A popular *dastgah* is **mahur**, marked by a characteristic optimistic mood that is unusual for much of Iranian classical improvisation. Some authors have commented that the name even sounds similar to the Western word "major," and indeed, the home scale of *mahur* is similar to the Western major scale, also associated with happy moods. Like all performances of the classical *dastgah*, this performance consists of a sequence of improvisations based on *gusheh* melodies of different character, but all having a unifying *mahur* sound. A full performance might include extended improvisations on ten to fifteen *gusheh* and last up to an hour. This short recording by Hussein Ali Zodeh playing the *tar* consists of just a few *gusheh* but preserves the overall form of a larger piece. Zodeh begins with a *daramad*, a *gusheh* with the specific function of starting a performance. He chooses subsequent *gusheh* for their contrasts in rhythm, mode, and character, and to achieve a gradual increase in tessitura. The final tone, or tonic, of *mahur* is called **ist** in Iran. The *tar*'s topmost string carries the melody, and the other three strings are used for drones and rhythmic ostinatos.

JEWISH MUSIC

20

It is difficult to generalize about Jewish music because of the diaspora which scattered the Jews from their original Middle Eastern home to other areas of the Middle East as well as North Africa, Europe, Russia, the United States, and elsewhere. Still, while Jewish musicians adopted many musical characteristics of their new countries, the segregation of Jewish communities in some areas helped to keep their culture and music distinct. Comparative studies have shown striking musical similarities between communities far removed in time and geography.

Religious Music

Sing to God our strength: make a joyful noise to the God of Jacob.
Raise a song and bring the drums, the harp, and the lyre.
Blow the trumpet at the new moon; at the full moon, and on our feast day.

—Psalm 81 [1]

The Bible records many such references to music, including folk songs and praise songs, many of which were apparently sung antiphonally (by alternating groups) or responsorially (by a leader alternating with the group). Especially important was the sacred music of the Temple, where *a hereditary caste of professional musicians*, the **Levites**, performed. The Bible mentions

---

[1] Translation adapted from the American Standard Version Bible.

a variety of instruments that have since been found in archeological sites. Of these the most important is the **shofar**, a ram's horn trumpet still used as a ritual instrument in Jewish ceremonies (Figure 20.1).

By about the fifth century BCE, **cantillation**, a standard method of chanting Biblical texts, had evolved. To sing these texts, which may vary widely in line length and meter, ancient Jewish singers used non-metrical melodic formulas, similar to those used by epic singers in Eastern Europe and the Near East. Lay singers, rather than Levites, sang the texts in small local places of worship known as synagogues. The many different melodic formulas for cantillation are indicated by signs called **ta'amim**, the first extant examples of which date from the ninth century. Later translations of these signs to European notation show remarkably consistent interpretations, even between widely separated traditions.

FIGURE **20.1**
The shofar, the ancient ram's horn trumpet, is still used as a ritual instrument in Jewish religious ceremonies.

Political uprisings led to the destruction of the Temple by the Romans in 70 CE. Within a short time, as many of the Jewish people gradually dispersed to other countries, the synagogue tradition replaced that of sacred music of the Temple. Today, a single singer called the **cantor** performs most cantillation in public services. Developing into professional singers, the cantors were soon entrusted with preserving the cantillation melodies through oral tradition.

The split of the Roman Empire into western and eastern states in 395 is reflected in the differing traditions of the diaspora communities. The Jews of the **Sephardic** tradition initially settled in Spain and Portugal, and after their expulsion in 1492 and 1497, respectively, they scattered throughout the Mediterranean region. The Jews of the **Ashkenazi** tradition eventually settled in Central and Eastern Europe, although they retained many of the non-diatonic modes of the Middle East.

The Ashkenazi Jews also retained a tradition of modal improvisation through sung prayers known as *hazzanut*, non-pulsatile songs based on certain scales and collections of melodic motives. The Jews had a system of modes, each of which had certain mystical associations, like the ancient Byzantine and Greek modes. The medieval Ashkenazim also composed metrically fixed, non-improvised chants, many influenced by European music. Some of these have become famous Jewish melodies, including the *Kol Nidre*.

The modes of the Ashkenazi cantoral traditions, called *shteygers*, are complex and include characteristic motives and tonal relationships used in *hazzanut* improvisations. Scales in Eastern Europe often included an augmented second, an interval consisting of three semitones, not found in the diatonic scales of Western Europe but common in Arabic *maqam*. This distinctive interval is common in klezmer music as well as popular folk melodies such as the famous *Hava nagila*.

One distinctive tradition of this region was the Hasidic movement, a mystical sect that arose in the eighteenth century and for whom music, even borrowed from folk sources, could represent an ecstatic union with the divine. Feeling that words limit the ineffable feeling of this joy, their songs, known as **nigun**, have only abstract syllables.

Klezmer

While ensembles of Jewish musicians have been common throughout the diaspora, those of the Ashkenazi tradition, particularly in Russia and Eastern Europe, became known for a distinctive style that distinguished them from non-Jewish bands. These folk musicians, known as **klezmorim** (the singular form is **klezmer**), typically played vigorous dance music for weddings and other events in small Jewish communities. The music of these ensembles featured characteristic syncopation (shifting of metrical accents) and non-diatonic scales. The ensembles typically included a pair of violins, a bass, a *cimbalom* (hammered dulcimer), and, later, a famously expressive clarinet. By the early twentieth century, bands sometimes added brass (buzzed lip) instruments and an accordion, although the instrumentation was never fixed.

Aside from dance music, klezmer bands sometimes accompanied popular songs or highly expressive unmetered introductions related to the Middle Eastern *taqsim* and the Eastern European **parlando rubato** tradition (see Chapter 44). By the end of the nineteenth century, many of these musicians were professionals who included European harmonies in their accompaniments. However, pogroms—systematic persecutions of Jews—in this region caused many of these musicians to emigrate, largely to the United States, between about 1880 and 1920.

Once in the United States, these groups absorbed influences from jazz and musical theater, but retained their distinctive sound. The use of the term "klezmer" to refer specifically to this music and the recognition of this music as a distinct tradition is a relatively recent phenomenon, associated mostly with the United States and, through further immigration, Israel. Since the 1970s, this music has undergone a revival in the United States with the popularity of such groups as the Klezmatics (Figure 20.2).

Modern Israeli Music

The modern state of Israel is home to immigrants from every extant Jewish musical tradition in the world. Since 1915, self-conscious attempts to create a national music and to encourage the use of the national language (Hebrew) in song lyrics have met with rather mixed success. Nevertheless, the diversity of these musical traditions, from Yemenite folk song to American jazz, creates an exciting mix.

FIGURE **20.2**
The Klezmatics, an American klezmer band.

One of the most popular genres among the Jews of the Sephardic (Mediterranean) tradition is the **romance** or **romancero**, which has its origins in Renaissance Spain. Like other songs of this tradition, it is sung in the Sephardic language, Ladino. These ballad-type folk songs were originally sung without accompaniment by women, although modern Ladino musicians often sing with guitar accompaniment.

Minority communities of Jews living in the Middle East have often been known for their distinctive music, but at the same time they have absorbed many attributes of Arabic culture. Israeli bands such as Bustan Abraham feature accompaniments by the *'ud, qanun, darrabukka*, and other Arabic or Turkish instruments.

REFERENCES

Discography

Arabic Music

Ensemble of Classical Arabic Music. *A Concert in the Nahda Style*. Beirut: Byblos BLCD 1023, 2002.

Kalthoum, Oum [Umm Kulthum]. *El Sett [The Lady]*. Paris: Buda 82244-2, 2002.

Ustad Massano Tazi. *Maroc: Musique classique andalouse de Fès*. Paris: Ocora C 559035, 1988.

Various artists. *Egypte: Les Musiciens du Nil*. Paris: Ocora HM CD83, 1987.

Various artists. *Music in the World of Islam* (3 CDs). London: Topic Records TSCD901-903, 1976/1994.

Music of Iran

Payvar, Faramarz. *Iran: Persian Classical Music*. New York: Elektra/Nonesuch 9 72060-2, 1974/1991.

Various artists. *Iran: The Masters of Traditional Music* (3 CDs). Paris: Ocora C 560024/25/26, 1979–1991.

Jewish Music

Bustan Abraham. *Pictures through the Painted Window*. Brussels: CramWorld CRAW 17, 1997.

Klezmatics. *Rhythm & Jews*. Chicago: Flying Fish, 1990.

Various artists. *Cantares y romances tradicionales Sefardíes de Marruecos y Oriente [Traditional Sephardic songs and ballads from Morocco and the Balkans]*. Madrid: Saga KPD(2)-10.202, 1994.

Various artists. *Israeli Songs and Dances*. Paris: Buda 82495, n. d.

Music of Turkey

Erguner, Kudsi and Soleyman Erguner. *Sufi Music of Turkey*. New York: CMP Records CMP 3005, 1990.

The Erkose ensemble. *Tzigane: The Gypsy Music of Turkey*. New York: CMP Records CMP 3010, 1991.

Various Artists. *Istanbul 1925*. New York: Traditional Crossroads 4266, 1994.

Bibliography

Danielson, Virginia. *The Voice of Egypt: Umm Kulthum, Arabic Song, and Egyptian Society in the Twentieth Century*. Chicago: University of Chicago Press, 1997.

During, Jean and Zia Mirabdolbaghi. *The Art of Persian Music*. Washington DC: Mage, 1991.

Farmer, Henry George. *A History of Arabian Music to the XIIIth Century*. London: Luzac, 1929.

Idelsohn, Abraham Z. *Jewish Music: In Its Historical Development*. New York: Schocken, 1929; rpt. 1967.

Racy, Ali Jihad. *Making Music in the Arab World: The Culture and Artistry of Tarab*. Cambridge: Cambridge University Press, 2003.

Rothmüller, Aron Marko. *The Music of the Jews: An Historical Appreciation*. Cranbury, NJ: A. S. Barnes & Company, 1967; rev. 1975.

Sendrey, Alfred. *Music in Ancient Israel*. London: Vision, 1969.

Shiloah, Amnon. *Music in the World of Islam: A Socio-cultural Study*. Detroit: Wayne State University Press, 1995.

Signell, Karl L. *Makam: Modal Practice in Turkish Art Music*. Seattle: Asian Music Publications, 1977.

Stokes, Martin. *The Arabesk Debate: Music and Musicians in Modern Turkey*. Oxford: Oxford University Press, 1992.

Touma, Habib. *The Music of the Arabs*. Portland, OR: Amadeus Press, 1996.

Zonis, Ella. *Classical Persian Music: An Introduction*. Cambridge, MA: Harvard University Press, 1973.

c. 200 BCE–1000 CE

Height of the Silk Road, a trade route that carries commerce and cultural influences between East and West. Through this trade, musical influences reach Central Asia, and Central Asian music influences other cultures, including the famous Tang dynasty in China.

661–750

Introduction of Islam brings Arabic and Iranian musical influences into large areas of Central Asia as far as Uighur (modern west China). Islamic courts patronize advanced traditions of art music.

7th–9th C

Buddhism becomes the dominant religion in Tibet, which becomes an influential empire in the region. Despite later isolationism, musical influences enter Tibet from China, India, and elsewhere.

1208–1242

Mongolian Empire spreads across China, Russia, Central Asia, and the Middle East. The re-opening of the Silk Road allows Marco Polo to travel from Europe to China in 1271. The Tibetan form of Buddhism is introduced to Mongolia, where it is firmly established by the sixteenth century.

PART 4

Central Asia

1365–1500

Timur's empire, establishing a golden age of scholarship, including music scholarship, centers at Samarkand (in modern Uzbekistan).

1731–1876

Russian annexation of Central Asian states brings new musical influences to these regions.

1917–1991

Soviet Union dominates region. The Soviet government largely ends nomadism and organizes people into collective farms or moves them to urban industrial areas. The socialist state controls much musical expression, and establishes professionalized "folk" ensembles. Similar state control and support of music occurs in communist China and Mongolia.

1924–1992

Mongolia becomes an independent communist state. Buddhism and Buddhist music are suppressed. After the transition to democracy in 1992, some traditional musical and religious practices return.

INTRODUCTION TO THE REGION

21

The awe-inspiring view from a Buddhist monastery on a Himalayan mountainside in Tibet, the "rooftop of the world," seems to extend forever (Figure 21.1). Many of the musical arts of Central Asia reflect this vastness, from the epic songs sung by horseback nomads on the steppes (flat grasslands) to the very slow "long songs" of the Mongols, whose long melodic lines and elaborate vocal ornamentation seem to be in no hurry.

In the Tibetan monastery, sound is expansive in another way. The *elaborate symmetrical paintings* called **mandalas** *that serve as objects of contemplation* for the monks depict multitudes of Buddhas, each representing a different deified manifestation of the transcendent truth (Figure 21.2). Associated with each manifestation is a particular sound which can become a part of this world through the chanting of those cosmic tones in *ritual formulas* called **mantra**.

🎵 **FIRST LISTEN**
CD 1:9
Invocation from Mahakala Puja,
The Monks of Sherab Ling Monastery, Tibet

───── 1950
Tibet annexed by China, which, especially during the period 1959–1978, suppresses practice and music of Buddhism.

To Westerners who may picture meditative music as quiet and relaxing, the crashing cymbals, raucous double reeds, and deep trumpets that accompany Tibetan Buddhist rituals may be startling. The most remarkable sound, however, comes from the deep-voiced chants themselves. Instead of melodies that traverse discrete pitches of a scale in a distinct beat, the melodies of some of these chants consist of slowly sliding pitches, gradually changing timbres, and beats that never stay constant. Some of these chants are sung in a special style that allows a single singer with a growl-like tone to create simultaneously two or three identifiable pitches, helping to create an overwhelming atmosphere filled with the luminescent sound of the cosmos.

To the Tibetan Buddhists, music is both a means to understanding and enlightenment as well as a reflection of the ultimate truth made briefly audible in this transitory world.

Geography The vast area of Central Asia consists of a variable geography inhabited by many different cultures. The largest empire the world has ever known arose here in the thirteenth and fourteenth centuries. The music of many of these regions—including the Central Asian steppes (Kazakhstan, Turkmenistan, Kyrgyzstan, and Uzbekistan, as well as the far western Xinjiang Uygur Autonomous Province of China) and the Central Asian western mountains (Afghanistan, Tajikistan, and far northern parts of Pakistan and India)—is most closely related to practices in the Middle East, which we heard in Part 3. Part 4 will focus on the distinctive musical practices of the Tibetans and Mongolians of Central Asia.

FIGURE **21.1**
Tibetan monks look out over a vast Himalayan valley from their monastery in the Zanskar Valley, Ladakh, India. They play *kungling*, a buzzed-lip instrument traditionally constructed of human femurs to remind us of the brevity of human existence. *Kungling* may also be constructed from metal and played in groups.

© Ric Ergenbright/CORBIS

FIGURE **21.2**
Here we see a *tanka*, a Tibetan painting of a mandala, a symbolic representation of the Buddhist spiritual universe. These paintings are hung in monasteries as objects of meditation.

© Alen MacWeeney/CORBIS

ELEMENTS AND CHARACTERISTICS
OF CENTRAL ASIAN MUSIC

22

Ethnic Mongolian people live not only in Mongolia proper (long ago known as "Outer" Mongolia), but also in neighboring regions of China ("Inner" Mongolia) and Russia. Tibet is currently an autonomous region within China, which claimed sovereignty over it in 1950. Many Tibetans live in expatriate communities in India, Nepal, Bhutan, and elsewhere. While Tibet is dominated by the Himalayan mountain range, Mongolia consists largely of immense plains through which herders have traditionally moved their animals from season to season. The musical instruments of nomads must be portable, and long treks provide excellent opportunities to develop long songs and sophisticated performance practices.

Characteristics of Tibetan music include the following:

■ **Epic Songs** Sung by specially trained bards, these *narrations of grand mythic poems* may last from hours to days. Related to similar traditions throughout Eurasia and perhaps introduced to China by the great Mongol conquerors, this ancient practice is dying out in many areas. (We will discuss epic singing from Eastern Europe in Part 9.)

■ **Multiphonic Singing** This is *a remarkable vocal technique in which a single singer can produce two or even three tones at once.* By growling very low tones and adjusting their vocal cavities in very specific ways, a singer can resonate certain *overtones* or **partials** to sound like a separate whistling sound. Although this practice is found in different forms throughout Tibet and Mongolia, the Western Mongols and neighboring Russian groups such as those from the Tuva region are especially known for this technique.

■ **Tone-Contour Melodies** Lacking a conventional melody made up of discrete variations in pitch, tone-contour melodies of chants follow subtle and continuous fluctuations of timbre, loudness, and slides between tiny pitch differences. Although this remarkable type of singing is only one type of Tibetan Buddhist chant, other Central Asian forms, such as the "long songs" of Mongolia, also focus attention on subtleties of pitch slides and shifts in timbre.

TIBETAN MUSIC

23 In mid-winter, stinging winds gust down the steep faces of the sky-kissing Himalayan peaks that rise above Dharamsala, India. The winds carry the sounds of prayers that are inscribed on hundreds of small flags hanging from ropes strung above the Buddhist temple. The winds also carry the sounds of enormous ten- to fifteen-foot metal *dung-chen* trumpets. These trumpets play profound, rumbling tones that the Buddhist monks of this famous monastery associate with the natural force of the winds. Music for these monks has two components: an external music, which is what we hear, and an internal music that accompanies the external in the musician's soul. In the same way, the *tantras, books of esoteric religious teachings central to Tibetan Buddhism,* speak of the external winds of nature and the *lung, winds of the inner spirit* that are the basis for consciousness.

Humanity's harmonious relationship to natural forces and the earth is a focus of *Tibet's indigenous religion,* known as *Bön,* and its practitioners, sometimes called **shamans**, often use music to help mediate between the spiritual forces of the earth and people. This tradition of shaman music is found in many areas of Central Asia, north to Mongolia, Siberia, and Korea, although these practices are extinct or increasingly rare in some regions. Around the seventh century, when Tibet became a powerful kingdom controlling trade routes, Buddhism entered from India. Though Bön and Buddhism have at times competed, today they peacefully coexist, Buddhism mediating the individual's relationship to the spiritual world's cycles of life and rebirth, and Bön his connection to the land.

In Tibet, Buddhism developed into a unique form emphasizing monasticism, an esoteric knowledge of the spiritual world, and elaborate rituals in which music plays a vital role. Despite important influences from China, India, and elsewhere, for centuries Tibet remained a kingdom isolated in the Himalayas and developed its own distinctive arts and traditions.

The Dharamsala monastery is the home of the Dalai Lama, the spiritual leader of Tibetan Buddhists, now the Tibetan leader in exile. In 1950, Communist Chinese troops suddenly invaded Tibet, but Chinese suppression of the indigenous culture and religion precipitated an uprising in 1959. The even more severe crackdown that followed led to the escape of the Dalai Lama and ultimately thousands of his followers to the neighboring countries of India, Nepal, and Bhutan. In the period that followed, especially during the Chinese Cultural Revolution of 1966–76, Tibetan Buddhism and its musical traditions, virtually eliminated from Tibet, survived only in expatriate communities like Dharamsala in India. Since the liberalization of religious tolerance in 1978, some Buddhist practices have returned to Tibet, although especially since a 1989 uprising, the Chinese authorities still strictly control them.

FIGURE 23.1

A *dung-chen* is a metal, straight, buzzed-lip instrument that creates a very low pitch. These highly revered objects are sometimes constructed in telescope fashion and may extend to fifteen feet. Often two or more play together in ritual contexts. Each plays a very low, sustained pitch, although, like the singers of low *dbyangs* chant, the player can vary the pitch slightly.

Ritual Music and Its Instruments in Tibet

The tuba-like tones of the enormous ***dung-chen*** trumpets (Figure 23.1) announce the evening prayers at the monastery. As the monks gather in an incense-filled hall, butter lamps dimly illuminate sacred images, including *mandalas*. Like the mandala paintings, the music of the prayer ritual also serves to focus the mind for meditation but lacks so many of the elements of conventional music we might expect—melody and beat, for example—that some writers have described it as "ritual sound" rather than music. Yet this powerful, otherworldly sound of deep trumpets, loud double reeds, clattering cymbals, and drums is as precisely organized as the detailed mandala images, creating (in the term of ethnomusicologist Ter Ellingson) a "mandala of sound."

Tradition so precisely prescribes the music that large books, specific to a particular monastic tradition, contain distinctive notation that allows virtually no improvisation in the music. The rhythm, controlled by *cymbals* called ***rul-mo*** (Figure 23.2), is often neither pulsatile nor non-pulsatile in the usual sense. Instead of beats represented as regularly spaced articulations in the sound, they are arranged in sections in which they gradually accelerate but are rarely static. Monks hold these bulbous brass cymbals in careful balance so that slight movements cause them to sizzle or strike together with precise control.

Tibetan ritual chant may take the form of conventional melodies (*rta*) or repetitive recitation (*'don*), but

FIGURE 23.2

Rul-mo, large metal cymbals with a prominent central boss (raised portion), are the leaders of the instrumental section of the rituals. These cymbals are carefully balanced in two hands so that the players can strike them along the edges in a variety of ways, ranging from a resounding crash to a delicate sizzle.

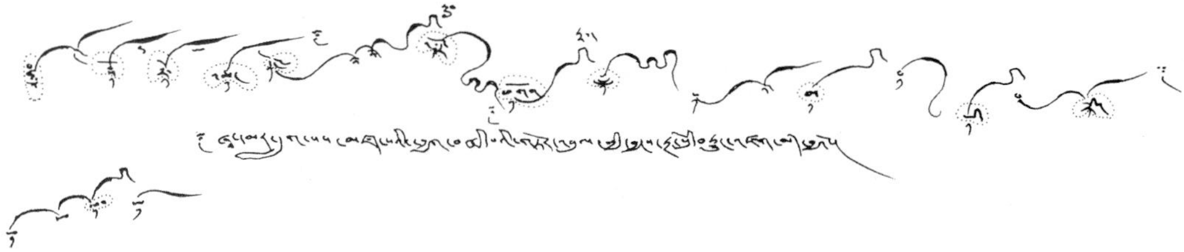

From Kaufman, Walter, *Tibetan Buddhist Chant*. Copyright © 1975 by Indiana University Press. Reprinted by permission.

FIGURE 23.3
Mahakala chant notation.

the most astonishing sounds come from a specialized style called ***dbyangs***, *chants where the "melodies" consist of subtle changes in timbre, loudness, and sliding pitches*. Different monasteries often write down these small slides and changes in pitch, although the details of the notational systems vary from one monastic tradition to another (Figure 23.3). The monks read from these sacred chant notations and use them to preserve ancient performing practices.

To produce differences in timbre, musicians have developed a wide repertory of techniques for achieving relatively bright, nasal, deep, or other vocal timbres. The monks may also interpolate meaningless syllables between the words of the chant for the sake of tone color variation.

The most remarkable vocal effect, though, is multiphonic singing, the singing of more than one pitch at a time. We will hear a related type of multiphonic singing from Mongolia, a region with strong historical ties to Tibet.

Only cymbals and ***nga chin***, a kind of *double-headed bass drum* (Figure 23.4) accompany the ritual chant. But the chant often alternates with a larger ensemble of instruments that may include the *dung-chen* trumpets, *rgya-gling* double reeds (Figure 23.5), and smaller *kungling* trumpets. These latter trumpets are traditionally made of a human leg bone, which remind

FIGURE 23.4
The *nga chin* is a cylindrical bass drum with two heads, often struck with a mallet shaped something like a question mark. Drums come in different sizes with specific names appropriate to specific rituals and traditions.

© Christine Kolisch/CORBIS

FIGURE **23.5**
Rgya-gling are large, very loud, conical double reeds, with a metal disc on which the lips rest and a flared bell. There are seven equidistant holes. The players practice circular breathing, a technique that allows for continuous sound. Two or more play elaborately ornamented melodies based on a few core tones.

© David Samuel Robbins /CORBIS

us of the transitory nature of human existence. The *kungling* we will hear are made of metal. Like the *dung-chen,* they play long extended tones that vary only slightly though quite deliberately in pitch and volume. This music, known as ***rul-mo*** (the same name as the cymbals) is filled with elements of special symbolic significance. The fact that this music rarely repeats may remind listeners of the Buddhas who have escaped from the cycles of death and rebirth. In one piece, ethnomusicologist Ter Ellingson showed how the placement of strikes and lines along which the two cymbals clatter against one another symbolically create a mandala image (Figure 23.6).

Chant and *rul-mo* instrumental music are not the only expressions of the spiritual mathematics of the mandala image. In the sacred dance known as *'cham,* each of the dancers assumes the identity of one of the deities of the mandala. Performed to the accompaniment of an ensemble similar to the *rul-mo,* *'cham* choreography is a highly stylized movement of high-stepping knees and precise hand gestures of symbolic significance, known as *mudra.*

A Tibetan Music Performance

At the end of each day, monks in the Kagyu tradition of Tibetan monasticism gather in a large incense-filled hall and chant an invocation and offering to their tradition's protector deity, Mahakala. Though depicted as a terrifying being surrounded by fire, this deity is an emanation of the compassionate Buddha Vajradhara; Mahakala directs his wrath towards obstacles to compassion and enlightenment (Figure 23.7). This ritual of chant, instruments, and offerings is called a *puja,* during which time the monks pray for the benefit of all sentient beings.

Our audio selection is an excerpt from a Mahakala invocation in hour-long *puja*. Here, as in other accompanied chants, the *rul-mo* cymbals carefully control the music's time dimension. The cymbals clatter with a gradually accelerating beat. This *whole series of accelerating strikes on the cymbal* is called a **brdung** (literally "beat"), and the *brdung* themselves are arranged in a set pattern for each section of this piece. Generally, in each pattern, the time between the *brdung* gradually shortens, creating an acceleration of the groups of beats, which themselves accelerate.

FIGURE 23.6
A *tanka* painting of Mahakala, the protector deity of Tibetan Buddhism, from the Kagyu tradition.

Collection of Shelley and Donald Rubin

Folk and Art Music in Tibet

As elsewhere in Central Asia, Tibetans have a rich repertory of folk songs associated with activities of daily life—nomadic or pastoral songs, agricultural work songs, love songs, and so on—that seem very different from the otherworldly sounds of religious ritual music. While many songs have conventional pentatonic (five-tone) scales like those of China (see Part 6), Tibetan modes and melody types are often

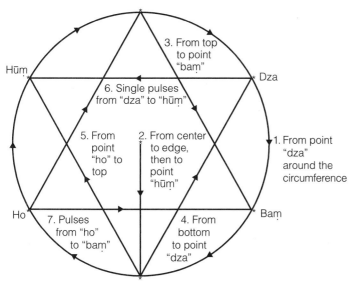

FIGURE 23.7
This schematic drawing shows how a succession of strikes between two *rul-mo* cymbals can symbolically create a mandala image. Four points along the rims of the cymbals are given Sanskrit syllables as names: *dza, bam, ho,* and *hūm.* At the beginning of the section, the player creates a series of accelerating pulses around the rims (1). During each succeeding *brdung* (lit. beat), a series of accelerating strikes on the cymbal, the player follows the pattern shown (single strikes and an accelerating series of strikes) to create a six-pointed mandala inscribed in a circle.

Listening Guide

CD 1:9. *Invocation from Mahakala Puja* (excerpt), The Monks of Sherab Ling Monastery

0:00	*Dung-chen* trumpets begin an interlude in the ritual. *Rul-mo* cymbals begin a series of accelerating strikes called a *brdung* (beat).
0:13	Second, loud *brdung*. The *nga chin* drum now follows the initial strike.
0:22	A softer intermediate strike without the drum follows 9 seconds after the last strike, which began 13 seconds after the first one, creating the effect of accelerating placement of the *brdung*.
0:30	Another pair of loud and short *brdung* repeat this pattern. This larger structure—introductory *brdung* followed by pairs of generally accelerating *brdung* and a concluding *brdung*—is a standard pattern used in the Mahakala *puja* in this tradition.
0:55	A special type of *brdung*, called a *bzhag rol*, announces the end of the pair structure with a much longer acceleration ending in a prolonged sizzle as the cymbals become so close as to rattle against each other until the player finally settles them in his lap. At this point *kungling*, the smaller trumpets, take over the wind instrument part. Like the *dung-chen*, they play long extended tones that vary only slightly though quite deliberately in pitch and volume.

Second Section—a pattern called *dgu brdung* (nine beats), referring to the number of *brdung*, not counting the introductory beat or the long, concluding, accelerating series.

1:17	A new pattern on the cymbals signals a new series of *brdungs*. A single drum beat announces each *brdung* and the time between each *brdung* gradually shortens—first 11 seconds, then 9, then 7, then 5, 4, 3, and so on. The *kungling* trumpets play dramatic crescendos (swelling of volume), often swooping down in pitch at the end of each crescendo, between *brdungs* 2 and 3, 5 and 6, 8 and 9, and during the concluding section.
1:51	By this time, the cymbal strikes happen every two seconds or so.
2:00	The time interval between cymbal strikes becomes so short that the line dividing the acceleration between *brdung* and the acceleration of strikes within the *brdung* gradually blurs. Cymbals and drums fade out.

Third Section

2:14 	*Rul-mo* cymbals introduce a third section and a lower-pitched *dung-chen* trumpet joins the texture. *Nga chin* drum plays along with the accelerating strikes of the cymbals (rather than just once, signaling a new *brdung* series). Again the sequence of *brdung* accelerates, with 20 seconds between the first two, then 13, then 7, then 4. Another accelerating sequence follows.
3:27 	The low *dung-chen* trumpets enter again to accompany the long accelerating *bzhag rol* that concludes this instrumental section.

Dbyangs chant

3:39 	Tone contour melody with subtle sliding pitches at the very bottom of the vocal range (see contour below) as well as shifts in timbre and loudness. Semi-regular cymbal and drum interjections, called *tshig rnga*, articulate and precisely control the timing. Each cymbal and drum strike corresponds to a change in syllables, so that the words unfold at a very slow pace, allowing the participants to meditate on them. 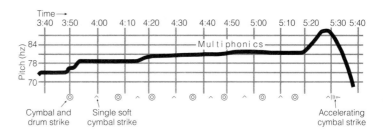
4:30	Listen closely here for multiphonic singing—a single singer producing the effect of two or more simultaneous pitches. Above the growling bass note that the singer chants (called the fundamental), you may hear a quiet whistling sound that moves up and down before the next cymbal strike. That pure sound is a partial (overtone) resonated by special treatment of the vocal tract. These changes in timbre are as important to the chant as the changes in pitch.

© David Samuel Robbins/CORBIS

FIGURE **23.8**
The *sgra-snyan* is a fretless long-necked lute with three to seven strings played with a plectrum (pick). Its resonator is often covered in snake skin. The number of strings depends on the geographical region.

quite different, and some songs may use six- or seven-tone (heptatonic) scales, like those in India. Pastoral or nomadic songs are known for their elaborate **melismas** (*many notes to a single syllable*), which, though common in Iran and Mongolia, are not as common in China. The *sgra-snyan* is *a lute with a long, unfretted neck* that sometimes accompanies folk songs (Figure 23.8). Folk songs are otherwise usually unaccompanied, although singers and other participants often dance.

In Tibet, as in Mongolia, there is an ancient tradition of extremely long epic songs. Tibetan epic songs are based on the mythic story of the ancient Tibetan king Gesar and his battles against evil. The lead performer narrates in stylized, heightened speech, while the characters sing from a repertory of stock melodies. Amateur troupes also perform stories from the Gesar epic in *a form of theater* known as **lhamo**, performances of which may last for a full day or more. In *lhamo* performances, narration in heightened speech alternates with action and songs, frequently accompanied only by cymbals and drums. Although the stories often include Buddhist elements and the form sometimes borrows from sacred dance ('*cham*), *lhamo*'s purpose is secular entertainment and celebration. Banned during the Cultural Revolution, *lhamo* was preserved mostly in expatriate communities, although new *lhamo* troupes have resumed performances in China since the 1980s.

Nangma and the related genre of **töshe** are sometimes called *the art music of Tibet*. Small instrumental ensembles prominently including a **yangqin**, the *hammered dulcimer of China* (Figure 35.5), accompany singers heterophonically. Because of its associations with the elite classes of old Tibet, the Chinese suppressed *nangma* in the 1960s, although groups such as the Tibetan Institute of Performing Arts in Dharamsala, India, preserved it as an art form. Since the liberalization of the 1980s, the Chinese have allowed *nangma* to return, but its traditional melodies now collide with popular music forms influenced by Chinese pentatonic songs, Indian film music, and Western pop. In contemporary Lhasa, the capital of Tibet, *nangma* clubs with disco lights and beer are as common as karaoke bars elsewhere. In these venues electric guitars have often replaced Tibetan and Chinese instruments, but traditional melodies still find a place, and many Tibetans view this new *nangma* with some pride as one of the unique cultural expressions of their country that is still allowed.

24 ⋰⋱ MONGOLIAN MUSIC

A Mongolian hosting a celebration (a *nair*) ritually greets visitors and conducts each to a special area in the **ger**, the *large round felt-covered tent that is the traditional home of Mongolians* (Figure 24.1). Every point inside the *ger* has meaning in symbolic social and spiritual space—the entrance is on the south side, men sit on the left (the west), women on the right. The most respected guests sit at the northern-most end, next to what in earlier times would have been a Buddhist shrine, but today is more likely a table of keepsakes and family photographs. At the center of the *nair* celebration is the performance of the **urtyn duu**, *a Mongolian long song*, whose expansive, non-pulsatile melodic elaborations recall the fenceless vastness of the Central Asian steppes.

Although most Mongolians now live in urban areas, many are still pastoral herders. In the spring, they move their herds of sheep or cattle to fertile mountain valleys and in the winter, to the lower grasslands. As their ancestors have done for centuries, they carry their *ger* homes with them. Long songs and portable instruments are well-suited to this semi-nomadic way of life, but celebrations and travel are not the only occasions for music. Men sing to move their herds, to coax animals to nurse, to calm animals, to accompany hunts, and so on. Songs are important accompaniments to traditional wrestling or archery contests at festivals. Herders also control their animals through whistling, a sophisticated musical art that symbolically connects the herders with the winds that gust over these immense plains and valleys. So closely is whistling identified with the spirit of the wind that it is

FIGURE 24.1
The professional Mongolian ensemble Tumbash sits in front of a Mongolian *ger* (round tent). From left to right, the instruments are the *yoochin* (a hammered dulcimer similar to the Chinese *yangqin*), the *morin huur* (the horsehead fiddle), the *limba* (transverse flute), and the *kuuchir* (spike fiddle, similar to the Chinese *hu*).

Courtesy of Face Music

considered bad luck to whistle indoors. In addition to the wind, the sounds of rivers and birds also serve as musical connections to the spirit world and inspire singing.

The subjects of Mongolian songs reflect the importance of animals and nature in the lives of the people, and songs about love for a horse are as common as songs about romantic love in other cultures. The point in a long song when a mythological horse sacrifices himself still brings tears to the eyes of those attending the *nair* celebration. While practices of Buddhism are gradually returning to Mongolian culture since the 1990s, spiritual beliefs known as shamanism still permeate traditional life, and music creates a symbolic opening to that supernatural world.

Traditional Songs

Like music in other nomadic cultures, the great majority of Mongolian music is vocal, and songs tend to share the same pentatonic modes that we hear in many other regions in Central Asia and in China. The **urtyn duu** *long songs* are so named not necessarily for their duration, but for their free, expansive rhythms, which the singer may draw out to any length. These highly expressive songs have wide ranges (up to three octaves) and melismas with highly developed ornamentation, especially pitch slides, wide vibratos (wavering pitches), and falsetto (a male high vocal tone).

Long song subjects may be heroes, myths, praise of nature, or praise of one's community; these songs are always serious and deeply felt. In some areas instruments heterophonically accompany the *long song* singers, while elsewhere they are always unaccompanied. Sometimes other celebrants or singers join in a refrain. Traditionally, only men perform *urtyn duu*, although this has changed somewhat in recent times.

Short songs, **bogino duu**, may in fact be rather long, but they differ from the *long songs* in their fixed meter and limited ornamentation. Whereas the *long songs* are associated with formal celebrations and rituals, *short songs* are often sung informally for different everyday situations. Also unlike the *long songs*, *short songs* tend to be lively and syllabic (one note per syllable), with relatively simple tunes that repeat (strophic form). A distinctive type of short song is the satirical song, which often pokes fun at drunk or rude people. However, the communist government effectively ended the tradition of such songs commenting on politics. Some short songs represent a dialogue between two speakers, and performers often dramatically act out the parts of those speakers in their voice, manner, and facial expressions. One is reminded of the similar Chinese *drum song* (see Chapter 38), a dramatic narrative said to have been introduced to China by the Mongols.

Also associated with the Mongols from a very early date are *epic songs*, generally known as **tuul'**, traditional performances of which could last hours or days. While such narrative songs entertained the courts of the great Khans, they were also frequently performed for special *nair* celebrations among the nomadic communities. While some of the epic stories are also found in Tibet, such as the Gesar story and its many derivative episodes, many epics are particular to a certain regional identity.

Each section of an epic is set **strophically** (that is, with *a repeating melody for the verses*) with pentatonic melodies of fixed types that the singer freely chooses from a traditional repertory. In some traditions, the singer usually accompanies himself heterophonically on an instrument, typically the ***morin huur*** fiddle. Between each section, the singer may insert dramatic spoken or non-pulsatile sung improvisations.

The specially trained singers of epics, sometimes called *bards* in the West, often belonged to families that traced their patrilineal heritage of training in this art back to the time of the Khans. Years of training often culminated in the young bard's examination by an expert panel. While modern urban industrialization and communist-era censorship have threatened this tradition, there remains a great interest in epic singing among many communities and state-sponsored folk art groups.

Höömii Singing

In Chapter 23, we saw how Tibetan monks produce more than one pitch simultaneously in **multiphonic singing**. In Tibet, the high, pure tones produced by this remarkable technique create a subtle shifting of timbre that is a part of the tone-contour melody. Some Mongolian groups have refined this technique, here called ***höömii*** or *khoomei*, to create extraordinary, clear melodies.

As in Tibetan *dbyangs*, the singer sings a low and timbrally rich, sometimes growling tone while contorting the vocal cavities to resonate certain partials. These overtones are normally present in a sound, but not heard as separate tones. Through the *höömii* technique, the overtones become so loud that they emerge as a kind of a whistle. As the singer further adjusts the shape of his mouth, different partials become prominent and create a melody even as the low sung pitch remains constant.

Different traditions identify different kinds of multiphonic singing, each distinguished by the timbre of the voice, the relative range of the sung pitch, the method of creating the partials, and other criteria. Traditionally it was taboo for women to perform *höömii*, ostensibly because some forms take great strength to perform and incorrect practices could lead to physical damage. Nevertheless, some women have taken up the practice in recent times.

While it is not possible to sing words on these tones, *höömii* may be inserted into songs, especially at the ends of phrases or verses. In some versions of *höömii*, the sounds are onomatopoeic, evoking the whistling winds of the steppes, the rushing sounds of rivers, and the songs of birds.

Instruments

While there are important instruments that require advanced techniques and virtuoso players, their traditional role is to provide accompaniment. Instrumental orchestras were found at the courts of the Mongolian empire, and,

Courtesy of Face Music

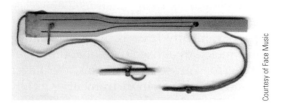

FIGURE 24.2
The *khomuz*, the Mongolian jaw's harp, has a stiff tongue of metal or wood that is plucked and resonated in the player's mouth.

while these groups influenced ensembles in China and vice versa, they died out with the disappearance of the courts themselves. Today purely instrumental music is not as common as songs, but there is a repertory of **program music** for solo instruments. In these works the music may describe part of an epic legend, such as the story of a mythological horse, or the origin of the instrument itself. Often these stories are so well known to the audience that they can recognize the story purely through the virtuoso performance. Modern conservatories and professional music groups have also reintroduced instrumental ensemble music as an independent art.

An important instrument in some regions is the ***khomuz***, a type of *jaw's harp*, a stiff tongue of metal or wood that is plucked and resonated in the player's mouth (Figure 24.2). By changing the shape of the mouth, different partials can be resonated, just as in *höömii*.

String instruments, relatively portable and useful for accompanying oneself when singing, are the most important Mongolian instruments. The ***morin huur*** or *hil huur* is a *large, bowed instrument of the lute type*. With a top carved in the shape of a horse's head, it is sometimes known as the horse-head fiddle (Figure 24.3). Although it is traditionally associated with Central and Eastern Mongolian groups, the government has elevated it to a national instrument. It is unfretted, with two horsehair strings and a large trapezoidal resonator usually covered with goat skin. The player changes the pitch with the unusual technique of pressing against the string laterally with the first knuckle of the index finger. Traditionally used to accompany epics and long songs in some regions, it also plays solo melodies at times.

FIGURE 24.3
Amarjargal of the Ensemble Temuzhin in Mongolia plays the *morin huur*, a lute-type instrument—the national instrument of Mongolia. A horse head carved on the top gives it its alternate name, the "horse-head fiddle."

In other areas, such as Western Mongolia, the primary string instrument for accompaniments is the ***topshuur***, also *a two-string unfretted lute, but held laterally and plucked* (Figure 24.4). The resonator may be oblong or circular and is also covered with skin. The ***limba***, *a small, portable, transverse bamboo flute*, may also accompany long songs.

Since the liberalization of the 1990s, Buddhists have reintroduced Tibetan ritual instruments to Mongolia. These buzzed-lip instruments, double reeds, and cymbals are otherwise uncommon. Many other instruments are direct counterparts of those found in China, where the name for fiddle, *hu*, may be related to the Mongolian word *huur*.

 ## REFERENCES

Discography

Tibet
Monks of Sherab Ling Monastery. *Sacred Tibetan Chant*. Franklin, TN: Naxos 76044-2, 2003.
Monks of Gyütö Tantric College, Dalhousie. *Tibetan Buddhism: Tantras of Gyütö: Sangwa Düpa*. New York/Los Angeles: Elektra/Nonesuch 9 79224-2, 1989.
Tibetan Institute of Performing Arts. *Nangma Toshey: Classical Music of Tibet*. Auckland, NZ: Voyager 1466, 1994.

Mongolia
Ganbold, Yavgaan and Tubsinjargal. *Mongolia: Höömii and Urtin Duu*. Tokyo: JVC VICG 5211.
Various artists. *Tuva: Voice from the Center of Asia*. Washington DC: Smithsonian Folkways CD SF 40017, 1990.

Elsewhere in Central Asia
Khushnawaz, Mohammad Rahim. *Afghanistan: The Rebab of Hérat*. Geneva: AIMP XXV/VDE 699, 1974/1993.
Various artists. *Instrumental Music of the Uighurs*. Tokyo: King Records KICC 5138, 1991.
Various artists. *Central Asia: Masters of the Dotar*. Geneva: AIMP XXVI/VDE 735, 1993.

FIGURE 24.4
The *topshuur* is a two-string unfretted lute held laterally and plucked.

Bibliography

See also books on music of China, the former Soviet Union, and Eastern Europe.
Haslund-Christensen, Henning. *The Music of the Mongols: Eastern Mongolia*. New York, Da Capo Press, 1971.
Levin, Theodore. *The Hundred Thousand Fools of God*. Bloomington, IN: Indiana University Press, 1996.
———. *Where Rivers and Mountains Sing: Sound, Music, and Nomadism in Tuva and Beyond*. Bloomington, IN: Indiana University Press, 2006.
Norbu, Jamyang, ed. *Zlos-gar: Performing Traditions of Tibet*. Dharamsala, H.P., India: Library of Tibetan Works & Archives, 1986.
Pegg, Carole. *Mongolian Music, Dance, and Oral Narrative*. Seattle: University of Washington Press, 2001.
Sakata, Hiromi Lorraine. *Music in the Mind: The Concepts of Music and Musician in Afghanistan*. Kent, OH: Kent State University Press, 1983.
Slobin, Mark. *Music in the Culture of Northern Afghanistan*. Tucson: University of Arizona Press, 1976.

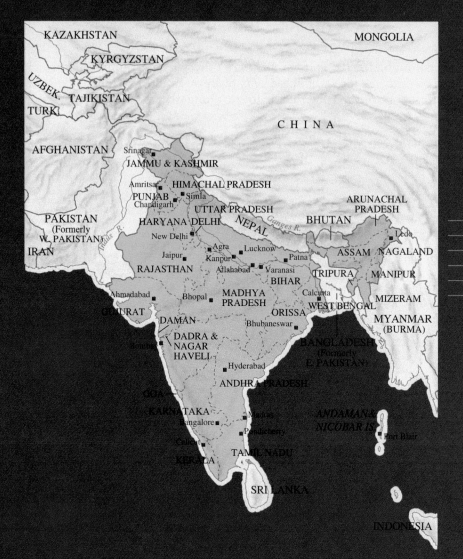

KAZAKHSTAN
KYRGYZSTAN
UZBEK.
TAJIKISTAN
TURK.
AFGHANISTAN
MONGOLIA
CHINA
Srinagar
JAMMU & KASHMIR
Amritsar HIMACHAL PRADESH
PUNJAB Simla
Chandigarh
UTTAR PRADESH
ARUNACHAL
PRADESH
PAKISTAN
(Formerly
W. PAKISTAN)
HARYANA DELHI
New Delhi
NEPAL
BHUTAN
Ganges R.
Ledo
IRAN
Agra Lucknow
Jaipur Kanpur Patna
ASSAM NAGALAND
RAJASTHAN Allahabad Varanasi
BIHAR
TRIPURA MANIPUR
Ahmadabad Bhopal
MADHYA
PRADESH
Calcutta
WEST BENGAL
MIZERAM
GUJURAT
DAMAN
ORISSA
Bhubaneswar
MYANMAR
(BURMA)
DADRA &
NAGAR
HAVELI
Bombay
BANGLADESH
(Formerly
E. PAKISTAN)
Hyderabad
GOA
KARNATAKA
ANDHRA PRADESH
ANDAMAN &
NICOBAR IS.
Bangalore
Madras
Calicut
Pondicherry
Port Blair
KERALA
TAMIL NADU
SRI LANKA
INDONESIA

GEOGRAPHY AND BRIEF HISTORY OF INDIA ■ GEOGRAPHY AND BRIEF

India, Pakistan, Bangladesh, Sri Lanka, and Nepal, all parts of the historical India.

c. 1800–c. 1200 BCE
Migration of Aryan-language peoples into India, development of caste system. The highest of these classes was that of the priests, the so-called Brahmins. Today castes have become a complex system indicating not only relative social placement but also occupation and one's place in religious rituals.

? 1500–1200 BCE
Development of early Hinduism and composition of the *Vedic* hymns, a series of holy books of rituals, prayers, and incantations that form the earliest literary basis for the Hindu religion. Brahmin priests chanted the oldest of the *Vedic* texts, the *Rig-Veda*, in a kind of heightened speech associated with the pitch levels given by certain diacritical marks. The *Sama-Veda* includes notation for chants, which now span octave scales.

563–483 BCE
Lifetime of Gautama Siddhartha, founder of Buddhism. By emphasizing personal enlightenment and inner peace, Buddhism has had a lasting influence on Indian culture, even though the practice of Buddhism mostly disappeared from its country of origin by 600 CE.

PART 5

India

c. 100 BCE

Composition of the *Mahabharata*, the long Hindu epic that is revered as a spiritual text of religious and moral lessons in its long tales of gods and ancient battles between good and evil. The stories of the *Mahabharata* have become the source for much drama and dance in India as well as areas touched by Hinduism, such as Southeast Asia and Indonesia.

5th C?

Natyasastra, the first important treatise on the arts, including music; some date it much earlier. It established many of the important premises of Indian music, including its devotional nature, its connections to the other arts, and perhaps the basis of its scales.

c. 1100–1400

Persian influence and introduction of Islam in the north. Eventually the courts of North India adopted the new religion, becoming sultanates, while southern peninsular areas retain Hinduism as the official religion. Although court music in the north retains a spiritual or devotional personal component, its context becomes secular.

1520–1590

Lifetime of Miyam Tansen, the most famous *Mughal* (Hindustani court) composer. The beginning of the golden age of arts patronage in the rich *Mughal* courts of North India.

PART 5 ■ INDIA

1660
Chaturdandi Prakasika by Venkatamakhi establishes the theory of the *Karnatic melakarta* scale system.

1764–1948
British colonial rule. Certain Western instruments and musical concepts are adopted during this period, such as the violin and the harmonium, *a portable reed organ.* British military bands inspired the tradition of bands of Western brass instruments (trumpets, trombones, tubas, and so on) now common in wedding processions.

c. 1780–1847
Period of the trinity of great composers in South India, including Tyagaraja.

19th C
The gradual acceptance of purely instrumental classical performances in North India, and the rise to prominence of the *sitar,* the *sarod,* and the *tabla.* Because of the association of classical music with the courts, it becomes largely an urban art.

INTRODUCTION TO THE REGION

25

The dusty streets of Varanasi in northern India resonate daily with the sounds of loudspeakers playing hits from the latest Hindi-language films, wedding bands, pop songs, and a collage of many other sounds. But this ancient city is also known as the traditional center of a ***gharana***, *a particular school of vocal or instrumental performance in India's classical music traditions*, which extend back to the times of the great medieval courts. Connoisseurs of Indian classical music still frequent the concerts and festivals of this very sophisticated art music tradition (Figure 25.1).

FIRST LISTEN
CD 1:10
Raga Khamaj. Sarod, Ali Akbar Khan; *tabla,* Pandit Mahapurush Misra.

© Michael Freeman/CORBIS

FIGURE 25.1
A performance on the *sitar* (left) and *tabla* (right). The drone instrument is not visible in this photograph.

1920s
Shift of patronage to public concerts, radio, and film. While this trend has resulted in the decline of the very complex, long, and refined forms favored at the courts, it has brought Indian classical music to much wider audiences.

1910–1932
V. N. Bhatkhande's *Hindustani-sangita-paddhati* music theory treatise. He and other Indian scholars sought to create a unified theoretical basis for North Indian music.

1947–1948
Independence from British rule and the partitioning of India into mostly Islamic Pakistan and Bangladesh and mostly Hindu India.

1950–1980
Golden age of *popular film music (filmi)*.

One of these performances, generally featuring a vocal or instrumental soloist and a drummer, begins very quietly, almost reverently, with an assistant playing a soft **drone** (*extended pitch*). Very slowly, without any perceptible beat, the melodic soloist, but not the drummer, starts to gradually expose the various notes of the mode and the characteristic melodic motives that will be used for the piece. Slowly the entire range of the instrument or voice unfolds. Moments of great beauty and passion emerge as the soloist withholds, then finally plays, important notes of the scale. After twenty minutes or more of this improvisation enveloping the audience in the mood of the piece, the drums dramatically enter for the first time. The rest of the performance, which may last an hour or more, consists of improvisations by the soloist and the drummer on the mode, the meter, the original melody (if there is one), or other standard melodic fragments.

Indian musicians trace the origins of these complex practices to holy traditions thousands of years old, the echoes of which can still be heard in chants greeting the first rays of sunrise on the steps down to the Ganges river in Varanasi. These chants are known as **mantras**, *repeated scriptures, prayers, or phonetic formulas that, through repetition, enhance one's karma or predisposition to goodness*. Mantras also represent the audible manifestation of the divine. This sonic dimension of the spiritual in life is apparent not only in the ritual chants that accompany the daily activities of Hindus of this area, but also in the sounds of nature, from the songs of birds to the thunder of the monsoons.

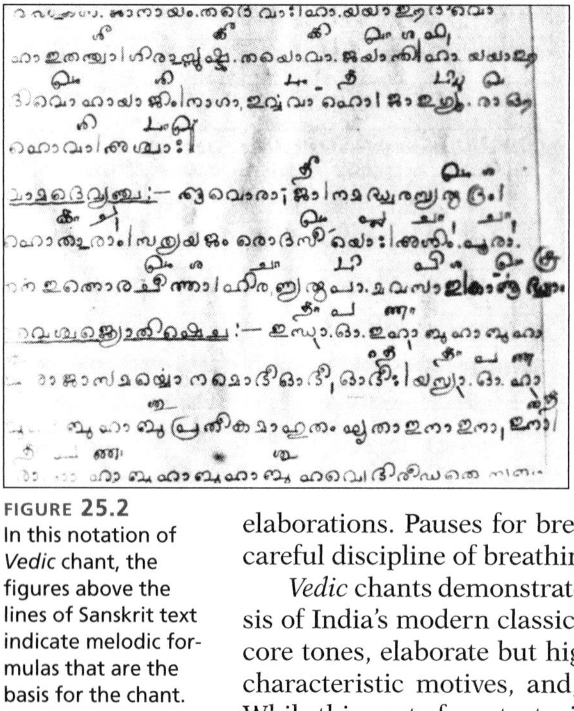

While lay people chant mantras every day to enhance their spirituality, in another part of the city, highly trained specialists sing the fluid chants of the *Sama-Veda* that also celebrate the divine nature of the sun and the cyclic rebirth of the morning. The **Vedas** are *unmetered songs of devotion and ritual that form the oldest books of the Hindu religion* (Figure 25.2). These chants center around a core tone that serves as an earthly foundation. Priests assemble the chants in mosaic fashion from carefully learned fragments, creating melodies that, while modest in their range, are stunning in their ornate elaborations. Pauses for breathing clearly separate the phrases, just as the careful discipline of breathing structures yoga meditation.

From *Samavedic Chant*, by Wayne Howard, 1977. Copyright © 1977 by Yale University Press. Reprinted by permission.

FIGURE 25.2
In this notation of *Vedic* chant, the figures above the lines of Sanskrit text indicate melodic formulas that are the basis for the chant. From Wayne Howard, *Samavedic Chant*.

Vedic chants demonstrate several elements that may have become the basis of India's modern classical traditions: a fixed foundation tone and other core tones, elaborate but highly codified melodic ornamentation practices, characteristic motives, and, above all, a devotional attitude towards art. While this part of our text will focus mainly on this classical tradition, it represents a small fraction of the region's day-to-day musical culture, which extends from diverse folk traditions to popular film music to wedding bands to the mantras that echo daily across the Ganges river.

Indian Geography   We will use "India" to refer to the entire region of South Asia, including the modern nation of India, but also Pakistan, Nepal, and Bangladesh. India is often divided into two large cultural regions that reflect different classical music traditions: *North India* or **Hindustani** India, and *South India* or **Karnatic** India. The country of India has several distinct languages and dialects, including Hindu, Urdu, Bengali, Tamil, and Telugu. The traditional language of scholarly and classical literature is Sanskrit, while English has become a common language of the government and national media. Although the large population of the country India is 80 percent Hindu, other important religions flourish, especially Islam, which is the majority religion in Pakistan and Bangladesh.

ELEMENTS OF INDIAN CLASSICAL MUSIC

26

The civilization of the sub-continent of India is one of the oldest in the world. Its huge population represents a great deal of diversity in culture and musical practice. The two classical music traditions known as Hindustani in the North and Karnatic in the South represent many differences in music theory, practice, and terminology, although both traditions have in common the following elements.

■ **Melodic Improvisation by a Soloist** Classical performances always feature improvisations by a single soloist, who may sing or play a melodic instrument.

■ **Accompaniment by a Drummer** A single drummer using palms and fingers (no sticks) plays elaborate patterns to accompany classical performances.

■ **Improvisation Based on *Raga*** *The collection of guidelines for a particular melodic improvisation* is called a ***raga***, which includes aspects of tuning, scales, functions of pitches, melodic motives, and ornamentation.

■ **Cyclic Conception of Meter** Meter is made up of *cycles of beat groups in systems* called ***tala***.

■ **Drone** A string instrument, such as a *tambura*, plays a **drone** (*constantly sounding pitch*) of the tonic and one other pitch. The drone accompanies performances and creates a tonal foundation for the *raga*.

The Nature of Improvisation in Indian Music

Some people associate the word improvisation with music that is without rules and left entirely up to the whims of the performer. In fact, improvisation rarely means something of that sort. The performance of any piece of music entails hundreds of decisions. A composer may determine such elements as the form, meter, tonality, on down to the individual notes of the melody and rhythm. For those elements that the composer has not determined, the performers use tradition and their sense of style to make decisions before the performance about how to play the precomposed elements. During the performance, a performer makes further decisions about the improvised elements. But these choices will be constrained by harmony, meter, tonality, and other complex and strict guidelines about what is and is not appropriate.

Some Indian musicians bristle at the term improvisation; they believe that what they do is so closely bound by rules and tradition that the term overstates the performer's ability to make spontaneous changes. An Indian musician makes decisions based on the form, the **raga**, the *melodic basis of the piece*, and the **tala**, the *metrical basis of the piece*.

Students of Indian music begin not by learning rules for improvisation, but by learning a *raga's precomposed* songs or *themes*, called **bandish** in the North and **gitam** in the South. Eventually, students will learn enough of a particular *raga's* themes to get an intuitive sense for the melodic characteristics of that *raga*. After presenting the *bandish* or a precomposed song more or less in its original form, students begin to weave its phrases together in new ways, perhaps with characteristic phrases learned from other songs in that *raga*. More advanced players are able to spontaneously compose new phrases in the same style as those songs, but only after truly internalizing the conventions, traditions, and spirit of that *raga*.

Training for Performance of Indian Music

As in many cultures, students of Indian music are traditionally taught not in schools, but by a **guru**, *an individual teacher*. Before the modern era of public schools and public concerts, young musicians were apprenticed to a guru, lived with him and, in between intensive music instruction, did chores like a member of the family. The decision to become a musician is not taken lightly, and the choice may not rest with the student. Family associations and caste still sometimes determine a person's role in society, and families of musicians commonly extend back many generations. Especially in North India, the guru most often is an exponent of a **gharana**, *a particular school of vocal or instrumental performance*, and the secrets of a *gharana's* instruction and compositions are kept within a literal or symbolic family of musicians.

While this form of exclusive apprenticeship from a young age is no longer common, the devotion of dedicated students to a particular guru and *gharana* remains. A *gharana* may no longer be associated with a family of blood relatives, but it is still strongly connected to a particular style and region. Dedicated students still proudly associate themselves with a particular guru, but they may also seek lessons from other teachers and study the recordings and public performances of musicians from other traditions.

Some students may study an instrument without intending to become professionals.

The institutionalized educational system of the British colonialists was the basis of India's modern system of schools and universities, where traditional music is often taught as well. Classical Indian music at universities is largely independent of any particular *gharana*, and instruction there may emphasize scholarship and the articulation of music theory.

Indian classical music performances generally include a small number of

INDIAN INSTRUMENTS AND THEIR FUNCTIONS

27

players; orchestral music is rare. Indian classical music generally comprises at least three elements: one or more soloists (singers or instrumentalists), drums, and a drone. While other parts may be added to these three elements (a second melodic instrument, for example), all three are necessary for a traditional music performance.

The Soloist

The focus of an Indian classical performance is the melodic soloist, who may play an instrument or sing. The most common of the many diverse melodic instruments are the **sitar** (*a plucked lute with frets*), the **sarod** (*a plucked lute without frets*), the **sarangi** (*a bowed lute*), the **bansri** (*a transverse flute*), the **bin** (*an ancient and venerated plucked stick-zither*), and the violin (borrowed from the West). (See Box, "Traditional Instruments of India.") Commonly used in accompaniment and as a solo instrument in the Karnatic music of South India, the violin is tuned differently from the way it is in the West. A seated performer holds the body of the violin on his left shoulder and the other end (the "scroll") against his ankle.

While each of these instruments has its own idiomatic qualities, including its own melodic characteristics, ornamentation, and so on, their roles in the course of a piece are roughly the same. The exception is the voice, which has the further complication of incorporating precomposed lyrics or improvised text or syllables.

Many performances include more than one melody instrument. A singer, for example, is often paired with a **harmonium** (*a portable reed organ*) or a *sarangi*. In these cases, the singer is the primary soloist, while the instrument plays a secondary melody that complements or imitates the singer's line. Although the harmonium is a keyboard instrument, it generally plays one pitch at a time.

TRADITIONAL INSTRUMENTS OF INDIA

Courtesy Ravi Shankar Foundation, photo by Vincent Limongelli

William Alves

FIGURE 27.1

The famous Indian musician Ravi Shankar (left) plays the *sitar* (an instrument of North India), *a plucked lute with a large neck and tall, metal, hoop-shaped frets; five metal melody strings; and two* chikari *or drone strings.* The strings are plucked with a metal plectrum (pick) attached to the index finger of the right hand. Approximately thirteen sympathetic strings run underneath the frets and over a second, smaller bridge.

Courtesy of Alam Madina Music Productions

FIGURE 27.2

Ali Akbar Khan is one of the most famous masters of the *sarod, a plucked lute with no frets but a metal-covered, tapered fingerboard, four metal melody strings, and* chikari *(drone) strings.* The strings are plucked with a single hand-held plectrum and are pressed to the slick metal fingerboard with the nails of the left hand, making long slides possible. The resonator is covered with skin, rather than wood, which helps give the instrument its highly reverberant timbre. The *sarod* has about fifteen sympathetic strings.

© Sophie Bassouls /CORBIS SYGMA

FIGURE 27.3

The **bin** or *rudra vina* (left) *is a highly revered and plucked stick-zither with frets, associated with the* dhrupad *and other old court forms.* It has two large gourds attached to the bottom of the soundboard which act as secondary resonators. The performer pictured here is the famour French ethnomusicologist Alain Danielou. The South Indian equivalent is the **vina** (below), which is more common today than the North Indian variety.

Courtesy of Gilbert Blount

© JAYANTA SHAW/Reuters /Corbis

FIGURE 27.4

The *sarangi* of North India is *a bowed fiddle with three gut melody strings, stopped with the upper fingernails of the left hand, and about thirty-five sympathetic strings.* Traditionally a secondary melodic instrument that accompanies singing, the *sarangi* has recently become recognized as a solo instrument in its own right.

William Alves

FIGURE 27.5
The *tambura* (*tanpura* in North India) is a *plucked chordophone whose only function is to provide a drone*. While shaped like a lute, it is more of a hybrid lute-zither because the resonator extends through the neck. The four open strings are lightly strummed with the flesh of the finger to provide a constant background drone.

© Arvind Garg/CORBIS

FIGURE 27.6
The *bansuri* (*venu* in South India) is a *transverse bamboo flute*. While still more common in folk music, the *bansuri* has become a classical instrument as well. A type of transverse flute known as the *murali* has been associated with the god Krishna since ancient times.

© Macduff Everton/CORBIS

FIGURE 27.7
The **harmonium** is *a portable, hand-pumped, reed organ with a small keyboard played by the right hand and a bellows operated by the left*. Adapted from the organs that European missionaries imported during British rule, this instrument has been controversial, partly because of its fixed tuning. It is nevertheless a popular instrument for accompanying singing. In India the harmonium is normally played monophonically—that is, one note at a time.

© E. O. Hoppé/CORBIS

FIGURE 27.8
The *nagasvaram* is a *loud, conical double reed in South India which can be up to a meter long:* Related to the *zurna* of the Middle East, these instruments are often played in ensembles at weddings and religious processions. The North Indian version, the **shahnai** (Figure 6.25, p. 40), has recently been used as a classical solo instrument, though it is also traditionally a folk instrument.

(continued)

TRADITIONAL INSTRUMENTS OF INDIA

FIGURE 27.9
The **tabla** is a *pair of drums used in North India—the wooden cylindrical* daya or tabla *(right) and the rounder metal* baya *(left).* The centers of several layers of drum heads are cut out in concentric circles to provide different playing surfaces. Leather straps along the slide of the body secure the heads. The drummer tunes the right drum to the pitch *sa* by hammering cylinders under the straps to tighten or loosen them and by the careful application of black paste in the middle of the drum head. The left drum is lower but has an indefinite pitch.

Courtesy of Gilbert Blount

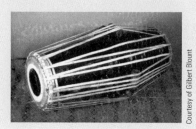

FIGURE 27.10
The **mrdangam** or mrdang, *a double-headed cylindrical drum held on the lap, is the standard classical drum of South India.* The North Indian equivalent, the *pakhavaj*, is used only in old court repertories.

Courtesy of Gilbert Blount

In the North, the emergence of instrumentalists as primary soloists, especially on the *sitar* and the *sarod*, has occurred mostly in the past century or two. Instruments that were primarily associated with vocal accompaniment, such as the *sarangi*, or folk or religious music, such as the *shahnai*, have found champions in the twentieth century who have promoted them as solo instruments in the classical tradition. In South India, all performances are based on composed songs, even those played by instruments alone.

The Drummer

Drumming is an indispensable part of an Indian classical music performance. While the melodic soloist is clearly the focus of the performance, the drummer is considered the soloist's equal as a musician. The drummer plays solos at times and, because his different strokes sound clearly identifiable pitches, even imitates the soloist's melodic phrases. In North India, the drummer usually plays the **tabla** (*a pair of small drums*) with palms and fingers. South Indian drummers play the **mrdangam**, *a single drum with two heads*. (See Box, "Traditional Instruments of India.")

From among a repertory of patterns, the drummer chooses those that fit into the meter and rhythmic scheme of the performance. The drummer's interaction with the soloist also determines the selection of patterns and the variations the drummer plays on them. A good soloist and drummer can be almost telepathic in their ability to improvise together and anticipate each other's music.

The Drone

A **drone** is *a very long* or *unchanging note*. In Indian music, a string instrument, the ***tambura*** (***tanpura*** in North India), normally plays the drone. The *tambura* player actually strums the strings continuously, but so gently that it sounds like a constant drone. The sound of the *tambura* is the familiar softly shifting background in Indian classical music. Because of its characteristic sound, some people mistake it for the more famous and similar-sounding *sitar*, but the *sitar* is a solo instrument with a very different function.

The drone functions as more than a background—it is a point of reference, the musical foundation on which the soloist's intricate melodies stand. The drone consists of two different pitches, usually the tonic pitch and another pitch five scale steps above. In certain *ragas*, the tonic pitch and the pitch a semitone lower may be used. This more dissonant interval gives the performance an aura of mystery that may be especially appropriate for evening *ragas*. The *tambura* player is often an apprentice and is not necessarily even acknowledged in the program. The soloist and drummer are the featured musicians. Sometimes singers play the *tambura* as they sing.

In South India a **sruti box**, *a specialized reed organ*, sometimes substitutes for the *tambura*. Modern musicians sometimes use an electronic version that continuously emits a tone like a *tambura* or a CD recording of a *tambura*. Such electronic substitutes can be very convenient for the working musician.

Chordophones in Indian Music

Chordophones—string instruments—have an ancient history in India and play a central role in classical music. Pitch-bending ornamentation, for example, is very important to the music. Thus, the bridges of some chordophones are broad and flat, a shape that enables the player to move a string side to side and change the pitch significantly. This type of bridge also helps create a characteristic slow timbral shift, a sort of "owowo" sound, as the end of the string buzzes along the top of the bridge. Most chordophones use metal strings, in part because the brighter tone helps to create this timbre.

Many chordophones in India also retain a feature called ***taraf***, meaning *sympathetic strings*. A performer can set a string in motion not only by playing it directly, but also by exposing it to the sound of the same pitch. Vibrations in the air corresponding to the pitch of the *taraf* string will cause it to vibrate very softly, a phenomenon known as **sympathetic vibration**. Sympathetic strings ring continually in response to the pitches played on the main strings. The player carefully tunes each of the perhaps dozens of sympathetic strings to the pitches of the scale being played, so that the notes of the *raga* are a constant presence in the music. This vibration sets up a subtle but unmistakable reverberation in the instrument that adds to the constant strumming of the *tambura*.

✲✿✍🔥Ⓖ *RAGA*—THE MELODIC DIMENSION OF INDIAN MUSIC

28

The most important guiding principle for melody in India is the concept known as **raga**. (*Raga* or *ragam* is the Sanskrit form of the word, and *rag* is the Hindi form of the word.) *Raga* includes the concept of mode as broadly defined in Chapter 2, but it implies much more than the usual Western use of the term. So complex a subject that some Indian musicians despair of ever arriving at a complete and accurate definition, the concept of *raga* includes at least the following components:

■ a tuning system, which may vary slightly among ragas that otherwise share the same scale

■ a scale system, which may be different in ascending and descending forms

■ a tonic, or starting point, within the scale as well as defined roles for some of the other pitches within the scale

■ certain melodic motives that are associated with a particular raga or are especially appropriate

■ certain ornamentation practices, although these may also vary according to the instrument playing

■ extramusical associations, such as the appropriateness of a particular raga for a particular time of day or for its ability to express certain emotions

Raga is sometimes broadly spoken of as the melodic dimension of Indian classical music, and, it is true that in performances that are entirely improvisational, raga is the ever-present force that guides the melodic instrument. While the bulk of a performance, often over an hour, is devoted to the metered section with the drum, the core of the feeling of the raga is best encapsulated in *the non-pulsatile introduction*, the **alap**, which we will discuss shortly.

The Tuning of Ragas

The history of ragas and their tuning has created a great deal of controversy among musicians and scholars. It seems that the theory, at least, of raga has developed considerably over time, although many writers have attempted to reconcile current theory with revered ancient sources such as the *Natyasastra*. The *Natyasastra* mentions a tuning system in which each octave is divided into twenty-two *sruti*; in this context **sruti** means *microtone*, that is, *a very small interval*. The intervals of each scale were constructed from different numbers of *sruti*. Although some writers have attempted to apply this tuning concept to modern practice, in reality musicians today use twelve pitches per octave.

The intervals between adjacent pitches are not necessarily the same, and the tuning of these intervals is neither fixed nor standardized, except in the case of the harmonium and string instruments with fixed frets. For other instruments playing twelve pitches per octave, the intervals between the pitches may vary slightly (but significantly) for different players and for different ragas. These differences can give different ragas a noticeably different flavor even when they share the same nominal pitches.

The Scales of Ragas

A raga most often uses *seven out of the twelve possible pitches* (**svara**). Some ragas, however, use as few as five pitches or as many as nine, and may use yet more pitches as auxiliary tones. Also, while there is a genre of performance in which ragas are mixed, musicians never modulate between keys in the Western sense.

Just as Western musicians may use solfege syllables—*do, re, mi, fa, sol, la*, and *ti*—to refer to the seven notes of a Western scale, the seven *svara* of Indian scales have names as well: *sa, re* (in the South *ri*), *ga, ma, pa, dha*, and *ni*. **Sa** (do) is *the tonic or home pitch*, though not necessarily the most important pitch. Pitches in different octaves can be indicated by placing a dot under the syllable indicating an octave down or over it for an octave up.

The seventeenth-century theorist Venkatamakhi was the first to create a system to enumerate all the possible seven-note scales that ragas could use, scales known as **melakarta**. Each of the different pitches in the scale, except for the tonic (the first pitch), may be altered by raising or lowering it by one semitone. We use the Western term **semitone** here as a convenience to indicate *the interval between any two adjacent notes in the complete twelve-tone per octave tuning system. A lowered tone* is called **komal** (the Western flat), and *a raised tone* **tivra** (the Western sharp), and, when it is necessary to distinguish an *unaltered tone* (neither *komal* nor *tivra*), it is referred to as **shuddh** (the Western natural). Venkatamakhi showed that there are seventy-two possible *melakarta* scales. The *melakarta* system is used mainly in South India, though only about twenty-four of the possible seventy-two scales are practically significant.

Classification of scale types became important in North India when Indian scholars in the early twentieth century sought to establish a theoretical basis for North Indian classical music. Influenced by the South Indian *melakarta* system, the theorist Vishnu Narayan Bhatkhande sought to classify the possible scale types in Hindustani music. He devised a system of thirty-two possible *heptatonic (seven-tone) scales* he called **that**. Of these, he found that the overwhelming majority of the hundreds of known ragas could be classified under just ten *that*.

Many musicians, however, never fully accepted these scale systems because of the simplifications and ambiguities they present when ragas are classified within them. First, in practice, many ragas have more than or fewer than seven *svara*. A raised version of the scale step may be used in ascent and a lowered version in descent. To classify the raga it is necessary to decide which version of that pitch is most characteristic. These classifications have resulted in many seemingly dissimilar ragas being grouped into the same category. In order to summarize more clearly the pitch material of a *raga*, musicians rely on a more complex demonstration of the pitches in a melodic context, called ***arohana/avarohana***.

Arohana/Avarohana (Ascending/Descending Scale)

While the *that* and *melakarta* are useful for classifying ragas, they do not describe the musical use of pitches. A pitch in the raga may occur only when the melody is descending. The melody may never descend from a certain pitch without immediately going up again. These factors are integral characteristics of the raga—as important as the scale itself. The construction called the ***arohana/avarohana***, the *ascending/descending scale*, shows the characteristics of the melody line.

For example, Bhatkande classified the *raga Desh* under the *that* (scale) *Khamaj*, even though it typically uses the *ni-komal* (lowered seventh scale step) found in *Khamaj* when descending, but *ni-shuddh* (unaltered *ni*) when ascending. Also, the simple scale by itself fails to demonstrate that *ga* and *dha*, the third and sixth pitches of the scale, are usually omitted in ascent, while *sa*, the tonic, is usually approached from *ni-shuddh*. Descending lines in *Desh* typically also have momentary changes of direction in them. The *arohana/avarohana* shows these elements.

In this graphic version of the *arohana/avarohana* of *raga Desh*, the syllables representing the pitches are arranged approximately proportional to their pitch. Unlike a simple seven-tone scale (*that*), the *arohana/avarohana* demonstrates the contour of the raga. *Raga Desh* avoids the pitches *ga* and *dha* when ascending the scale, and approaches *sa* (the tonic) from *ni*. When descending the player uses *ni-komal*, a lowered version of *ni*.

GRAPHIC **28.1**
The *arohana/avaro-hana* of *raga Desh*. The tonic pitch, *sa*, is in boldface. A dot above or below the pitch name indicates an octave displacement.

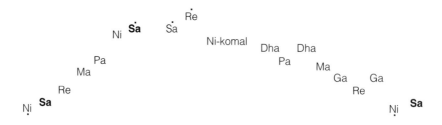

Bhatkande classified the *raga Khamaj* under the same *that*—in fact, he named the *that* scale for this raga. Like *raga Desh*, it uses both forms of pitch *ni*, but its *arohana* and *avarohana* are quite distinct and give the *raga Khamaj* a character quite different from the character of *Desh*. In Graphic 28.2, the pitch *re* (second scale degree) is absent in the ascent, but

TABLE 28.1
The ten *that* of Bhatkande

Kalyan that:	sa	re	ga	ma-tivra	pa	dha	ni	sa
Western equivalents:	C	D	E	F♯	G	A	B	C
Bilaval that:	sa	re	ga	ma	pa	dha	ni	sa
Western equivalents:	C	D	E	F	G	A	B	C
Khamaj that:	sa	re	ga	ma	pa	dha	ni-komal	sa
Western equivalents:	C	D	E	F	G	A	B♭	C
Bhairav that:	sa	re-komal	ga	ma	pa	dha-komal	ni	sa
Western equivalents:	C	D♭	E	F	G	A♭	B	C
Purvi that:	sa	re-komal	ga	ma-tivra	pa	dha-komal	ni	sa
Western equivalents:	C	D♭	E	F♯	G	A♭	B	C
Marva that:	sa	re-komal	ga	ma-tivra	pa	dha	ni	sa
Western equivalents:	C	D♭	E	F♯	G	A	B	C
Kafi that:	sa	re	ga-komal	ma	pa	dha	ni-komal	sa
Western equivalents:	C	D	E♭	F	G	A	B♭	C
Asavri that:	sa	re	ga-komal	ma	pa	dha-komal	ni-komal	sa
Western equivalents:	C	D	E♭	F	G	A♭	B♭	C
Bhairvi that:	sa	re-komal	ga-komal	ma	pa	dha-komal	ni-komal	sa
Western equivalents:	C	D♭	E♭	F	G	A♭	B♭	C
Tori that:	sa	re-komal	ga-komal	ma-tivra	pa	dha-komal	ni	sa
Western equivalents:	C	D♭	E♭	F♯	G	A♭	B	C

the descending scales can be direct, without the momentary changes of direction of *raga Desh*.

GRAPHIC **28.2**
The *arohana/avarohana* for *raga Khamaj*

The details of the *arohana/avarohana* may vary from musician to musician, and especially between schools of performers and different instruments. Nevertheless, in the ear of the educated listener, the *arohana/avarohana* creates the unmistakable sound of a particular raga. The **chalan** is a *yet more expanded representation of a raga's characteristic rising and falling melody that includes its characteristic motives. A chalan, such as the follow-*

ing one for *raga Khamaj*, begins to resemble a musical phrase more than a scale and is used as a basis for improvisation.

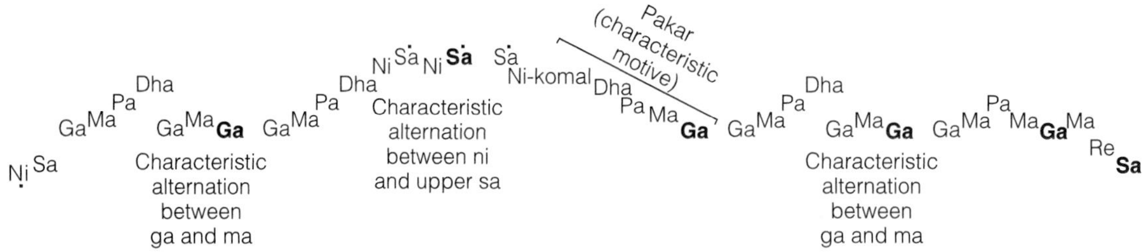

Ni Sà Ni **Sà** Sà Ni-komal Dha Pa Ma **Ga** GaMa Ga Pa Dha GaMa**Ga** GaMa Pa MaGaMa Re **Sa**

Dha Pa GaMa GaMa**Ga** GaMa Ni Sa

Dha Pa Characteristic alternation between ni and upper sa

Pakar (characteristic motive)

Dha Pa GaMa**Ga** GaMa

Characteristic alternation between ga and ma

Ni Sa Characteristic alternation between ga and ma

Characteristic alternation between ga and ma

GRAPHIC **28.3**
The *chalan* for *raga Khamaj*

The Hierarchy of Pitches

In tonal music, the tonic, or home pitch, is often spoken of as being the most important of the pitches, but such a statement may be misleading. It is often the relationships among all of the pitches that are really important, and none could really be dropped. The tonic is best described as the pitch that provides the foundation, the home base, for the melody. Usually the melody comes to rest on the tonic at the end, although not always.

In addition to the tonic, *sa*, Indian theory also specifies *a principal tone* (which might, with more justification, be called the most important tone) called the **vadi**, and *a secondary principal tone* called the **samvadi**. Neither corresponds to the tonic *sa*. Instead, they are pitches on which the musician is likely to dwell in a performance of a raga, and differences between them can give very different sounds to ragas that otherwise share the same basic scale.

The **samvadi** is normally three or four *svara* (pitches) above the *vadi*. While not emphasized as much as the *vadi*, the *samvadi* is relatively prominent and is often used as a cadence pitch, that is, the pitch on which the melody comes to rest at the ends of phrases. Given differences in performance practice and interpretation, *vadi* and *samvadi* are not universally agreed upon for all ragas. Indeed, many different scale degrees are emphasized during the course of a performance, and it is sometimes difficult to assign them all to a consistent hierarchy.

Gamak (Ornamentation)

Another characteristic that helps distinguish one raga from another is the *characteristic ornamentation*, called **gamak** or **gamaka**. Ornamentation and embellishment may be misleading terms, because they imply that these melodic figures are optional and may be played or not according to the player's will. But in Indian classical music, *gamak* are the life of the melodic line. They provide graceful and smooth transitions from one core pitch to another, creating interest in the nuanced character they give to the melody, just as subtle shading and filled-in curves give life to much Indian art.

Certain *gamak* are as indispensable as the notes of the raga scale. Not only do they help give a raga a characteristic sound, but their absence at specific points would disturb listeners or even suggest another raga. Many *gamak* are idiomatic to a particular instrument, and pitch bends, slides, and occasional wide vibratos are characteristic of most prominent solo instruments in India. The lack of the capability to produce these continuous changes in pitch has relegated to secondary status such instruments as the *santuri* zither and most keyboard instruments.

Pakar—Important Motives in Indian Music

One of the first ways that an experienced listener of Indian classical music recognizes a raga is not through its scale, which many ragas share, nor even through the *arohana/avarohana*, which may not be immediately apparent, but through *certain motives* (short melodies) called **pakar** *that are uniquely associated with certain ragas*. Frequently the *pakar* is represented in the *chalan*, the concise summary of the melodic material of a raga. A performer often features the *pakar* prominently at the beginning of a **gat** (*metered section*) and returns to it in many different forms throughout the performance, particularly at *the ends of phrases* (**cadences**).

A performance of a raga will, of course, include many motives, but most will be inventions of the performer. Each of these motives is developed in sophisticated ways throughout the piece, especially in the metered section.

Extramusical Associations

Musicians often quote an old Sanskrit saying: "Raga is that which colors the mind." That is, musicians first think of raga not as a scale, a characteristic melodic contour, or a set of motives, but as the emotional effect that this combination of attributes produces.

Writers as far back as the *Natyasastra* codified a set of *specific feelings that art can express*—the **rasa**. By tradition the basic *rasa* are nine in number: tragic, romantic/joyful, heroic, comic, furious, fearful, odious, surprising, and peaceful. But the nine basic *rasa* are only starting points for the much more complex emotional associations and symbolism of a raga. In addition to expressing more specific emotions than can the general *rasa* categories, a performance of a raga may take the listener on an emotional journey through different *rasas* characteristically associated with the raga. The characteristics became so specific, especially in the North, that schools of painting and poetry arose to symbolically represent various ragas. These paintings, known as **ragamala**, traditionally depict certain scenes that illustrate the mood of a raga and provide insights into its emotional and symbolic associations (see Figure 30.1).

One of the best known of a raga's extramusical associations is the time of day that is appropriate to the raga's performance. While the practice is not always observed today, now that concerts take place mostly in the evening, and radio broadcasts and recording sessions take place at unalterable times, knowledge of this association is important to truly understanding a raga. While South Indian ragas no longer are associated with time of day, they still carry specific connotations of mood and tradition.

For example, the name *raga Darbari Kanada* means "of the court of Kanada," and it is one of the most majestic and grand of all ragas. It is a nighttime raga, meant to be performed around midnight. In the *ragamala* painting tradition, the *raga Darbari Kanada* symbolizes strength, heroism, and nobility and is usually portrayed as a victorious king who has killed an elephant.

The North Indian *raga Desh* literally means "of the country," which indicates its origin as a regional or folk raga. Therefore, most musicians do not treat it with the weightiness as, for example, *raga Darbari Kanada. Raga Desh* is a late night raga, and *ragamala* paintings illustrate it as two lovers lying on a bed underneath an awning at night, the woman watching her sleeping mate.

29 TALA—THE RHYTHMIC DIMENSION OF INDIAN MUSIC

Mantra are textual formulas chanted over and over. Their repetition creates not only a sense of spiritual quietude and goodness, but captures the cyclic nature of time, an important attribute of Hindu cosmology. Whereas other traditions may treat time as an inexorable progression, Hinduism sees existence as bound up in cycles of death and rebirth, not only of individuals, but also of days, seasons, and civilizations. The careful periodic breathing of **yoga** (*spiritual discipline*) also reflects these wheels within wheels, as well as the breathing between the lines of Vedic chant, which is otherwise unmeasured.

The meters of classical Sanskrit poetry are also built on repeating patterns, and their rhythmic nature is emphasized by the fact that the words have **quantitative accents**, that is, *syllables are accented not through loudness* (as in English) *but by holding them twice as long as unaccented syllables*. Therefore the elaborate and subtle rhythms of this poetry already give it a very musical sound.

These cycling rhythms eventually came to define the repeating meters of all classical music as the concept of *tala* (*tal* in Hindi). In the same way that the concept of raga governs the melodic dimension of Indian music, so tala governs the rhythmic dimension. Tala includes the concept of meter discussed in Chapter 3, but it may also imply the way beats lie within this framework.

Tala has a hierarchy of pulses, that is, ways of grouping and subdividing beats. It has a system of subdivisions of beats, beats themselves, *groupings of beats* (called *vibhag* in the North or *anga* in the South), *groupings of groupings of beats* (called *avarta* or *avritti*, or, more informally, the *tala* cycle).

The numbers by which beats and groups may be grouped is sometimes considerably complex in the Indian system. In addition to groupings of twos and threes, groupings of fours, fives, and even one-and-a-half occur. Sometimes different sizes of groupings are mixed in asymmetrical patterns. For example, in the North Indian tala called *Jhampa*, each *avarta* or large cycle has four *vibhag* (groupings of beats), the first and third *vibhag* consisting of two beats each, and the second and fourth consisting of three beats. A shorthand way of writing this meter would be 2 + 3 + 2 + 3. An even more complex meter is the *tala* called *Upatal Jhampak*, which is 2 + 3 + 2 + 1½. In this case the last *vibhag* contains one-and-a-half beats—unusual, but still possible.

Traditions elsewhere in the world occasionally use complex meters. However, assuming that Indian metrical concepts are the same as those of the West, for example, would cause us to overlook subtle but crucial differences in the ways that musicians in the two cultures think about meter, especially in the ways that drummers and melodic soloists establish and treat patterns of beats.

Patterns of Beats in the Tala

In a tala, stress is usually placed on the first beat (**sam**) of the cycle. However, this doesn't necessarily mean that any note falling on that beat is automatically louder. Rather than thinking about the *sam* in terms of loudness, it is better to think of it as the rhythmic equivalent of *sa*, the tonal center in the melodic dimension of music. In the same way that the listener expects a return to *sa*, so we anticipate the completion of the *tala* cycle on *sam*. However, just as it is common for the melodic player to withhold *sa* in order to create tension, the drummer may de-emphasize *sam* for the same reason. Its structural importance remains in the performers' minds, and presumably in the minds of the audience, or else this artful play of expectations would have no effect.

On the other hand, the polar opposite to the *sam* beat is the de-emphasized beat of the cycle, called **khali**, meaning *empty*. It often comes about halfway through the cycle. Normally, low or loud beats are avoided on *khali* beats, but this, too, may be changed for musical effects. Both *sam* and *khali* normally occur at the beginnings of *vibhag*, and, on a higher level, these *vibhag* are also considered emphasized or de-emphasized, respectively. The first beats of *vibhag* that are neither *sam* nor *khali* are called **tali**.

When musicians, or often audience members, count along with the tala, they use special hand signs. *Sam* and *tali* beats are indicated by a hand clap or a hand beating on the thigh; the word *tala* itself refers to this clapping. *Khali* (empty) beats are indicated by waving the right hand away from the left or by beating the back of the hand on the palm or thigh. The remaining beats are counted off on the fingers by touching fingers to the thumb. In notation now commonly used, X stands for a clap, O for *khali*, and numbers for the beat within the *vibhag*.

The *tala tintal* is the most frequently used *tala* today; more than three-quarters of all performances are in *tintal*. It consists of a cycle containing sixteen beats divided 4 + 4 + 4 + 4. The first beat of the third *vibhag*, beat nine, is *khali*. It would thus be notated like this.

Tintal tala

Vibhag number	1	2	3	4
Beat number	1 2 3 4	5 6 7 8	9 10 11 12	13 14 15 16
Notation	X 2 3 4	X 2 3 4	O 2 3 4	X 2 3 4
Action	clap (count)	clap (count)	wave (count)	clap (count)

At a further level of detail, musicians assign different characteristic *tabla* strokes to each beat. These strokes are useful as a guide to the different characteristics and importance of each of the individual beats but do not represent the actual part the drummer plays. Each of the different types of strokes are known by syllables called **bols**. The use of mnemonic syllables is common in complex drumming in music around the world—in Africa, Indonesia, Japan, and so on. The four most basic beats are *dha, dhin, ta,* and *tin;* their names are onomatopoeic. *Dha* and *dhin* are played with both drums and are thus lower and more resonant, while *ta* and *tin* are played by the smaller drum alone. Different *bols* may represent many other types of strokes. The *bols* assigned to the beats of *tintal tala* are as follows.

Tintal tala

Vibhag number	1	2	3	4
Beat number	1 2 3 4	5 6 7 8	9 10 11 12	13 14 15 16
Notation	X 2 3 4	X 2 3 4	O 2 3 4	X 2 3 4
Action	clap (count)	clap (count)	wave (count)	clap (count)
Bols	dha dhin dhin dha	dha dhin dhin dha	dha tin tin ta	ta dhin dhin dha

A pattern of *bols* is called a **theka** (North) or **sokattu** (South). The *theka* for *tintal* shows that the *tala* is far more than a simple foursquare pattern. The predominance of the higher *bols* that begin with the T sound toward the end of the pattern create a sense of expectation for the resolution of *sam* that is reflected in the drumming patterns in a performance.

For performances, students memorize complex *theka* patterns, and, just as the melodic soloists create variations on known phrases and motives in a raga improvisation, a drummer improvises variations based on a wide variety of such patterns. Of course the musical situation, the interaction with the soloist, and the player's personal taste will always guide such improvisations. The Indian musician feels syllables cycling around as though strung together like beads on a necklace.

PERFORMANCE OF *RAGA KHAMAJ*

30

Raga Khamaj

In the **alap**, *the non-pulsatile section that begins a classical Indian performance*, the melodic soloist gradually reveals the characteristics of the raga as if folding back the petals of a flower. A skilled performer, such as Ali Akbar Khan in this recording, creates moments of delight or great drama as he slowly builds this melodic world by withholding, then artfully exposing, the raga's tones, motives, and ornaments. Thus the *alap* is the section in which we can hear the characteristics of the raga in their purest form.

Raga khamaj is traditionally associated with sensuality and feminine beauty. Ragamala paintings depict *khamaj* in different ways, but most include a beautiful woman (Figure 30.1). Romantic songs in light classical genres thus often use this raga, although it can also express deep emotions. It is a late night raga, meant to be performed between about midnight and 3 AM.

Raga khamaj uses an unaltered seventh scale step (*ni-shuddh* or simply *ni*) in ascent and lowered seventh step (*ni-komal*) in descent and avoids the second scale step (*re*) in ascent (see Graphic 28.2, page 139). The *vadi*, or stressed tone, in *khamaj* is *ni*, the seventh scale step. Because it lies just a semitone below the tonic, it often seems to be striving to resolve to the tonic (*sa*). By stressing this tone, the musician creates a sense of yearning or striving that is part of the mood of *khamaj*. The *samvadi* (secondary stressed tone) is the third scale step (*ga*), which is a semitone below scale step four (*ma*). Characteristic of *khamaj* is the way in which players create mirror-like motives of moving up and back the semitone from *ni* to *sa* and down and back the semitone from *ga* to *ma*. These patterns are prominent in the more extended melodic outline called the *chalan* (see Graphic 28.3, page 140).

The *alap* is generally divided into at least two parts, called the *sthai* and the *antara*. In each part the player gradually explores different parts of the scale, often beginning with the four notes below *sa*, then the notes below that, then gradually the octave above *sa*, increasing excitement and tension as he does. In a full performance, in which the *alap* could last half an hour, these sections are followed by sections called the **jor** and **jhala**, which are quasi-pulsatile, though still without the accompaniment of the drums.

British Library [mhii 021 0001546, Add.Or.28]

FIGURE 30.1
This *ragamala* painting illustrates *raga Kambhavati*, an earlier form of the *raga Khamaj* that we hear on CD 1:10. It depicts a beautiful woman making an offering of fire to the god Brahma.

CD 1:10 & 1:11. *Raga Khamaj. Sarod*, Ali Akbar Khan; *tabla*, Pandit Mahapurush Misra.

Alap: sthai section

0:00 	*Tampura* softly strums scale tones one and five (*sa* and *pa*), the most common drone pitches, but also adds the third scale step (*ga*), the *samvadi* in this *raga*. *Sarod* plays drone strings (*chikari*) throughout the performance, especially in between major melodic phrases.
0:10 	*Sarod* quickly ascends to the high tonic (*sa*) and then alternates, with elaboration, between *sa* and *ni*, the semitone just below—an alternation characteristic of *raga Khamaj*. The alternation introduces us to the *vadi*, *ni*, and its role as a stressed note in this *raga*. 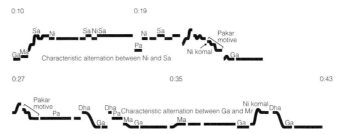
0:22 	*Sarod* descends the scale to *ga*, the *samvadi*. Listen for the lower scale tone seven (*ni-komal*) used in the descending scale. This descent with *ni-komal*, often with a slide, becomes a central motive, or *pakar*, for this performance.
0:35 	With the melody settled on *ga*, the *sarod* elaborates on a characteristic oscillation between the third and fourth scale steps, *ga* and *ma*. The phrase ends on the lower tonic (*sa*), completing the exposition of the entire octave below our starting point.
0:47	The first half of the *alap* (the *sthai*), ends with a statement of the entire ascending scale. Note that the second scale step, *re*, is missing in the ascending scale of *raga Khamaj*. The melody comes down again with the *pakar* motive and cadences on the *samvadi*, *ga*.

Alap: antara section

0:55 	The *pakar* motive again, but this time in the lower octave. *Sarod* explores and retraces some of the important *Khamaj* motives, but now in a lower octave and with increasing motion and diversity. Once again *sarod* emphasizes the alternation between *ni* and *sa*, at times dramatically lingering on *ni* to create a sense of yearning for resolution to the tonic, *sa*.
1:32	Another statement of the *pakar* brings us down to the bottom of the scale and another exploration of the *ga-ma* semitone.
2:36	One more statement of the *pakar* precedes our ascent back to the central tonic and a short ending section emphasizing *ni-sa* and a final cadence on upper *ga*, the *samvadi* again.

Gat (metered section)

2:56 	*Tabla* plays a short roll.

Sarod and *tabla* both land on the first beat, *sam*. This *tala* is *chachar*, a metrical pattern of 3 + 4 + 3 + 4, for a total of fourteen beats per cycle. The eighth beat (the beginning of the second half) is *khali* or the unstressed beat. *Sarod* expresses these two halves of the cycle by landing on the fifth scale step (*pa*) at the beginning and the third scale step (*ga*, the *samvadi*) at the halfway point, often anticipating or delaying their appearance. These phrases are variations of the theme (*gat*) of the first part of the metered section. 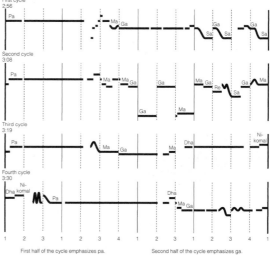 |

(continued)

Saval-Javab (question-answer) section CD 1 : 11	
0:00	Tempo has become much faster; typically, instrumental performances get gradually faster. For the second half of the metered section, the *tala* has changed to *tintal*, a 16-beat pattern of 4 + 4 + 4 + 4. Melodic soloist improvises a phrase and the drummer spontaneously imitates the phrase's rhythm and melodic contour. It is an exciting game of question-answer that increases in tension as the phrases become more complex and then more compressed.

Jhala section

2:03 	*Sarod* launches the climactic final section. Fast repeating notes alternate between melody tones and strokes on the *chikari* (drone) strings—a technique called *jhala*. This technique allows a speed suitable to the finale and emphasizes rhythm.
3:17 	As the tempo speeds up yet again, *sarod* uses the *jhala* technique of *thok jhala*. *Thok* literally means "hit," and refers to the fact that three successive down plucks ("hits") on the melody string follow a stroke on the *chikari* drone string. Other variations follow as the strokes become faster and more virtuosic. *Sarod* recapitulates several important melodies, including the *gat* theme from the beginning of the metered section and the *pakar* motive.
5:30	By unspoken agreement, Khan on *sarod* and Misra on *tabla* arrive at the very last *tala* cycle with a dramatic unison rhythm, without *jhala*, that recapitulates the important alternation between the seventh scale step (*ni*) and the high tonic (*sa*) that began the performance.

 CD1, Track 12 Raga Desh examples (that, arohana/avarohana, chalan)
   Track 13 Raga Khamaj examples (that, arohana/avarohana, chalan)

This performance, like many recordings, is rather abbreviated, the *alap* itself lasting less than three minutes. Therefore there are no *jor* or *jhala* sections and the unfolding of the raga is somewhat compressed. In addition, the famous *sarod* virtuoso Ali Akbar Khan inverts the usual practice of moving from the lowest part of the scale up and instead exposes the upper octave first, then the lower. Because the *sarod* has a metal fingerboard and no frets, its great strength as a solo instrument is that it allows continuous slides between pitches. Instead of separately plucking many of the pitches, the player deftly slides his fingernail to them after the initial pluck, sometimes stopping at several notes after a single pluck.

Because we do not have room here for the entire twenty-one-minute performance, we include two excerpts, the first from the *alap* and the beginning of the *gat* or metered section, the second from the very end of the piece.

VOCAL MUSIC IN INDIA

31

Because of the legacy in the United States and Europe of legendary performers such as Ravi Shankar and Ali Akbar Khan, it is easy to form the impression that most Indian music is instrumental. However, the voice is traditionally the most important instrument in India, since it is the only instrument that can convey text. Writers from the *Natyasastra* to the present day have traced this primacy of song back to the Vedic hymns, which they consider to be the source of many fundamental concepts of Indian music, including the cyclic philosophy now reflected in the concept of tala, the concept of melodic types now codified as raga, ornamentation practices (*gamak*), and the idea that music for any purpose is fundamentally devotional and spiritual in nature.

Because most vocal forms rely on a preexisting text, the structure of improvisation in vocal performances has to be carefully controlled. The singer can elaborate on phrases of an existing song, extending notes, interpolating tones, and adding ornamentation according to the rules of the raga. At other times, the singer may improvise without the restriction of having to set a text. Just as jazz vocalists improvise using so-called **scat** syllables, Indian singers may sing neutral syllables such as *ah*, solfege syllables (*sa, re, ga, ma, pa, dha,* and *ni*), or the rhythmic patterns of syllables used by the drummer (*theka*).

North Indian Vocal Music

From the time of the Vedas through the Middle Ages, the primary source for song texts was devotional religious poetry, first in Sanskrit and later in regional languages. As patronage in North India shifted to the Islamic courts,

FIGURE **31.1**
Nusrat Fateh Ali Khan (left) performing *qawwali*. Among the instruments accompanying him are two harmoniums in the foreground.

© Kapoor Baldev/Sygma/CORBIS

the song texts sometimes, though not always, shifted from praise of gods to praise of kings and sultans and romantic subjects.

Despite this general rule, one important type of religious song emerged from the **Qawal**, *wandering Sufi mystics who sang devotional Islamic songs known as **qawwali**.* Today the *Qawal* are generally professional musicians who give concerts that are still primarily devotional and religious. Before his death in 1997, Nusrat Fateh Ali Khan did much to popularize this art form in the West (Figure 31.1). *Qawwali* share some Indian concepts of raga and tala, but they also show characteristics of Middle Eastern vocal music such as florid melismas. A *qawwali* ensemble may include one or more harmoniums, a **dholak** (*small hand-held drum*), and melody instruments such as the *bansri*, *tabla*, and *tambura*.

From at least the fifteenth century until their decline in the early twentieth century, the Hindustani courts provided the primary patronage for classical music in the North. With the support of a ruler, a musician could devote himself to music full-time and apprentices could learn their craft over years without having to worry about earning a living. Recitals were intimate and only for the educated elite. In this context, composers could develop long and sophisticated musical forms without having to worry about appealing to large audiences or arranging concert schedules.

The primary musical form associated with this period is the grand but austere vocal form called **dhrupad**. The majestic *dhrupad* is the musical equivalent of that other famous icon of the Mughal period—the palace known as the Taj Mahal. A performance of *dhrupad* is a vocal tour de force that can last up to three hours and include accompaniment by the *bin*, *tampura*, and the **pakhavaj**, the *ancient double-headed drum* (instead of the modern *tabla*). Though rarely performed today, the *dhrupad* was an important influence on many subsequent forms, including instrumental performances.

The *dhrupad* begins with an unmeasured *alap* sung on neutral syllables derived from mantra chants, moving into a quasi-pulsatile section called the *jor*. When the drummer enters, the audience hears the precomposed song that is the basis for the performance, followed by elaborate improvisations on sections of the song. While the song may be either devotional or secular, it is always serious and profound. In keeping with the reverence and austerity of the form, the performance is only lightly ornamented, and self-indulgent displays of virtuosity are definitely out of place.

Today, the **khyal** is *the most prominent vocal genre* in Hindustani concerts. Some writers credit the invention of the *khyal* to the influence of the florid and melismatic *qawwali* on *dhrupad* singers of the Mughal courts. Highly ornamented in comparison to the relatively unadorned lines of the *dhrupad*, *khyal* creates elegant and ornate lines suited to the lighter and often romantic texts. Men most often sing *khyal*, accompanied by the *tabla* and *tambura*, or sometimes with an added melodic instrument such as the *sarangi* or harmonium. Unlike Hindustani instrumental performances, in *khyal* performances the tempo does not gradually increase, but the *tala* cycle may be suddenly halved at some point, in effect doubling the tempo. Adding to the excitement toward the end of the performance are *fast scalar runs*, called **tans**, or sometimes fast scat sections derived from a related form known as **tarana**.

Thumri is the most important light classical Hindustani vocal genre; these are lyrical songs of love or lost romance. Unlike the virtuosic *khyal*, the focus is not on the virtuosity of the singer, but on the poignancy of the text. Thus the raga and tala are usually relatively simple, and *thumri* are especially popular as short closing pieces for concerts.

South Indian Vocal Music

Kriti are the most popular of the major vocal forms of South Indian performances. Although their length can be variable, they are often, like the Hindustani *khyal*, the long centerpiece of a concert. Both men and women may sing *kriti*, most often accompanied by a single melody instrument, usually a violin, in addition to the *tambura* and *mrdangam* (drum). The form of the song on which a *kriti* is based is similar to the verse/refrain form of many Western songs; the *refrain* is called the **pallavi** and the *verse* the **caranam**. A *contrasting section* known as the **anupallavi** is also common. The singer may repeat each section several times, with different elaborations and ornamentation.

Improvisational sections may follow the song or may be inserted between each *pallavi-caranam* or *pallavi-anupallavi* pair. In addition to free elaborations on preceding phrases of the song, there are a number of standard improvisation types, including *svara kalpana*, improvisation using solfege syllables, and *niraval*, improvisation using extemporaneous variations on text that may be unrelated to the text of the *kriti*. An opportunity for the drummer to take a solo usually arises.

The **ragam-tanam-pallavi** is a long and virtuosic form associated with court patronage, much like the northern *dhrupad*. Rather than featuring elaborations on fixed devotional song, the *ragam-tanam-pallavi* is nearly entirely free improvisation with very little text. The *ragam* of the title refers to the first part of the performance, consisting of an *alapana* section performed by the singer and the violinist (or other instrumentalist) in turn. The quasi-pulsatile *tanam* section follows the *ragam*, then metered improvisations on the *pallavi*, or fixed text.

Relatively fixed songs are popular everywhere in Indian musical culture. **Bhajan**, for example, are well-known popular devotional songs that frequently close a South Indian concert. **Tillana**, a form used to accompany dance, consists entirely of *bols* (drum syllables); the Hindustani equivalent is *tarana*. **Kirtana** are songs that include improvisation and form an intermediate step for the student singer between non-improvised forms and long virtuoso forms such as *kriti*. *Kirtana* are nevertheless popular concert works, though generally shorter and less elaborate than *kriti*.

Performance of the *Kriti, Ninnada nela*

Tyagaraja (1767–1847) is probably South India's most famous composer. To the people of this region he represents much more than a composer of songs or a great poet in the Telugu language, although he was both of these. He is remembered as a holy person for whom music was a means of devotion and spiritual enlightenment. Tyagaraja was a devotee of the god Rama, whom his lyrics address in a startlingly personal and emotional tone, often expressing the disappointments and failures of the composer's own life—as they do in our audio selection.

The form Tyagaraja chose for most of his compositions was the *kriti*. The performer on our recording sings the melody of the *kriti* substantially as Tyagaraja composed it (as far as we know), but with extensive ornamental variations and extemporaneous repeats. The *kriti* itself may be introduced with an unmetered *alapana* and followed by more improvisatory sections, but this performance consists of only the *kriti* proper—the *pallavi*, *anupallavi*, and *caranam*. The singer's variations of the melody are extremely ornate and recall the elaborations of some traditions of *Sama-veda* chant. Such fluid lines are characteristic of much South Indian vocal music, especially when compared to similar forms in the North. Given this ornamentation, it is surprising that most of the time the violinist follows the singer very closely, but the violinist is as familiar with the composition as the singer and listens very closely so he can anticipate the singer.

Tyagaraja wrote a total of three *caranam* sections, the balance of which would normally follow the last refrain on our recording, but this is an abbreviated performance. Singers may perform several such short *kriti* before a concert's centerpiece of a full performance with *alapana* and improvisation. Tyagaraja composed *Ninnada nela* in *raga Kannada*. The *arohana/avarohana* shows how in this raga pitch *ri* (the second scale degree) is avoided in ascent and *ni* (seventh scale degree) is avoided in descent. There is also a characteristic turn around pitch *ma* (fourth scale degree) in both ascent and descent.

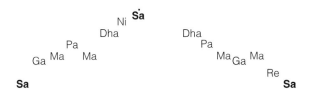

GRAPHIC **31.1**
Arohana/avarohana
of *raga Kannada*

Folk Song in India

Despite the prominence of its large cities, the vast majority of India's population lives in rural villages. Few of these people have any contact with the classical tradition of Indian music. The ethnic diversity of the subcontinent is reflected in the many different styles and instruments of folk music. Some versions of the instruments have found their way into the classical tradition, although, as exemplified by the *sarangi* fiddle and the *shahnai* double reed, they are now built in much more finely crafted and standardized forms.

Although prerecorded cassettes and movies have replaced some of the traditional roles of folk music, traditional performances are still common, especially for festivals, weddings, and performances for tourists, where one can still find the so-called snake charmer. Folk traditions are especially well known in the northwestern state of Rajasthan, where a special caste of Muslim folk musicians known as Langa play for festivals and celebrations and in restaurants. Among the many folk ensembles in the south is the **cinna melm** instrumental ensemble of the Kerala state, who accompany certain ritual dances with the powerful sound of massed barrel-shaped drums, double reeds or flutes, and drones. One of the most famous folk traditions, however, comes from the culture of the Bauls of Bengal.

Baul Music

One very distinctive folk tradition is the music of the Bauls, a minority religious sect in Bengal, a state in eastern India, and Bangladesh. The Bauls are a distinct cultural group whose unique blend of mystical Hinduism and Islam emphasizes simplicity and social equality; they often come from the poorest segments of society. Although their songs are not usually explicitly religious, their texts usually consist of religious or moral allegories, the meanings of which are often obscure.

Listening Guide

CD 1:14. *Ninnada nela* ("Why should I blame you"),[1] Tyagaraja. Singer, Ramnad Krishnan; violin, V. Thyagarajan; *mrdangam*, T. Ranganathan; *kanjira* (a kind of tambourine), V. Nagarajan.

Pallavi section

0:00	*Tambura* drone enters (some preliminary tuning)
0:15	*Pallavi* begins. The first phrase of the *pallavi*, on the words *"Ninnada nela,"* ("Why should I blame you?") lasts one cycle of *adi tala*, which has a form of 4 + 2 + 2. However, the sung phrase begins and ends somewhat before *sam* (the first beat of the cycle).
	Ornate vocal variations on the melody, with violinist following closely. Florid exploration of the tetrachord (four notes) below *sa* (the tonic).
	Try to match the actual vocal performance with the graphic representation of the ascent, descent, and turn in the ascent and descent (Graphic 31.1). The singer sings this phrase six times in different variations, increasing the range towards the end.
0:46	The next phrase of the *pallavi* "nirajaksha Sri Rama" ("Lord Rama") makes it clear that the poet is addressing the god Rama in a personal, nearly blasphemous tone, that leads the listener to wonder, "Why does the singer blame the benevolent god Rama?"
1:06	A sudden emptying of the texture through an unspoken coordination among the singer, violinist, and drummer leads to a short ending section that wraps up the *pallavi*.
	The drummer twice interpolates a new threefold repeat that finally lands on the first beat of the next section, the *anupallavi*.

Anupallavi section

1:17	Vocalist's next phrase, "kannavari paini kaka seya nela?" ("Is it fair for a child to be angry with his parents?"), offers, if not a justification, a way to consider this most human reaction to despair.
	The *anupallavi*'s long notes centering around *sa* (the tonic) provide dramatic contrast to the florid character of the *pallavi*.
	Vocalist repeats the first half of the *anupallavi* a total of seven times, each with more elaborate deviations from *sa* and opening up the register above *sa*.

[1] Translation adapted from C. Ramanujachari, *The Spiritual Heritage of Tyagaraja* (Madras: The Ramakrishna Mission Students' Home, 1957); 261.

1:54 	Vocalist begins the *anupallavi*'s second half—the dramatic centerpiece of the *kriti*—with a melody that now extends in striking sweeps. *Kanjira* (tambourine) joins the ensemble, doubles the *mrdangam* (drum) part.
Pallavi refrain	
2:04	The *pallavi* returns as a refrain to round out the first large section of the *kriti*.
Caranam section	
2:25 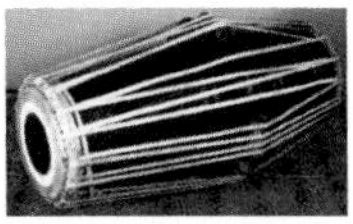	The poetry of this section answers the questions previously posed: "Sattva rupa ninnu sannuti jesi tattvamu telisina tyagarajuniki" ("Tyagaraja [the composer] has learned the secret of success in spiritual fulfillment comes only at a cost"). He resigns himself to the uselessness of anger in the face of *dharma* (fate) and accepts the spiritual truth that comes through devotion. The *mrdangam* takes a more active part that culminates in . . . Tense series of high subdivisions of the beat during the ending part of this line.
2:55	The second line of the *caranam*, now joined by the *kanjira*.
Pallavi refrain	
3:30 	Violinist joins the singer once again for the final coda. Three powerful strokes on the *mrdangam* and *kanjira* end the performance.

FIGURE **31.2**
A Baul singer (center) in Kenduli, India, accompanies himself with a *khamak*, a drum with a string attached to the head. The musician on the left plays a *khol*, a double-headed drum with a clay body, and the musician on the right plays a *dotara* lute.

© Chris Lisle/CORBIS

On the streets of Bengal, in celebrations and festivals, the Baul singer is often a one-person band who plays, for example, a drone chordophone in one hand and a small drum in the other and jingles ankle bells to movements of a dance, all while singing. A distinctive instrument of the tradition is the *string-drum* known as the **khamak**. A drum membrane resonates a long string that can generate swooping sounds as the player varies the string tension by squeezing two flexible pieces of wood forming the neck to which the string is attached. In professional concerts or radio broadcasts, other musicians may join in the accompaniment, playing flutes, plucked lutes, or other drums, but the focus is still on the singer (Figure 31.2).

The singing style is full, expressive, and open-throated. Recognizing its surprising similarities to American blues singing, the Paul Butterfield Blues Band presented a Baul ensemble as an intermission feature during their 1969 tour. Charles Capwell, whose book *The Music of the Bauls of Bengal* is the best study of this music, relates an interesting anecdote about this relationship.

> By chance, Laksman [a famous Baul singer] once heard a recording of Janis Joplin when he was visiting an American friend at her hotel in Calcutta. Listening with surprising intentness, he occasionally murmured a word of approval. After the song was over, he inquired about the meaning of the text, and when he learned that the text concerned a woman's desire that her lover [actually God] buy her a Mercedes-Benz automobile, he asked, slightly puzzled, if there were not mention of yoga or some other spiritual-physical discipline; he was incredulous to think that such emotional energy as Joplin put into her performance could be expended on such a trivial matter as the desire for a car.[2]

---

[2] Charles Capwell, *The Music of the Bauls of Bengal* (Kent, OH: Kent State University Press, 1986); 48–49.

THE INFLUENCE OF INDIAN MUSIC ON CONTEMPORARY WESTERN MUSIC

32

In 1967, at the height of the counterculture movement, the Indian sitarist Ravi Shankar (Figure 27.1) electrified the audience at the Monterey Pop Festival with his performance of the afternoon raga *Bhimpalasi*, introducing Indian classical music to Western popular audiences. In many ways, Shankar's unique career made him the ideal musical emissary. The son of a Bengali Brahmin (high-caste) family, Shankar was educated in both India and Europe, and spent his teenage years participating in an innovative dance troupe organized by his older brother Uday. Uday's new choreography and music fused European and Indian influences, but Shankar was drawn to the resurgence of Indian nationalism, then at the height of its resistance to British colonial rule.

At age eighteen he apprenticed himself to the famous Alauddin Khan, whose eclectic musical background included study within the *gharana* of Tansen, the famous Mughal-period composer. During Shankar's seven years of intensive study, he befriended a fellow student, Alauddin Khan's son, Ali Akbar Khan, who specialized in the *sarod*. While retaining great respect for and command of the classical traditions, Shankar also composed film scores using combinations of Western and Indian instruments. He toured Europe and America extensively in the 1950s, and by the 1960s, his recordings brought him to the attention of jazz musicians and, most famously, George Harrison of the Beatles.

Certainly many Western writers had expressed respect for and interest in Indian classical music through the colonial period and saw in it correspondences to the European classical tradition. Both are sophisticated traditions performed by professionals dedicated to the subtleties of emotional expression. At the same time the two seemed very far apart. Indian music is largely improvised and was not deemed compatible with Western-harmonic progressions and modulations.

Those limitations were less of an issue with Harrison, whose "Within You Without You" used a *sitar*, melismas, and slow changes in harmony to imitate surface elements of an Indian performance. Although the Beatles were later disillusioned with their study with a spiritual guru on a trip to India, Harrison befriended Shankar, who gave him some lessons on the *sitar*. The Monterey Pop Festival and other large concerts followed. While Shankar respected Harrison and other Western musicians he met, he was ambivalent about some of the concert venues, believing that many of the young people in these audiences did not properly respect the music or its spiritual basis.

The melodic and improvisational basis of Indian classical music was an inspiration rather than a limitation for many jazz musicians, especially with the popularity of so-called modal jazz in the 1960s. In these works, performers such as John Coltrane and Miles Davis, like Indian musicians, focused mainly on the resources of the scale as a basis for improvisation, rather than the usual harmonic progression. Davis's guitarist John McLaughlin studied Indian music, and some Indian-influenced pieces appeared on Davis's album *Big Fun* from 1969. McLaughlin went on to produce a number of solo albums with Indian collaborators, and formed the group Shakti in the 1970s with South Indian violinist L. Shankar and percussionists Zakir Hussain and T. H. Vinayakram. Other groups who adopted Indian influences in the 1970s included the Paul Winter Consort and Oregon, a jazz ensemble devoted to Indian fusion.

Indian music's deep meditations on the worlds within the sounds of the raga also impressed some musicians of the classical avant-garde. The American composer La Monte Young was especially impressed with the modal improvisations of Coltrane and recordings of Ali Akbar Khan. In the mid-1960s he began studying with North Indian vocalist Pandit Pran Nath. Among the elements of Indian music that influenced Young were its tuning systems, the drone, the exploration of a single scale, and improvisation. Because these elements could be left unchanged literally for hours, Young became one of the first composers associated with the label **minimalism**, *a style in which composers experimented with a minimum of means.*

Another composer known as a minimalist was Young's friend Terry Riley (Figure 32.1), who also studied with Pran Nath. In the 1970s, he performed improvisations based on his own raga-like scales and melodic formulations for hours. He also used Eastern drums, Indian-style singing, and other South Asian elements. Unlike some of the less successful jazz and rock fusion pieces, there is nothing about these works that suggest mere exoticism or a superficial imitation of Indian elements.

Many Indian musicians have also written compositions involving both Western and Indian instruments and concepts. Both Ravi Shankar and Ali

FIGURE **32.1**
Terry Riley in performance at Intermedia '68. Riley used tape loops to create drones and ostinati over which he improvised raga-like melodies on this soprano saxophone.

Courtesy of Terry Riley, via Tom Welsh, Elision Fields. Reprinted with permission.

Akbar Khan opened music schools in California to which they brought the ideals of devotion, discipline, and spiritual peace through music to new generations of dedicated students from many countries.

 REFERENCES

Discography

North India

Khan, Ali Akbar. *Signature Series* (4 vol.). San Anselmo, CA: AMMP CD 9001–9004, 1968–73/1990–94.

Narayan, Ram. *North India: Pandit Ram Narayan, sarangi*. Paris: Ocora C 559060, 1989.

Shankar, Ravi. *The Sounds of India*. New York: Columbia CK 9296, 1966/1989.

Shankar, Ravi. *Three Ragas*. New York: Angel CD 67310, 1956/2000.

South India

Balachander. *Veena Virtuoso*. Tokyo: King Record Co. KICC 5199, 1982.

Ramnad Krishnan, Vidwan. *Music of South India: Songs of the Carnatic Tradition*. New York/Los Angeles: Elektra/Nonesuch 9 72023-2, 1968/1988.

Subramaniam, L. *Le violon de l'Inde du sud*. Paris: Ocora C559029, 1980/1988.

Other Traditions

Khan, Nusrat Fateh Ali. *Shahen-Shah*. Beverly Hills, CA: RealWorld, 1989.

Purna Chandra Das Baul. *The Bengal Minstrel: Music of the Bauls*. New York: Nonesuch 72068, 1975.

Shakti. *Handful of Beauty*. New York: Sony SRCS 7015, 1977/1999.

Bibliography

Bor, Joep, ed. *The Raga Guide: A Survey of 74 Hindustani Ragas*. Netherlands: Nimbus Records, 1999.

Capwell, Charles. *The Music of the Bauls of Bengal*. Kent, OH: Kent State University Press, 1986.

Jairazbhoy, Nazir. *The Ragas of North Indian Music: Their Structure and Evolution*. Middletown, CT: Wesleyan University Press, 1971.

Neuman, Daniel M. *The Life of Music in North India: The Organization of an Artistic Tradition*. Detroit: Wayne State University Press, 1980.

Pesch, Ludwig. *The Illustrated Companion to South Indian Classical Music*. Delhi: Oxford University Press, 1999.

Ruckert, George E. *Music in North India*. Oxford: Oxford University Press, 2004.

Shankar, Ravi. *My Music, My Life*. New York: Simon and Schuster, 1968.

Sorrell, Neil. *Indian Music in Performance: A Practical Introduction*. New York: New York University Press, 1980.

Viswanathan, T. and Matthew Harp Allen. *Music in South India*. Oxford: Oxford University Press, 2004.

Wade, Bonnie C. *Music in India: The Classical Traditions*. Englewood Cliffs, NJ: Prentice-Hall, 1979.

——— c. 2205–c. 1766 BCE
Xia Dynasty. According to legend, Huang Di (the "Yellow Emperor") ordered his court entertainer, Ling Lun, to create a standard system for music. Ling Lun traveled until he found suitable bamboo for fashioning a pipe. He fixed the pitch according to the song of the phoenix bird, and this pitch, called the Yellow Bell, *huang zhong*, became the basis for the Chinese musical system.

——— c. 1766–c. 1030 BCE
Shang Dynasty. The first surviving musical instruments include bone whistles, bronze bells (*zhong*), globular flutes (*xun*), and stone chimes (*qing*). Pitch measurements of the extant instruments have been inconclusive, although it is clear that the pentatonic system of Chinese music was established at a very early date.

——— c. 1030–256 BCE
Zhou Dynasty. Period of Lao Zi (604–517 BCE), founder of Daoism and Kong Fuzi "Confucius" (551–479 BCE), founder of Confucianism. Confucius is especially associated with the introspective music of the *guqin* and the *se* (zithers).

——— 221–207 BCE
Qin Dynasty. To fight the influence of the Confucians, Emperor Shi Huangdi orders destruction of all books, including music books. This meant the loss of most of the music theory and notation from the earlier periods. Much Confucianist music and theory from later periods is based on attempts to recover this ancient heritage.

PART 6

China

202 BCE–220 CE
Han Dynasty. Period of re-building and Confucian influence, including development of tuning systems, musical symbolism and codification of court rituals. Establishment of imperial music bureau.

c. 64 CE
Buddhism brings new philosophies of music, rituals, and Central Asian and Indian influences. Buddhist rituals, including chant, were established in great monasteries that became meccas for Buddhist monks and scholars from throughout China as well as other countries.

221–581
Period of Three Kingdoms and Southern and Northern Dynasties. Influence of Central Asian kingdoms and the Silk Road (trade route to Europe) leads to the importation of musical styles and instruments, including the *pipa* lute. By the end of this period, the northern imperial music bureau recorded ten separate court music groups from different regions. The tradition of court orchestral music is retained in Korea and Japan, though not China.

PART 6 ■ CHINA

⟨decorative glyphs⟩ INTRODUCTION TO THE REGION

33

FIRST LISTEN
CD 1:15
Ping sha lo yen
("Wild Geese
Descending onto
the Sandbank"),
Li Xiang-Ting

Although they are rare in today's People's Republic, one hundred years ago the homes of the intellectual class were found by idyllic streams and mountainsides in China, their seclusion symbolizing the scholar's withdrawal from the human world and closeness to nature. It might be more accurate to say that they viewed themselves as a part of nature, ideally in harmony with it. The sparse furnishings of their dwellings would have included such emblems of the intelligentsia as a brush and ink, a carefully crafted arrangement of flowers, and a number of books. Foremost among these items would be the *ancient Chinese zither* known as the **guqin** (pronounced goo-chin).

581–906			
Sui and Tang Dynasties. An era representing the greatest extent of internationalism and cultural interchange, later seen as a classical period for music as well as poetry and other arts. Chinese music greatly influences music in Korea and Japan.			

581–906
Sui and Tang Dynasties. An era representing the greatest extent of internationalism and cultural interchange, later seen as a classical period for music as well as poetry and other arts. Chinese music greatly influences music in Korea and Japan.

960–1279
Song Dynasty. Period of a more nationalistic and isolationist character. Theatrical schools established.

1260–1368
Yuan (Mongol) Dynasty. Period of rule by Genghis Khan and his Mongolian successors.

1368–1644
Ming Dynasty. Development of dramatic forms, including *kunqu, gaoqiang,* and *banziqiang.* These become the basis for *jingxi* or Beijing (Peking) opera and other regional theatrical forms.

The *guqin* has seven strings, traditionally made of silk, but no frets (Figure 36.1, page 174). It is a curved board about four feet long set on a low table and plucked. The sound is very soft. When a scholar played the instrument, he would play for a few friends in his home or perhaps out in the woods for his own pleasure.

Such a performance would be an extraordinary experience. The delicate, floating tones are played very slowly, even reverently, so that one's attention focuses not so much on the melody, but on each sound as an individual event. The contemplative attitude of the performer gives little hint of the extremely compli-cated and difficult performance technique the instru-ment requires. Each tone requires a precise method of plucking, holding, touching, moving, or otherwise manipulating the string with both hands. As the sounds of the instrument drift across the quiet surroundings of bamboo and flowers, they are meant to evoke beautiful images of nature and trans-port the listeners through a kind of mystic journey.

Because of its refinement and sophistication, *guqin* music is cultivated by relatively few. The panorama of styles in this large country includes ex-citing, fast, earthy, and dramatic traditional music, and in many ways *guqin* music is not as representative as some repertories of Chinese traditional music. Yet in many ways the *guqin* represents ideals not only of Chinese clas-sical music and art, but also of a way of life.

The ideas of spiritual connection with nature, beauty in simplicity, and art as inward contemplation are all closely associated with the mystic Chi-nese religion of Daoism. The tones of the *guqin* are sometimes described as "the sound of emptiness," referring to the Daoist goal of freeing one's mind through the contemplation of nothingness, a goal it shares with Buddhism.

© Asian Art & Archaeology, Inc./CORBIS

FIGURE **33.1**
This *guqin* player figurine is from the later Han dynasty (c. 25–220 CE), a time of reaffirmation of Confucian values.

1644–1911
Qing (Manchu) Dynasty. As in the Yuan period, Northern invaders, this time from Manchuria, take control of China, only to become sinicized themselves. This is a pe-riod of isolationism and struggles with European imperialism.

Late 19th C
Christian missionaries teach European music in some regions; military music and political songs with European harmonies also become popular.

1911–1949
Republic. Period of war-lords is followed by a government under the Nationalist party. Ancient court rituals and music as-sociated with them near extinction. Western popu-lar songs are common in urban areas, and Songs for the Masses are com-posed on Western models.

1931–1945
Japanese take Manchuria and later invade most of China.

But most of all, the *guqin* is associated with the Confucian religion and its social class of literati who cultivate the ideals of balance, harmony, and moderation. *Guqin* texts often point out that in Chinese, a homonym of *qin* (zither) is the word meaning "restraint."

For the most part, class distinctions and their various emblems, such as the library in the cottage by the stream, have not survived the social leveling of communism, especially the attack on intellectuals during the Cultural Revolution (1966–76), but the *guqin* is enjoying a modest resurgence of interest in recent times. And while the trappings of class distinction are no longer a prerequisite for the study of the *guqin*, its historical association with devotion and contemplation, harmony and balance remain a crucial part of its legacy.

Geography   China today is the world's most populous country, with well over one billion people, of whom 94 percent are of the Han ethnic group. This vast population has a great variety of languages and customs, as well as music. Mandarin Chinese is the language of the People's Republic of China, and major regional dialects, such as Cantonese, are largely unintelligible to people of other regions. The system of writing, however, using classical Chinese ideographic characters, is understood throughout the empire and has always allowed the Chinese to transmit laws, rituals, and philosophy, forging a unity across thousands of miles. This section will primarily cover the music of the Han people.

1945–1949
After defeat of Japanese at the end of World War II, Mao Zedong leads a communist revolution. The republican government flees to Taiwan.

1949
People's Republic. The communist government of Mao Zedong institutes socialist realism, censorship in the arts, and surveys of folk music. Western musical influence appears in workers' songs, political songs, and orchestras of traditional instruments.

1966–1776
The Cultural Revolution sends many musicians, composers, and intellectuals to labor camps and begins strict censorship in the arts. Chinese opera theaters are closed or allowed to present only approved operas in the style of socialist realism.

1976
After the death of Mao Zedong, foreign contact resumes, censorship relaxes, and composers and musicologists associate more freely with their counterparts in other countries. By the 1980s, religious music and rituals are tolerated.

CHARACTERISTICS OF TRADITIONAL CHINESE MUSIC

34

Composers and performers emphasize the melodic aspects of composition, in which balance and harmonious proportions are especially important.

■ **Monophonic, Heterophonic Textures** Much of the traditional art music of China was written for a single instrument; when more than one instrument plays, heterophony enriches the texture while still emphasizing the original melody.

■ **Importance of Ornamentation** Ornamentation is highly developed, as might be expected in a melodic tradition, and much of an instrument's performance technique rests on knowledge of the appropriate use of ornaments.

■ **Timbre as a Compositional Element** Variations in timbre, effected through subtle distinctions in performance technique or changes in singing style, can be as important as melodic ornamentation to the character of a melody.

■ **Variation Form** The forms of many pieces, from folk songs to *guqin* performances, are based on a series of elaborate variations of a basic melody.

Religion and Music in China

Despite the official support of atheism in the People's Republic, the three historical religions of China—Daoism, Confucianism, and Buddhism—have occupied an important position in the culture and music of China. While not necessarily mutually exclusive, each religion emphasizes different ideas.

Founded by Lao Zi in the sixth century BCE, Daoism, or Taoism, is the first major religion of China. It is essentially a mystical and inward-looking philosophy overlaid by a variety of later rituals. Music is used in its rituals, but Daoism in its pure form has no use for stimulation of the senses. As suggested by the following passage from Lao Zi, music for entertainment is looked upon with suspicion.

> The five colors blind our eyes.
> The five tones deafen our ears.
> The five flavors confuse our taste.
> Racing and hunting madden our minds.
> Possessing rare treasures brings about harmful behavior.
> Therefore the sage regards his center, and not his eyes.
> —Translation by Charles Muller.
> Reprinted by permission of Barnes & Noble Publishing, Inc.

Nevertheless, the influence of Daoism is clear in the contemplative nature of much Chinese music, its emphasis on simplicity, and its connection with the natural world.

The sixth-century BCE philosopher Kong Fuzi, known to the West as Confucius, established the second great Chinese religion. Because Confucius was especially concerned with establishing strict norms of moral behavior, social classes, theories of government, and ritual traditions, Confucianism is especially associated with the intellectual class. Like his near-contemporary Plato, Confucius saw music's ability to influence behavior as a powerful tool that should be controlled by the state. He encouraged the cultivation of music that inspired noble sentiments and other emotions useful to society, and he advocated state censorship for music for entertainment or music that inspired harmful emotions.

Books about and attributed to Confucius are full of references to the power of music and its proper place in society. In particular, music had an important place in ritual and in the personal expression of ideals of goodness and propriety. Confucius himself was said to have been a player of the *guqin*, sometimes moving people to tears with the emotions his playing could express. Among the poems attributed to Confucius is the following:

> When one has a loving wife,
> It's like the playing of *guqin* and *se*,
> When there is congeniality between brothers,
> It resembles the beautiful music that gathers.
> —Translation by Hsu Wen-Ying

Since the time of Confucius, Chinese music has maintained a clear demarcation between the refined and elegant *art music of the court and rituals*, known as **yayue**, and *common entertainment and folk music*, known as **suyue**. An elaborate layer of metaphysics and cosmology was later added to Confucian thought, which continued to control many aspects of court life and court decisions until the end of dynastic China in 1911. Each of the twelve pitches in the Chinese tuning system was associated with one of the twelve months of the year and one of the twelve hours into which the Chinese traditionally divide both the day and the night. The five pitches of the pentatonic modes were related to five metals, five planets, and so on. Intimate knowledge of these associations helps composers craft music to heal, to instill warlike feelings, to inspire noble behavior, and so on.

The third main religion of China is Buddhism, which entered China through its trade with South and Central Asia in the first century of the Current Era. By the third and fourth centuries, Buddhism had become very prominent and had brought not only new philosophies and metaphysics, but also new instruments, rituals, and music.

Like Daoism, Buddhism emphasizes meditation and inner knowledge. Because much traditional Chinese art music is intended for a single instrument, playing it is similar to meditation. The presence of an audience is incidental. It is the relationship of the performer to the sound that is important.

While Buddhism and Daoism were not outlawed under the Communist government, religious practice, including music, was suspect, and temples were sometimes closed, even plundered. Since the 1980s, the government's attitude towards religion has grown more tolerant, temples have reopened, and many traditional religious practices are allowed without interference.

Traditional Music Theory in China

In many musical cultures, music theorists are writers who attempt to articulate and elucidate the often unspoken and complex processes underlying musical composition and performance. While there may always be a gap between practice and theory, the goal of theory is to codify what musicians do and why. In China, however, the purpose of music theory has been to find music's philosophical basis and its relationship to the cosmos. If musical practice does not completely agree with music theory, then those performances are considered vulgar, ill-informed, or out of balance.

A document from the third century BCE describes a tuning system in which successive pitch ratios of 3:2 derive a scale of twelve pitches per octave. This method was probably known long before that time in many ancient societies, including Europe, where it became known as Pythagorean tuning. Chinese theorists, like later musicians in Europe, extended this tuning system to derive a twelve-tone scale. *Each of the twelve pitches* is known as **lü**. Traditional zithers, such as the *guqin*, are still tuned this way, although most modern versions of Chinese instruments adopt the compromise of twelve-tone equal temperament so that, like their European counterparts, they can easily transpose and be grouped into larger orchestras.

From this theoretical set of twelve pitches, theorists next derived various heptatonic (seven-pitch) scales that are basically the same as the diatonic scales of Europe. However, as far as we know, most traditional Chinese music was pentatonic, not heptatonic; the two extra notes, called **bianyin** (*changing tones*), were sometimes used as auxiliary pitches. These pentatonic scales left out the semitones (small intervals) of the heptatonic scales. Thus the pentatonic scales are sometimes called **anhemitonic** (without semitones) scales. The black keys of the piano keyboard approximate these scales.

There are five possible *anhemitonic pentatonic modes*, **diao**, one for each possible tonic or home pitch. Musicologists often name these pentatonic scales by numbering them within the heptatonic system, leaving out those numbers corresponding to the two absent notes. The pitches are numbered so that 1 always represents the tonic. Therefore the five possible pentatonic modes are:

gongdiao	1	2	3	–	5	6	–
shangdiao	1	2	–	4	5	–	7
juediao	1	–	3	4	–	6	7
zidiao	1	2	–	4	5	6	–
yudiao	1	–	3	4	5	–	7

Gongdiao and *zidiao* are the most common modes in use. As we see in Table 34.1, a great deal of classical writing in Chinese music theory was

TABLE **34.1**
Table of the Notes of the Chinese Musical Scales and Their Symbolic Connections

Musical Notes	*Gongdiao*	*Shangdiao*	*Juediao*	*Zidiao*	*Yudiao*
Cardinal Points	center	west	east	south	north
Political Structure	king	minister	people	national affairs	natural world
Virtues	faith	righteousness	benevolence	respect	knowledge
Colors	yellow	white	blue	red	black
Elements	earth	metal	wood	fire	water
Heavenly Bodies	constellations	earth	stars	sun	moon
Planets	Saturn	Venus	Jupiter	Mars	Mercury
Flavors	sweet	pungent	sour	bitter	salty
Emotions	desire	melancholy	anger	joy	fear
Sounds	song	weeping	shouting	laughter	mourning

devoted to the cosmological significance of such musical components as these modes. Clearly, the tonic pitch affects the symbolism of a piece as well as its relationship to the other pitches.

In Chinese opera, many different aspects of a performance may characterize a mode apart from its scale—the sequence of pitches that end phrases (cadential pitches), the music's relative range, even the instruments. The character of the mode makes it most appropriate to the rhythms and meters, the degree of ornamentation or melisma, and the characters in the opera.

TRADITIONAL CHINESE INSTRUMENTS

35

Chordophones

Despite the historical existence of orchestras and chamber music (small groups of musicians), China's musical traditions have emphasized the role of the solitary performer. Each classical instrument has developed its own tradition, idiomatic techniques, and sometimes, notation. Each instrument is often associated with a particular social class, context for performance, and character of piece. For example, while the ancient and revered *guqin* is associated with Confucian rituals and the literati class, another curved board zither, the **zheng** (Figure 35.1), was associated historically with the household and romantic songs. While on a *guqin* the player plays different pitches by pressing the string down to the resonator, the *zheng* has a different string for each pitch, although pitches can also be bent by pressing down behind the bridge after plucking.

During the period of Northern and Southern dynasties (265–581 CE), China engaged in considerable contact with Central Asian cultures. Orchestras from several of these cultures were installed in Northern courts, and many of their invigorating styles and instruments were quite popular. Among the instruments the Chinese adopted was the *pear-shaped lute* now known as the **pipa** (Figure 35.2). Because of its origins, the *pipa* does not have the same place in the Chinese tradition as the *guqin*, but respect for its evocative power is clear from the famous poem "Song of the Pipa Player" by Bai Juyi (772–846):

> Strong and loud, the thick string sounded like a sudden shower;
> Weak and soft, the thin string whispered in your ear.
> When strong and weak, loud and soft sounds were mixed,
> They were like big and tiny pearls falling on a jade plate.
>
> —From T. C. Lai and Robert Mok, *Jade: The Story of Chinese Music*,
> © 1985 Schocken Books

The *pipa* has traditionally been associated with banquet music and storytelling. The style of its music is much more extroverted and dynamic than traditional Confucian music. While the tradition of epic narratives for banquets has all but died out, much of the *pipa*'s repertory still consists of pieces intended to represent historical or mythological scenes. The pictorial nature of its performance technique is much more explicit than the *guqin*'s or the *zheng*'s. For example, the player may hit the instrument body to effect sounds representing battle. A string may be plucked so hard that it ricochets against the sound body and produces a loud snap. A galloping horse may be evoked by accelerating strums, and so on. Descriptive solo pieces are the specialty of Northern *pipa* players today, while the Southern school concentrates on *pipa* ensemble music.

Hu or **huqin** has become a generic name for *traditional bowed lutes* in China, although it originally meant "foreign" because the bowed fiddle was introduced from Central Asia. Mentioned as early as the twelfth century, bowed fiddles are especially associated with the Mongols who ruled China during the Yuan dynasty (1260–1368). Bowed fiddles are common throughout Islamic countries and in Central Asia, where they are held vertically.

The most important *hu* type is the **erhu** (Figure 35.3). It is primarily a solo instrument, although it is also featured in the *sizhu* ensemble (discussed below). While the *erhu* may sometimes be used in opera performances, the lead instrument in Beijing opera (*jingxi*) is the **jinghu**, a fiddle pitched an octave higher. Other variants are used in other regional opera forms. In the 1950s, larger *hu* were invented to function like the viola, cello, and bass of the Western symphony orchestra. They are used in modern orchestras of traditional instruments, and the larger versions have four strings and fingerboards like their Western counterparts.

The **sanxian** is *a lute with a very long fretless fingerboard and a shallow box resonator covered in snake skin*. Its three strings can be tuned to suit the range of a singer. It is used in opera (usually the smaller *sanxian*) and to accompany musical storytelling and epic narratives (usually the larger *sanxian*). While it is associated with the Yuan (Mongol) dynasty (1260–1368), its earlier history is obscure, probably because it was a folk instrument.

Courtesy Minnesota Chinese Music Ensemble

FIGURE **35.1**

The *zheng* is a *curved board zither with approximately twenty-one metal or nylon strings*. The strings are supported by intermediate bridges that can be moved to tune the strings to the desired mode. Plectra are taped to three fingers of the player's right hand and the left hand effects pitch bends and vibratos by pressing down on the string behind the bridge.

Courtesy Danlee Mitchell

FIGURE **35.2**

The *pipa* is a *four-string pear-shaped fretted lute held nearly upright*. The sound body is solid, not hollow, and hewn from a single piece of wood. This gives the *pipa* a bright and dry timbre. The frets are raised high above the fingerboard so that it is possible to obtain both fixed pitches (by placing the finger directly on the fret) and sizable pitch bends (by placing the finger on the string behind the fret). Plectra (picks) were used when the instrument first appeared in China; today players use artificial fingernails.

Courtesy Danlee Mitchell

FIGURE **35.3**

The *erhu* is a *two-string bowed spike fiddle with a cylindrical or hexagonal resonator covered with snake skin or hide*. Like the Islamic spike fiddle (*rabab*, Figure 16.4), the *erhu* has a cylindrical neck but no fingerboard. The player stops the string with pressure from the fingers of the left hand, which do not press the string all the way down to the neck, thus facilitating pitch slides and bends. An unusual feature is that the hair of the bow is threaded between the strings. The hair is loose, so that the player holds it taut against one of the strings with a right-hand finger.

Courtesy Minnesota Chinese Music Ensemble

FIGURE **35.4**

The *ruan* is a *four-string fretted lute with a large circular resonator*. The resonator is hollow and covered with thin wood.

FIGURE **35.5**

The *yangqin* is a *trapezoidal hammered box-zither*. It was adapted from the Middle Eastern *santur* (Figure 16.5) brought by traders to China's southern coast in the seventeenth century. As with the *santur*, each string is stretched over an intermediate bridge, but the strings alternate on the right and left side. The strings are struck with light and thin bamboo sticks or "hammers." It is a relatively soft instrument used primarily for solo pieces and to accompany songs.

Courtesy Minnesota Chinese Music Ensemble

FIGURE **35.6**

The *paixiao* is a *set of end-blown bamboo panpipes*. The *dizi* is a *transverse bamboo flute with six fingerholes*. In addition, this flute has a hole covered with a thin rice paper membrane that buzzes when the flute is played, giving it a distinctively rich, reedy timbre. It is a common solo and small ensemble instrument and is the principal carrier of the melody in *kunqu* (classical opera). The *xun* is a globular flute made of clay.

Courtesy Gilbert Blount

FIGURE **35.7**

The *xiao* bamboo flute comes in different sizes; this one is relatively long.

Courtesy Minnesota Chinese Music Ensemble

FIGURE **35.8**

The *suona* or *laba* is a *loud double reed with a conical bore and a trumpet-like flared bell*. The player places the reeds in his mouth, not between the lips. It is derived from the Middle Eastern *zurna* (Figure 16.8) through Central Asia and is usually associated with outdoor processions and folk music.

© Michael S. Yamashita/CORBIS

(continued)

TRADITIONAL CHINESE INSTRUMENTS

Courtesy Danlee Mitchell

FIGURE 35.9
The *sheng* has multiple pipes, each with a single reed connected to an air chamber. The player both blows into and sucks air from the mouthpiece, like a harmonica, and allows air into the various pipes by uncovering holes. Unlike the Japanese counterpart, the *sho*, the *sheng* plays single melodies, not chords, although the melodies are usually played in parallel fourths or fifths, thickening the texture.

© Asian Art & Archaeology, Inc. /CORBIS

FIGURE 35.10
The *bianzhong* is a collection of bronze bells suspended from a wooden stand. The bells do not use clappers and have a distinctive shape—cylindrical or elliptical. The most famous set was recovered from the tomb of the Marquis of Zeng (433 BCE). This replica of that set is played at the Wuban Music Academy in China.

Another plucked lute is the **yueqin**, also known as *the "moon lute"* because of its distinctive circular resonator. Like the *sanxian*, it also comes in different sizes and is used in regional opera and storytelling genres. According to traditional history, the earliest version of this instrument, the **ruan** (Figure 35.4), was invented in the third century.

Wind Instruments

The legendary creator of music, Ling Lun, established the **huang zhong** (Yellow Bell) pitch by blowing over a piece of bamboo. Such a simple instrument is common wherever bamboo grows. A piece of bamboo is stopped at one end and blown over at the other, like a bottle. In China, as elsewhere, several bamboo tubes of different pitch were tied together to form the **paixiao** (Figure 35.6), *bamboo pipes arranged to resemble the wings of the phoenix bird*, Ling Lun's inspiration.

Related to this instrument is the *bamboo vertical flute*, the **xiao** (Figure 35.7) which, of course, is basically a single tube of the *paixiao* with fingerholes and an open end. The mouth end is mostly covered, except for a small notch carved into the side into which the player blows. While the *paixiao* is no longer commonly used, the *xiao* is frequently found as a solo instrument or in chamber ensembles. The most common of the several types of Chinese transverse flutes is the **dizi** (Figure 35.6). The *dizi* has a higher range than the *xiao* and a much brighter timbre.

There are two varieties of traditional double-reed instruments: the **guan** is a *short, cylindrical double reed* and the **suona** or **laba** (Figure 35.8) is a loud outdoor instrument. The **sheng** (Figure 35.9) is a multiple pipe instrument, like the *paixiao*, but with single reeds and an air chamber.

Percussion

Expert bronze casting was already practiced in southern China in the second millennium BCE. Among the artifacts surviving from this period are bronze bells, some very large, and bronze drums. Bronze drums are actually idiophones, not membranophones, since the head is made of metal. Similar instruments in Vietnam, Burma, and Indonesia possibly developed into gongs. *Gongs*, **luo**, in China are often used in folk bands and Chinese opera. Although they don't generally have a definite pitch like those of Southeast Asia and Indonesia, Chinese gongs are often built so that the pitch swoops up or down when the gong is hit. A *collection of dish-shaped gongs on a stand*, sometimes used in theater music, is called **yunluo**.

Bronze bells have been recovered from many imperial graves dating back to 1500 BCE. Traditionally sixteen or more of these bells are collected in a set called a **bianzhong**. Sixty-five bronze bells dating from 433 BCE were part of the spectacular discovery of the tomb of the Marquis of Zeng in Suixian, Hubei province (Figure 35.10), proving that sets of such bells were associated with imperial courts from the time of Kong Fuzi; they are still found in Confucian temples.

Another very early instrument found in Suixian and elsewhere is the **qing**, a *stone chime* that gives a mellow, dry sound when tapped by hammers. Sets of these L-shaped carved stones, called **bianqing**, were also associated with imperial courts and Confucianist rituals.

Although drums are not often used in modern Chinese classical music, there were apparently many different kinds in ancient times. A *large, barrel-shaped drum with riveted heads*, the **dagu**, is commonly used in folk music, religious music, and some repertories of court music. It is set horizontally in a stand in front of the player, who plays with two sticks. Drums of a wide variety are used in folk music, and drumming ensembles can be found in folk processionals. The player of the **xiaogu**, *a small horizontal drum on a stand*, serves as the conductor in many forms of Chinese opera and in *sizhu* chamber ensembles. He also sets tempos with an idiophone called a **ban**, *a set of small wooden slats tied together on a string*. With a flick of the wrist, the conductor can make the slats come together in a powerful "pak!"

36 GUQIN MUSIC

The **guqin**, or simply **qin**, the Chinese zither (see Figure 36.1), is the most revered instrument in China. An ancient instrument known in the time before Confucius, the earliest surviving *guqin* are from the Han dynasty (202 BCE–220 CE). Since then, the *guqin* has been associated with the Confucianist social class and represents the epitome of the Chinese ideal of music as meditation. Formerly used in Confucian ritual orchestras and to accompany songs, the *guqin* is primarily an extremely sophisticated solo instrument.

Courtesy Minnesota Chinese Music Ensemble

FIGURE 36.1
China's most revered instrument, the *guqin* has seven strings, traditionally made of silk but today generally made of steel-wound nylon. The body of the *guqin* is a long curved board with bridges on either end over which the strings are stretched. Unlike most other East Asian zithers (see the photo of the *zheng* on page 170), however, the *guqin* has no frets or movable bridges. The performer changes pitch by pressing the finger of the left hand to the soundboard; small dots of inlaid mother-of-pearl called *hui* along the table of the instrument serve as a guide. This difficult performance technique makes possible a wide variety of ornaments and nuances.

Solo *guqin* music is almost always peaceful, serene, and balanced; the meter is relatively free and slow. Typically, a free and expressive introduction is followed by a series of variations based on a traditional melody or series of melodies. Books of *guqin* notation sometimes give the player a scene or idea to contemplate as he plays each variation: "The autumn river is glossy like silk" or "Ascending into pure emptiness."[1]

Even though *guqin* pieces are often slow, the *guqin* is one of the most difficult Chinese instruments to master because of the huge number of ways in which a tone can be generated. The pitch of a note can be bent up or down by sliding the finger of the left hand. No fewer than thirty-three types of vibrato are codified. In addition, a note can be played with the fleshy part of the finger, with the fingernail, as a **harmonic**, as an open string, or as a stopped (fingered) note. When all of these possibilities are combined, there can be over a hundred different ways of playing a single pitch. Much of the interest in a *guqin* performance comes from the artistic exploitation of these tiny nuances.

The invention of a notation system that specifies the string to be plucked, the manner of the plucking, and the action of the left hand for each note

---

[1] These examples are from translations by R. H. van Gulik, *The Lore of the Chinese Lute* (Tokyo: Sophia University, 1940); 89, 92.

helped to codify these subtle complexities. This notation system was in place by about 1200, although earlier pieces that have been handed down, perhaps by earlier notation systems, date back to the year 589.

A *Guqin* Performance

The composition of the famous *guqin* classic *Ping sha lo yen* ("Wild Geese Descending onto the Sandbank") is attributed to Prince Ning Xian (d. 1448), though the earliest surviving publication is from 1634. Geese in Chinese poetry have a number of symbolic connotations, including devotion. Geese mate for life, and even the death of one will not cause its mate to seek another. Thus the image of a lonely flying goose may be symbolic of the loss of a loved one, as in the following poem by Li Ching-tsao (1080–?), who lost her husband during the collapse of the Northern Sung Dynasty.

> *Slow Sound*
> Seeking, searching,
> Icy, sparkling,
> Aching sadness deepen,
> Time of mild warmth and lingering cold,
> Is the hardest to hold
> Scanty wine two, three cups bit by bit,
> Fierce wind blowing at night, how can I stand it?
> Wild geese fly by fast,
> Oh, miserable heart!
> A reminiscence of the past.
> Petals of yellow flowers are piling,
> Freshness fading,
> Who will care picking?
> By the window I harden,
> Solitarily waiting till the day does darken.
> Leaves of *wu-tung* and misty rain,
> At dusk dripping and dropping,
> As it is,
> How can I put the word, "grief," in restraint?
> —Li Ching-tsao, translated by Hsu Wen-Ying[2]

An early *guqin* publication suggested various pictorial descriptions to be associated with each section of the piece. For example, the writer suggests that during the first section the player contemplate the following image [translation by Liang Mingyue]: "Autumn wild geese in flight crossing the river; as the first goose alights on the sandy shore, the other geese—singly, in pairs, and more—follow suit."

---

[2] Hsu Wen-Ying, *The Ku-Ch'in* (Pasadena, CA: Wen Ying Studio, 1978); 427–28.

Listening Guide

Introduction	
0:00	Opens with high, pure sounds symbolic of the heavens, the sky, and geese flying before they alight on a sandbank (*fan yin* performance technique).
	Introduction introduces the mode which, in this performance, seems to imply the scale of 1–3 4 5–7 (*yudiao*), although sources differ on the mode of this piece.
Variation 1	
0:45	Just the skeletal core tones of the theme are stated, beginning with a characteristic ornament of a scoop up in pitch, which can be heard throughout the performance. Notice how the tone of the string subtly changes through left hand manipulations after it has been plucked. The focus is not on a continuous melody, but on the delicate ornamentation of single notes.
1:06	Listen for the technique in which the right hand plucks a string and the left hand moves while the string is still vibrating, so that several notes of the melody sound without the right hand replucking the string. This technique will become common in the rest of the performance.
Variation 2	
2:07	As the melody becomes more elaborate, it begins to expose the key melodic motives of the piece.
Variation 3	
3:11	Although the rhythm is still somewhat free, note how the tempo has gradually increased since variation 2.
Ending section	
4:20	New material emphasizing pitch 3 replaces familiar tune and builds to a climax in this first part of the closing section.
4:39	Dramatic damped strum marks the emotional climax of the piece and leaves us hanging, expecting a return to the tonic (pitch 1).
4:41	Emphasis on pitches 3 and 7, fragments of familiar motives—as if the poet's thoughts are now wandering back to the peaceful scene of the geese.
5:39	The *fan yin* (harmonics) return, the tonality of the opening returns, and we end on the opening pitch with a sense of closure. While ending with harmonics is a common device in *guqin* pieces, here one can imagine it representing the geese flying like a departed loved one back up into the heavens.

Like many classical *guqin* works, the performance on our audio selection (CD 1:15) opens with a playing technique known as **fan yin** (*harmonics*). In this technique the left hand lightly touches the vibrating string at certain points (marked by inlaid dots on the soundboard), but does not completely stop the vibration. *Fan yin* allows only certain vibrations in the string and creates a crystalline timbre that, depending on where the left hand touches the string, can sound at least an octave higher than the open string.

After this introduction, this piece presents a series of variations. The first of these includes only the fundamental core tones that define the melody. Each subsequent variation fills in many more notes around those core tones, like the intricate designs of jade carvings. The following graphic illustrates this process by overlaying a schematic representation of the first statement of the core tones (blue) with the following variation (red). The numbers refer to the pitches in the scale (here transcribed as a 1–345–7 mode).

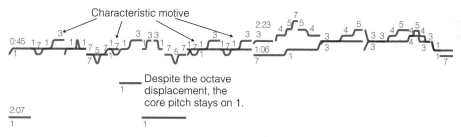

GRAPHIC **36.1**

The rhythm and meter of *guqin* pieces are known mainly from oral tradition and may vary from one performance to the next. The rhythm is not as crucial to the variation as the melody and ornamentation.

FOLK AND CONTEMPORARY MUSIC

37

Although the classical traditions of solo instrumental performance, opera, and orchestras are the best known of China's music, by far the most extensive repertories here, as elsewhere, are found in the folk music tradition. Aside from the many work songs, entertainment songs, lullabies, and other typical folk songs, instrumental ensembles play an important role in traditional Chinese life, especially in rural areas.

Instrumental Folk Ensembles

Outside of the urban centers, major life events and holidays are nearly always accompanied by music, especially as performed by instrumental ensembles. While the instrumentation varies in different regions, these bands usually provide music for ceremony and music for processions. At its simplest, such an ensemble includes one or more riveted-head barrel drums (*dagu*), gongs (*luo*), and *small cymbals* (**bo**). Such *gong-and-drum ensembles* (**luogu**) are very common in rural areas.

If two *suona* double reeds are added, the ensemble is called **guchui**, and the loud *suona*, carry the melody. More instruments can be added, but the *suonas* still tend to dominate. The pieces these ensembles play are usually improvised variations of familiar tunes, sometimes folk songs or traditional instrumental pieces, and sometimes pieces borrowed from **wu** (*military operas*).

Sizhu

In teahouses and people's homes, ensemble music of a more subdued and refined sort was played for entertainment. These ensembles, traditionally known as **sizhu**, *silk-and-bamboo* ensembles (Figure 37.1), generally feature a *dizi, sanxian, erhu,* and perhaps other soft instruments such as the *xiao, sheng, yueqin,* or *yangqin.* These ensembles play traditional tunes in an elaborate heterophonic tapestry with a soft drum or *clappers* (*ban*) to keep the beat.

Sizhu pieces, like classical works, are frequently based on a sequence of variations of a core tune. Musicians may vary a tune by lengthening the time between the core tones to allow for denser elaborations. This process, poetically known as "slowing and adding flowers," is similar to the process found in Javanese gamelan music (see Chapter 46) and elsewhere. The technique can result in the creation of new compositions or entire families of compositions related in different ways to a single parent tune.

FIGURE **37.1**
This historical photograph of a traditional chamber ensemble includes, from left to right, *xiaogu* (played with the right hand), *ban* (in the player's left hand), *sanxian, yangqin, sihu* (four-string fiddle), and *pipa.*

© Roger Viollet / Topham / The Image Works

Although the repertories, techniques, and level of refinement of these ensembles overlap with those of the classical traditions, and the players who cultivated the silk-and-bamboo tradition tended to be from the upper intellectual class, this is music by amateurs for everyday entertainment. The popularity of *sizhu* has declined, but informal *sizhu* clubs still regularly meet at teahouses, especially in southern regions around Shanghai.

Reform and Popular Music

In the late nineteenth century, European missionaries in many regions of China taught Christian music with group singing and Western harmonies. Because of the compatibility of European and Chinese tuning systems, harmonization of Chinese songs was a straightforward process and was often adopted to create new "modern" school and military songs. After the fall of the empire (1911) and the subsequent rejection of old Confucian values, reformers created "Songs for the Masses" with European modes and harmonies, often based on models from the Soviet Union. At the same time, Western popular music could be heard in many urban areas. As reformers condemned traditional music associated with the court and the old intellectual class, many of the old practices neared extinction.

When Mao Zedong and the communists assumed power in 1949, they adopted a policy of socialist realism in the arts—that is, all art should serve the state and be a genuine expression of the masses rather than entertainment for the elite. The government supported the collection of traditional folk songs and other ethnomusicological research, and, at state-sponsored music conservatories, some of the traditional practices, such as solo instrument repertories, were refined and notated. At the same time, the government suppressed religious music, music of shamanism, and other traditions that were contrary to official atheism.

Possibly the most visible innovation during this period was the establishment of orchestras modeled on European orchestras, but with Chinese instruments. The creation of these Chinese orchestras required the standardization of instruments to conform to a single tuning based on twelve-tone equal temperament and the invention of some new instruments, such as large versions of the *hu* bowed lutes that were the counterparts of the European cello and double bass. Professional composers often adapted traditional melodies to Western harmonies, but without the experimentation or intensely personal expression that has characterized much Western orchestral music. This music is very familiar in modern China through concerts, film scores, and radio broadcasts.

During the Cultural Revolution of 1966–1976, conservatories were closed, most musical institutions disbanded, and many composers and performers were sent to rural re-education camps. This was a time of great hardship for these artists, but many returned with a greater understanding and appreciation of the folk music they encountered. After 1980, a liberalization of artistic expression was accompanied by a reduction in state sponsorship of music conservatories and other institutions. Western popular music is now commonly sold and performed, and Hong Kong and Taiwanese pop stars are well known from films. The government still treats indigenous rock and roll bands with suspicion, especially after their perceived role in the 1989 Tiananmen uprising.

38 CHINESE DRAMATIC MUSIC

Narrative Song and Folk Dramas

By the tenth century, Central Asians brought to China a love of epic story-telling with musical accompaniment. Over a period of months, professional storytellers, accompanied on the *pipa* or *sanxian*, depending on the region, would narrate their stories in one- or two-hour episodes of nightly enter-tainment. Many of these regional genres of epic storytelling have died out since the Cultural Revolution.

A shorter type of sung narrative is **guqu**, the *drum song* so named be-cause the singer accompanies himself or herself with a clapper and wooden frame drum (*dagu*). An ensemble may also accompany songs and play inter-ludes. Each presentation of *guqu* lasts about fifteen to twenty minutes, and performances may be strung together for an evening's entertainment or placed in between acts of another drama or variety show.

While court entertainments have a long history in China, the center of theatrical activity moved to the public stage after the fall of the Tang dynasty (960). As is common throughout East Asia, the actors in Chinese folk dra-mas do not use a script, but instead improvise the dialogue from their inti-mate knowledge of the story and certain standardized ways of speaking for each character type. The music usually consists of well-known folk songs adapted for use in a particular drama.

Regional Opera

By the thirteenth century, dramas in the Song and Mongol courts developed into sophisticated forms with precomposed songs and lyrics. These and later types of Chinese musical drama have been called operas by Western writers, even though they differ in many ways from Western opera. In Chinese opera, spoken dialogue, mime, and acrobatics combine with singing to produce a unique synthesis. The staging often lacks the elaborate and realistic sets and props found in the West.

Many of the elements in these forms have become conventionalized and are well known to the cognoscenti. Actors learn elaborate codified move-ments and expressions to indicate the emotions of a particular character type, and actors tend to specialize in only one sort of character—old men, for example, or military heroes. Most stories derive from episodes contained within a handful of medieval novels and traditional tales, usually classified either as military (heroic historical tales) or civilian (typically romantic stories), although most stories include elements of both.

As in folk drama, these sophisticated genres are highly regionalized, so that today one hears references to Canton opera, Sichuan opera, Shanghai opera, and so on. Each of these forms shares many fundamental concepts but differs in dialect and conventions such as gestures, costumes, acrobatics, singing styles, melody types, modes, and instruments. One of the oldest of these genres that still exists is **kunqu**, which appeared in the sixteenth century. Like contemporary Shakespearean drama, *kunqu* is today considered *a classical dramatic form known for its ornate sophistication*.

Jingxi—Beijing Opera

Those who could afford the best tickets to an opera performance in 1920s Beijing sat at one of the tables that surrounded the stage on three sides and were served tea and snacks. Others sat or stood on the surrounding balconies. The stage, a large wooden platform with corner columns supporting a sloping roof, was bare, except for a small table and two chairs in front of a large elaborate curtain. A small orchestra sat off to one side. Audiences were noisy, conversing during lulls in the action or enthusiastically applauding and shouting after an actor's featured solo. These connoisseurs often found the greatest beauty in the graceful curves expressed in every theatrical detail from an actor's gestures and walk to his speech and melodies.

Rather than a complete drama full of conflict and resolution, an evening's entertainment might consist of a series of unconnected episodes from various operas and culminate in an acrobatic battle scene late in the evening. Troupes were normally all-male, and some of the most famous actors were those who cultivated a high falsetto and sang female roles. Some character types had faces painted with striking symbolic patterns, and the elaborate nature of the costumes more than made up for the sparse sets.

This was *jingxi* theater, better known in the West as **Beijing Opera** or Peking Opera, the most popular of the regional opera styles. Its origins reflect the cosmopolitan nature of the capital at the end of the eighteenth century, when the city's opera drew upon *kunqu* and elements from other folk and regional opera styles. Within a hundred years, its increasing popularity and imperial patronage made it into a national theater, and *jingxi* theaters could be found in many cities outside of the capital.

The Japanese occupation of World War II and the subsequent communist revolution created drastic changes in *jingxi*. Women now performed, and theaters began to use realistic staging and proscenium stages. In the People's Republic, *jingxi* was adapted to socialist realism, and Mao's wife Jiang Qing, a former singer, led a movement during the Cultural Revolution (1966–76) to completely reform Chinese theater. All traditional and modern opera companies were shut down. In their place, Jiang commissioned eight new "model dramas" based partly on Western dramatic conventions and harmonies, but with Chinese instruments. Only these model dramas were allowed during this period.

After Mao's death and the fall of Jiang Qing, *jingxi* returned, but without its former popularity and some of its conventions. New experimentation has resulted in more elaborate staging and newly composed stories, some, for example, based on Shakespeare. Today, Beijing has four *jingxi* companies, catering mostly to audiences of connoisseurs and tourists, and one can also see performances on television and video (Figure 38.1).

A *jingxi* play is divided into dialogue, songs, dances, pantomimes, and musical interludes. About ten *standard rhythmic types* (**ban**) classify *jingxi* songs not just by meter, but also tempo, rhythmic density (notes per beat), and the relationship of the poetry to the meter. At one end of the spectrum are songs in *manban*, slow beat, an expansive and highly melismatic style appropriate for a character's expressive introspection and often an emotional high point in the opera. *Yuanban*, primary beat, is a moderate tempo that accompanies simple narration or description. *Liushuiban*, flowing water beat, is a fast tempo often used for exciting scenes and sung with little or no melisma.

In much Chinese opera there is a distinctive terminology and complex theory of modes, and *jingxi* operas are based entirely on two modes, *xipi* and *erhuang*. **Xipi** is similar to *gongdiao* (page 167) in that it uses a 123–56–mode, but mode includes many other concepts in addition to the scale. For example, the setting of a couplet of text typically traverses a certain series of internal cadence pitches. Further *xipi* subtypes are characterized by typical melodic contours, the text's relationship to the rhythm, and the rhythmic types appropriate for the mode, although these characteristics are further adjusted depending on the gender of the character. Whereas *xipi* is considered bright and happy, **erhuang**, a 12–45–7 mode, is usually more serious and introspective.

The instrumentation of the *jingxi* orchestra varies according to the troupe and the needs of a particular drama, but the core instruments of the ensemble include *jinghu* (high fiddle), *erhu* (lower fiddle), *yueqin* (moon

FIGURE **38.1**
A performance of *The Monkey King*, a favorite *jingxi* play, takes place in Beijing, 1981, shortly after Chinese opera resumed following the death of Mao. Unlike more traditional staging, this one uses a proscenium with a projected background.

© Dean Conger/CORBIS

FIGURE **38.2**
In this orchestra practicing for a *jingxi* performance, the front row instruments include (left to right) the *ruan*, *yueqin*, *sheng*, and two *dizi*. Just visible behind the *yueqin* is a *hu* player. In the back stand three percussionists.

lute), *ban* (wooden clappers), *xiaogu* (a small drum), *luo* (gongs), and *naobo* (cymbals). The conductor of the ensemble, a percussionist playing the *ban* with the left hand and the *xiaogu* with the right, plays important cues, starts the group, and establishes tempos. As the most prominent melodic instrument, the *jinghu* forms a nearly constant heterophonic accompaniment of the voice. In the classical opera form of *kunqu*, and whenever the *jingxi* orchestra adopts *kunqu* melodies, the *dizi* flute takes on the vocal accompaniment role.

Other instruments may be added for specific occasions, such as a *suona* double reed to accompany processions or to imitate horses, large drums for military scenes, and so on. In addition to articulating the rhythmic structure of the songs, the percussion also provides many sound effects during both songs and stage action not otherwise accompanied by music. The characteristic swooping pitch of the *luo* gongs is a nearly constant accompaniment to blows in battle scenes and other important dramatic actions.

A *Jingxi* Performance: *The Drunken Concubine*

Probably the most famous *jingxi* performer of all time was Mei Lanfang (1894–1961), a man known for his refinement and innovation playing leading *female roles* (**dan**). One of his signature roles was the title character in the short opera *The Drunken Concubine* (*Guifei zui jiu*).

The play opens with the emperor's favorite concubine, Yang Guifei, and her attendants processing through the imperial gardens to a grand pavilion, where she has ordered a great feast for herself and the emperor. As she sits and the wine is poured for two, word comes that the emperor will not attend. He is spending the night with another woman.

Crushed and furious, but too proud to display these emotions in front of her attendants, Yang Guifei drinks both glasses of wine. As the glasses are refilled, anger and jealousy give way to bitterness and abandon, expressed largely through a series of remarkable dances. Finally, her sorrow breaks through her pride, and she expresses her loneliness and grief in a poignant series of songs. Accepting her fate, she and her entourage leave the banquet hall without having seen the emperor.

CD 1:16. "An Island in the Sea," *The Drunken Concubine*, **Mei Lanfang with the National Opera of China**

0:00	Instrumental music (excerpted here) for the *jinghu* fiddle, the *erhu* (low fiddle), *yueqin* (moon lute), *ban* (wooden clappers), and *xiaogu* (a small drum) opens the play.

0:01 & **0:08** 	The *luo* gong punctuates the gestures of the concubine, Yang Guifei, as the actor (Mei Lanfang) enters. Graceful movement of his sleeves was a highly regarded part of Mei Lanfang's artistry.
0:16	Yang Guifei sings: *An island in the sea*, to an important motive, which we will call motive a, consisting of pitches 7, up to 1, and then down to 6, 5, and 4 (sometimes they are numbered differently). Pitch 6 is a *bianyin*, an alternate pitch outside the basic pentatonic scale. Motives such as this help unify this extensive melody. Listen to how the *jinghu* closely shadows the voice and the *ban* clappers help establish the dignified walking tempo of *yuanban* (primary rhythmic type) as the characters progress through the garden.
0:35	*The water wheel begins to turn and rise*, is sung to another important motive, which we will call b. Motive a then returns, like the water wheel coming around. Beginning with the third line, the melody follows the same core tones as the first two, as is appropriate for *sipingdiao*, a subtype of the *erhuang* mode.
0:51 **1:04**	*See the scared rabbit.* *The rabbit again turns east and leaps.* *The water wheel leaves the island in the sea.*

	Motive b is again followed by motive a. Musically and textually, this resolves the first 3 lines.
1:28	*All heaven and earth shine brilliantly,* *The bright moon is in the middle of the sky,* Motive a returns to accompany this lyric.
1:59	*It looks just like Chang-E going to the moon palace.* *This concubine is like Chang-E going to the moon palace.* The melody of 0:51 repeats. One level of meaning in the lyric now becomes apparent. Chang-E is the legendary goddess who drank the elixir of immortality and flew to the moon, where her companion is a rabbit. The moon, like an island in the sea of night, brilliantly illuminates the Emperor's garden. By comparing herself to this goddess and symbol of the female principle, Yang Guifei not only metaphorically expresses her pride but also foreshadows her isolation and downfall. The song ends on pitch 5, cadence for *sipingdiao*.
2:37	Prominent strikes on the *xiaogu* drum set a new tempo as the percussionist-conductor leads the orchestra directly into an interlude.
2:57	Stylized dialogue. The *sheng*, Yang Guifei's male attendant, and the *chou*, the clown attendant, introduce themselves in speech and bow to their lady. She answers in the stylized speaking voice of a *dan* (female role) which like her gestures consist of graceful sweeps of pitch with no sharp points. (The continuation of their dialogue after the end of the interlude is not included in this recording. There follows a reprise of the previous song, also not included here.)

(continued)

3:25	*Ban* clappers signal the beginning of the next piece *In the limitless sky, a wild goose.* The rhythm suddenly changes to a non-pulsatile rhythmic type known as *sanban* ("dispersed rhythm"), as if Yang Guifei's breath is taken away by the unexpected sight of the wild goose, a good omen. The instruments, primarily the *jinghu* and *erhu*, play the core tones heterophonically with the voice, ornamenting the long tones with periodic quick slides from the scale tone below.
3:47	Accelerating strikes from the *ban* clappers and a strike from the *luo* gong end the section and then introduce the next song: *A wild goose flies.* *Oh! The wild goose is scared.* Although this section is again metered in *yuanban* (primary rhythmic type), the tempo is somewhat faster than before, reflecting Yang Guifei's building excitement.
4:14 **4:17**	*The wild goose also flies up,* *Hearing me, then falls in the shade of the willow tree.* The repeat of motives b and a here connect the previous mention of the scared rabbit with the wild goose. The image of rise and descent in the lyric foreshadows Yang Guifei's own downfall.
4:31	*This scenery is almost intoxicating.* A more obvious foreshadowing of Yang Guifei's own intoxication.
4:38	A shout from the attendant signals that they have reached the Hundred-Flower Pavilion where the banquet will be served. Woken from her musings, Yang Guifei also remarks that they have arrived. The melody of the phrase emphasizes the core tone of pitch 5, which ends the melody on a more serious but not yet settled tone.
4:47	The tempo increases yet again in a brief orchestral postlude as Yang Guifei sits at the banquet table to await the emperor.

The Drunken Concubine is entirely in the *erhuang* mode, as befits its serious and thoughtful subject. Different rhythmic types (*ban*) and subtypes of *erhuang* provide the contrast among the opera's musical pieces. The play opens in the primary rhythmic type (*yuanban*), the leader of the orchestra sounding the clappers every two beats. The first series of songs is in the subtype of the *erhuang* mode known as *sipingdiao*, which, in company with the primary rhythmic type, expresses an atmosphere of dignity and confidence that appropriately establishes Yang Guifei's pride and power.

In the first song, as she anticipates her dinner with the emperor, Yang Guifei's poetic descriptions of the imperial gardens evoke her emotional state of optimism, satisfaction, and pride. Most *jingxi* text is in couplets, and the musical phrases reflect the unsettled end of the first line resolving in the second line. *Sipingdiao* sets a conventional sequence of core tones at important metrical points, although these may not be immediately obvious in the song's elaborate melodies, especially as ornamented by a singer such as Mei Lanfang.

 ## REFERENCES

Discography

Chinese Orchestra of Shanghai Music Conservatory et al. *Sword Dance: Chinese Plucked String Music*. Hong Kong: Hugo HRP 724-2, 1988.

Lanfang, Mei, and others. *Guifei Zui Jiu* [*The Drunken Concubine*]. Video CD, Beijing Audio-Visual Production Ltd ISRC CN-A08-99-0114-0/V.J8, 1999.

Li, Xiangting. *Soul of China: Guqin Recital*. Voyager CD SV 1337, 1993.

Wu Man. *Pipa: Chinese Traditional and Contemporary Music*. Wyastone Leys, Monmouth, UK: Nimbus Records NI 5368, 1993.

Various artists. *China: Classical music*. Paris: Ocora C 559039, 2001.

Various artists. *China: Music of the First Moon: Shawms from Northeast China*. Paris: Buda Musique 92612-2, 1994.

Bibliography

Gulik, Robert Hans van. *The Lore of the Chinese Lute: An Essay in Ch'in Ideology*. Tokyo: Sophia University, 1940.

Hsu, Wen-Ying. *The Guqin: A Chinese Stringed Instrument, Its History and Theory*. Los Angeles: Wen Ying Studies, 1978.

Jones, Stephen. *Folk Music of China: Living Instrumental Traditions*. Oxford: Clarendon Press; New York: Oxford University Press, 1995.

Lai, T. C. *Jade Flute: The Story of Chinese Music*. New York: Schocken Books, 1981.

Mingyueh, Liang. *Music of the Billion: An Introduction to Chinese Musical Culture*. New York: Heinrichshofen Edition, 1985.

Wiant, Bliss. *The Music of China*. Hong Kong: Chung Chi Publications, Chung Chi College, Chinese University of Hong Kong, 1965.

Wichmann, Elizabeth. *Listening to Theatre: The Aural Dimension of Beijing Opera*. Honolulu: University of Hawaii Press, 1991.

Yung, Bell, ed. *Celestial Airs of Antiquity: Music of the Seven-String Zither of China*. Madison, WI: A-R Editions, 1997.

---

c. 100–553

Yamato period: Japanese courts adopt pictographic characters and other Chinese ideas by the fifth and sixth centuries. The introduction of Buddhism inspires Japanese monks to travel to China and India, bringing back musical instruments and other influences.

553–794

Nara period: Beginnings of *gagaku* (Japanese court orchestral music). The first extant native literature from the eighth century shows that court musicians at this time were Chinese or trained in the Confucian *yayue* court music tradition of China.

9th C

Heian period (794–1185). The *koto* zither is adapted from the Chinese *zheng*.

10th C

Tradition of blind priests singing and playing *biwa* (*moso-biwa*).

PART 7

Japan

—— **11th–12th C**
Rise of the samurai warrior. The courts of this period tend to be isolated from the world and extremely refined. The most respected pursuits for aristocracy are the arts and contemplation of beauty through music, poetry, calligraphy, painting, moon-viewing and other pastimes.

—— **12th–13th C**
Kamakura period (1185–1333). Rise to dominance of Zen Buddhism and the Shogun as ruler of Japan.

—— **1300s**
Beginning of *komuso*, wandering Zen priest *shakuhachi* players, who use the *shakuhachi* as an aid to meditation. By the 17th century, the Fuke sect of *komuso* is officially recognized by the government, establishing the first of several *shakuhachi* schools.

—— **c. 1370**
Muromachi period (1333–1615). Creation of Noh drama (based on earlier forms), which becomes a refined theatrical form largely influenced by Zen.

▶

INTRODUCTION TO THE REGION

39

FIRST LISTEN
CD 2:1
Daiwa gaku,
Jin Nyodo
(1891–1966);
Shakuhachi, Bill
Shozan Shultz

Watching and listening to a performance on the **shakuhachi**, the *traditional vertical bamboo flute of Japan* (Figure 39.1), one notices the transported state of the musician as much as the sound of the instrument. The music quietly and slowly enfolds you in this contemplative state, one in which time seems nearly suspended. The music of the *shakuhachi* is often compared to the sound of a breeze blowing through a bamboo forest, and, while such an explicit connection with nature is common in the contemplative music of China as well, here this music has at once a spacious and melancholy quality that is distinctively Japanese.

This quality of necessary emptiness within a space is an integral part of traditional Japanese art, a principle known as **ma**. In much traditional Jap-

---

1552
First sustained contact with West: Portuguese sailors introduce firearms.

1500s
Establishment of first *koto* school (Tsukushi) and the introduction of the *shamisen* from China. Both are largely associated with the rise of the mercantile class.

1603
Traditional date for the invention of Kabuki theater.

1614–1685
Lifetime of composer Yatsuhashi Kengyo, a composer who nearly single-handedly invented the solo school of koto playing, including a new and decidedly un-Chinese scale with semitones, known as *in*.

anese art, the composition does not fill the canvas to the edges of the frame. Instead, the subtle but strategic placement of a few isolated elements serves to suggest the space through their very sparsity. The same principle appears in room decoration, architecture, and music, which is often very slow, with suggestive pauses that let the sounds breathe.

Scholars of Zen, the distinctive sect of Buddhism which is the major religion of Japan, often speak similarly of emptiness, the void achieved when meditation takes one beyond sensory experience to a deeper, wordless truth. Zen Buddhist monks sometimes use the disciplined breathing required to play the *shakuhachi* as an aid to this meditation. The other major Japanese religion is Shinto, a tradition of prayer and ritual associated with an ancient body of music also connected with Buddhism.

Just as Shinto, the indigenous religion of Japan, and Buddhism, a religion of foreign origin, represent two sides of spiritual practice for the Japanese, many other aspects of Japanese culture demonstrate the enthusiastic adaptation of foreign ideas that coexist with native elements in a unique synthesis. Historically, alternating periods of isolationism and the embrace of foreign ideas, including music, have shaped Japan's national identity.

Even as video game music and pop fill Japan's airwaves, the introspective and serene tones of the *shakuhachi* still represent qualities which are as essential to the Japanese character now as they were in centuries past.

Geography Japan consists of four main islands—Honshu (the mainland), Kyushu, Hokkaido, and Shikoku—and about 3000 smaller islands (see map). Almost the entire population is ethnically homogenous, except for

Courtesy of Bill Shozan Schultz

FIGURE 39.1
The *shakuhachi* is the traditional vertical bamboo flute of Japan. Its melancholy, almost otherworldly sound and the controlled breathing required by its performance seem perfectly suited to attaining the meditative state sought by Buddhist monks who made it their own. (See also Figure 42.4.)

1638
All foreigners expelled at the beginning of a period of isolationism that characterized the Edo, or Tokugawa, period (1615–1868).

c. **1690**
Establishment of Gidayu school of Bunraku puppetry.

1700s
Development of the *shamisen* repertory and styles of playing.

1800s
Establishment of classical chamber music known as *sankyoku*.

small groups on the islands of Hokkaido and Okinawa. A single language, Japanese, traditionally written in pictographic characters adapted from Chinese, unites the country.

CHARACTERISTICS OF JAPANESE MUSIC

40

Despite the impressive musical diversity of Japan, highly refined and often remarkably consistent traditions in the classical arts have evolved from the country's ethnic homogeneity and occasional historical isolation. Common elements that are distinctively Japanese and help distinguish their arts from those of China or Korea include the following.

■ **Scales with Semitones** Many of the most prominent genres of classical music in Japan use scales that include relatively large as well as very small intervals called semitones, although their tuning may vary somewhat. Like Chinese scales, Japanese scales are pentatonic (five pitches per octave), but they sound very different because of the presence of semitones.

■ **Slow Tempos** Some prominent genres of traditional Japanese music have tempos so slow they may at first seem non-pulsatile. Other genres are in fact non-pulsatile but also unfold at a very slow pace.

■ **Sense of Space** Sometimes the temporal space between notes is cultivated as much as the notes themselves. This space is known as *ma*. These spaces help create a musical architecture of understated simplicity and balance.

■ **Prominent Classical Solo Repertories** Despite the importance of orchestral court and dramatic music, some of the most prominent traditions in Japanese classical music have developed within schools of solo instrumental performance, each with its own repertory and style, and frequently its own notation and terminology.

1868
Meiji period (1868–1912). Constitutional monarchy established, ending feudalism and isolationism; opening to Western trade and cultural influences. Imported musical influences include European harmonies and scales, especially through popular music. Music conservatories are established that teach both Western and Japanese classical music.

1910
Korea invaded and annexed.

1920s
Contemporary Japan (c. 1912–present). Beginnings of *shinkyoku* (new music) style through the innovations of composer Miyagi Michio (1894–1956).

1931–1945
Manchuria, later China and Southeast Asia, are invaded and annexed. After Japan's loss in World War II, Allies impose a government which becomes a constitutional democracy.

Kagura—Shinto Music

The rituals and music that are a part of the Shinto religion have their roots in the purification rites, pantheism, and ancestor worship of prehistoric Japan. *Shinto music* is generically known as **kagura**. Today the most visible form of *kagura* takes place in the colorful folk festivals held for various occasions, especially in the harvest season. These *festival performances* are called *satokagura* and are especially popular in rural areas. A festival may consist of several parts, including a procession to the shrine, purification ceremonies, and so on, but dances are performed at seemingly impromptu times. They become part of the celebratory atmosphere.

A popular *satokagura* dance is the *lion dance* (**shishi-mai**). Like the dragon costumes in festivals in China and elsewhere in East Asia, the lion costume covers one or several people inside the lion's body and a carved wooden head with jaws that clack together ferociously. Bringing good luck to the inhabitants and to the dancers themselves, the lion dances through the village and visits stores and homes.

The dances are accompanied by a *small folk ensemble* generically known as **hayashi**. It may include one or more *transverse flutes*, usually known as **takebue**; one or more *small, shallow drums* called **taiko**; a *very large barrel drum with riveted heads* called **o-daiko**; and small cymbals or gongs. The flute plays a high, piercing melody with abundant ornaments between the extended notes, but the real interest is in the lively drum parts. While the *o-daiko* keeps a steady rhythm, the *taiko* plays fast, elaborate rhythms against it. Quite frequently these rhythms are syncopated—that is, metric stress shifts away from the expected beat—as are many of the rhythms of Japan's distinctive folk songs.

More recently these rhythms have served as an inspiration for a new type of drum ensemble. In 1971 the musician Den Tagayasu formed such an ensemble, not only to revitalize Japanese folk traditions, but to return to Shinto's spiritual asceticism. Living on a remote island, his performers

---

1950s–present

Remarkable economic growth makes Japan a world economic superpower. Western jazz, rock, pop, and techno music have a tremendous impact on Japan, and these styles provide the overwhelming majority of the music heard in everyday Japan. Distinctively Japanese styles of popular music known as j-pop and video game music have become popular in the West as well. Some Japanese composers in the Western classical tradition, such as Toru Takemitsu (1930–1996), have sought to merge Japanese aesthetics and instruments with those of the West, and some traditional Japanese musicians have adopted influences of Western classical music.

meditated, trained athletically, and rehearsed drumming. The group became known as Kodo and has toured widely throughout the world. Since their popularity, many other groups have imitated their instrumentation and playing style, now known as **taiko drumming**, which includes precise choreography of the drummers' movements. Even though it lacks the polyrhythms of Africa and the complex improvisations of India, *taiko* drumming is overwhelming in its sheer power and precision.

Another form of Shinto music is **mikagura**, the *ancient music for imperial court rituals* (distinct from the *gagaku* court orchestra music that we discuss later). The music of *mikagura* is very different in instrumentation and style from the music of Shinto folk celebrations. Like most court music, it is very reserved and refined. Three or four instrumentalists often accompany a chorus and traditionally perform for special court rituals or prior to an emperor's pronouncements.

Shomyo—Buddhist Chants

In Japan, Buddhism and Shintoism are not considered mutually exclusive. In fact, it is often difficult to separate the Buddhist and Shinto elements in some festivals and rituals. However, the main musical expression of Japanese Buddhism is found in the chants sung by various schools of monks. These *chants*, generically called **shomyo**, were imported from China and Korea in the early eighth century, perhaps earlier (Figure 40.1).

A service is announced by the ringing of *a giant cylindrical bell* called a **densho** (Figure 2.2, page 7). It has no clapper, but is rung with a hammer or a log suspended perpendicular to the bell. The music is performed responsorially—that is, a lead singer intones a part and is answered by the rest of the monks. At certain times small ceremonial bells may be rung. The music is often non-pulsatile, but the impression is that it is very slow. The starting pitch may be left up to each monk, resulting in tone clusters similar to those heard in some Tibetan Buddhist chants.

Despite the apparent flexibility of tuning, *shomyo* is the source of classical Japanese modal theory, and ancient Buddhist texts discuss music theory in some detail. The modes of *shomyo* were eventually adopted in *gagaku* court music and other genres; these modes are distinct from the indigenous modes found in folk music and solo instrumental music.

Modes in Japanese Music

Buddhist chant brought Chinese music theory to Japan, and, although this theory was later modified, Japanese *modes* called **choshi** are *modeled on Chinese modes lacking semitones* (see page 169). The pentatonic modes the Japanese eventually adopted are the **ryo** 1 2 3–5 6– scale and the **ritsu** 1 2–4 5 6– (see Graphic 40.1). Each mode consists of five pitches in the octave with two gaps where auxiliary pitches called *hennon* are occasionally inserted; in our graphic, the auxiliary pitch names are shown in parentheses. The three

© Michael S. Yamashita/CORBIS

FIGURE **40.1**
In a Tokyo monastery, a Japanese Buddhist monk of the Fuke sect chants *shomyo*, very slow, repetitive, non-pulsatile recitations of sacred texts. The monks behind him play *shakuhachi* (flutes) to foster disciplined breathing and meditation. In front of them are the traditional baskets the monks wear on their heads. In the left foreground are two *mokugyo* (large woodblocks carved in the shape of fish) whose sounds accompany chants and call the monks to prayer.

scales differ most clearly in the placement of these gaps. *Ryo* and *ritsu* may be transposed into different keys. But each transposition may vary the traditional melodies and result in different treatments on various instruments with limited ranges. *Choshi* modes, then, are distinguished not only by the basic scale, but also by range, tones emphasized, and melodic contours. *Ryo* and *ritsu* still form the basis for *gagaku* court music and Buddhist music traditions. Another pentatonic mode, **yo**, is associated with folk music rather than the classical *choshi*.

GRAPHIC **40.1**
A Schematic Diagram of Various Japanese Scales

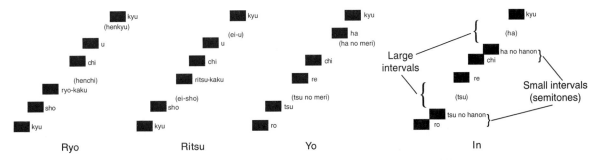

The most distinctive of Japanese modes—and the one that clearly distinguishes most Japanese classical music from Chinese music—is the **in** mode (see Graphic 40.1). Unlike Japan's other pentatonic modes, the *in* mode has a distinctive scale that includes two semitones balanced by larger intervals. The invention of the *in* mode, which is associated with music outside the court tradition, is attributed to the famous seventeenth-century composer Yatsuhashi Kengyo, who first established it as a tuning for the *koto*, discussed in Chapter 42. The *in* mode has also become associated with music for the *shamisen* and *shakuhachi*.

The names of the pitches in the scales differ from one instrument or tradition to another—those given here for *yo* and *in* come from *shakuhachi* (flute) terminology. The exact tuning of each of these pitches may vary, even within the same performance, and some pitches may be substituted or left out of the scale. For example, some songs use pitch 5 (*chi*) in the *yo* mode so infrequently that it is considered another auxiliary tone. Often pitch 7 (*ha*) of the *in* scale is used in ascending melodies, and pitch 6 (*ha no hanon*) in descending.

The indigenous population of Okinawa, one of the few groups ethnically distinct from the majority of Japanese, uses another *pentatonic mode* known as **ryukyu**. While different from *in*, this distinctive mode also includes semitones, and resembles some modes found in Southeast Asia.

 CD2, Track 2, Japanese scales (*ryo, ritsu, yo, in, ryukyu*) and demonstrations of *shakuhachi* ornamentation and playing techniques

41   *GAGAKU*—ANCIENT COURT ORCHESTRAL MUSIC

The ancient court orchestras of China found their way to Korea, where they still exist, and on to Japan, where, beginning in the sixth century, the art of **gagaku**, *the ancient orchestral court music of Japan*, took root. With the introduction of Indian Buddhist melodies and indigenous Japanese compositions, the repertory of Chinese and Korean melodies expanded into two basic genres: **togaku** (*music of the left* or old melodies), a repertory that includes Chinese and Indian influences, and **komagaku** (*music of the right*), a repertory that includes Korean, Manchurian, and indigenous melodies. The distinctive choreography and costumes for **bugaku**, the *graceful and controlled dances that sometimes accompany gagaku*, also distinguish the two repertories. Probably the oldest continuous tradition of orchestral art music in the world, *gagaku* has survived apparently with little change for over a thousand years. Many of the musicians of today's imperial *gagaku* orchestra in Tokyo (Figure 41.6 on page 198) can trace their ancestry back through hundreds of years' membership in *gagaku* orchestras.

The *gagaku* orchestra divides its instruments into three main groups—wind instruments, string instruments, and percussion—seen in "Instruments of the Gagaku Orchestra." The wind instruments include three *ryuteki* flutes and three *hichiriki* double reeds, all of which have the responsibility of carrying the melody. Players of both of these instruments can bend their

INSTRUMENTS OF THE *GAGAKU* ORCHESTRA

Kenneth Hamm/Photo Japan

FIGURE **41.1**

The *sho* (left) is a *collection of seventeen single-reed pipes connected to an air chamber.* The player manipulates fingerholes to allow air into the pipes, usually creating chords consisting of up to seven notes. Like a harmonica, the *sho* can be played by both inhaling and exhaling, enabling it to sustain chords for a long time. It is the Japanese counterpart to the Chinese *sheng* (Figure35.9). The *hichiriki* (second from left) is a *small cylindrical-bore double reed* similar to the Chinese *guan* but much louder. The *ryuteki* (third from left) is a *transverse bamboo flute used in gagaku.* In some repertories it may be replaced with the slightly smaller *koma-bue.*

Courtesy of Bill Shozan Shultz

FIGURE **41.2**

The *biwa* is a *four-string, fretted, pear-shaped lute.* While similar in form to the Chinese *pipa* (Figure 35.2), it is held horizontally and constructed so that the relatively loose strings rattle against the neck. It has long been used to accompany narrative songs and play melodies associated with a group of blind priests. However, the version of the instrument pictured here, the *gaku-biwa*, is used exclusively in *gagaku.* Periodically, the player forcefully plucks the strings with a very large plectrum, resulting in a loud, dry tone. The black leather strap extending across the resonator protects the wood of the body from these powerful hits.

Courtesy of Gilbert Blount

FIGURE **41.3**

The player of the *kakko*, a *small double-headed cylindrical drum*, is the conductor of the *gagaku* orchestra. The drummer plays the *kakko* with two mallets, one for each side, and the drum rests on a stand in front of the drummer, who sits cross-legged in front of it. By playing accelerating rolls and carefully timed taps, the *kakko* player controls the tempo and coordinates the performance. In some repertories, a slightly larger hourglass-shaped drum called the *san-no-tsuzumi* replaces the *kakko.*

Courtesy of Gilbert Blount

FIGURE **41.4**

The *tsuri-daiko* is a *large vertically suspended bass drum* with an elaborately painted drum head. Some *gagaku* repertories use other sizes of hanging drums which regularly interpunctuate the melody.

Courtesy of Gilbert Blount

FIGURE **41.5**

The *shoko* is a *small metal disc hung vertically from a stand.* The player strikes the *shoko* on the concave side (the side opposite that showing in this picture) with two metal-tipped mallets, one slightly ahead of the other. Its high, dry sound punctuates the melody just after the beginning of every four-beat metrical unit.

FIGURE 41.6
In the *gagaku* court orchestra, the front row includes (left to right) the *shoko*, the *tsuri-daiko*, and the *kakko*. Behind them are the string players, two *gaku-so* (a version of the *koto* zither) on the left and two *gaku-biwa* on the right. In the back row are the aerophones, including (left to right) *ryuteki* (three), *hichiriki* (usually three, but only one is visible here), and *sho* (usually three, but two are visible here).

© Mitsuru Kanamori/HAGA/The Image Works

pitches substantially. Carefully coordinated scoops up to a pitch and slides between pitches are characteristic of their performance style. Another aerophone, the *sho*, is a mouth organ that plays constant background chords. The bottom notes of these chords form a skeletal version of the melody. The string instruments consist of two each of special forms of the *biwa* and *koto*, which interpolate short fragments between phrases of the melody. The percussion instruments include the large *tsuri-daiko* hanging drum and the small *shoko* gong, both of which divide the melodic phrases at regular points. The tempo is set by another drummer who plays the *kakko*, an hourglass drum.

A *gagaku* piece, which may last from five to twenty or more minutes, is generally performed in three large sections, a tripartite division common in Japanese arts. Different melodic phrases, rather than dramatic changes in texture, distinguish the three sections. These sections are called **jo** (*introduction*), **ha** (*exposition*), and **kyu** (*ending*), and each section repeats. *Gagaku* music unfolds so slowly that it may at first seem non-pulsatile, but when one becomes attuned to its extremely slow tempos, it can envelope the listener, producing an experience of weightless refinement, balance, and serenity.

A *Gagaku* Performance

The work *Etenraku, Nokorigaku Sunben* is one of the oldest and best known pieces in the *gagaku* repertory. It is especially associated with New Year celebrations and other symbols of new beginnings, and Shinto rituals also use its tune. Despite its composition in *hyojo*, a *ritsu* mode with no semitones, the *hichiriki* and *ryuteki* parts have gravitated over the years toward alternate pitches that allow the occasional semitones so characteristic of Japanese music outside the *gagaku* court tradition. *Etenraku* is a *togaku* piece from the old repertory "of the left." A *short prelude*, known as a **netori**, not heard on our recording, sometimes precedes a *gagaku* performance.

In the following graphic we show the texture of *Etenraku* in a diagram of the first half of section A. In this opening section, as each instrument enters the texture builds. The diagram shows the beats as vertical lines; the beginning of each four-beat metric unit is a solid line. Though carefully controlled, the exact timings of these beats are somewhat flexible, and not all instruments line up as precisely as shown here. The *ryuteki* flute and *hichiriki* double reed (in red) carry the melody; the strings (green horizontal lines) interject short notes and patterns at the beginning of each four-beat unit; the *shoko* gong (light blue) plays just after the beginning of each four-beat unit; and the *kakko* drum (medium blue) controls the timing with an accelerating roll around the middle of the phrase and a constant roll at the end of the phrase. The *sho* mouth organ (pink) provides a constant chordal background throughout with complex movements from one chord to another, indicated only generally in the graphic.

GRAPHIC **41.1**
CD 2:3. Texture
of *Etenraku*

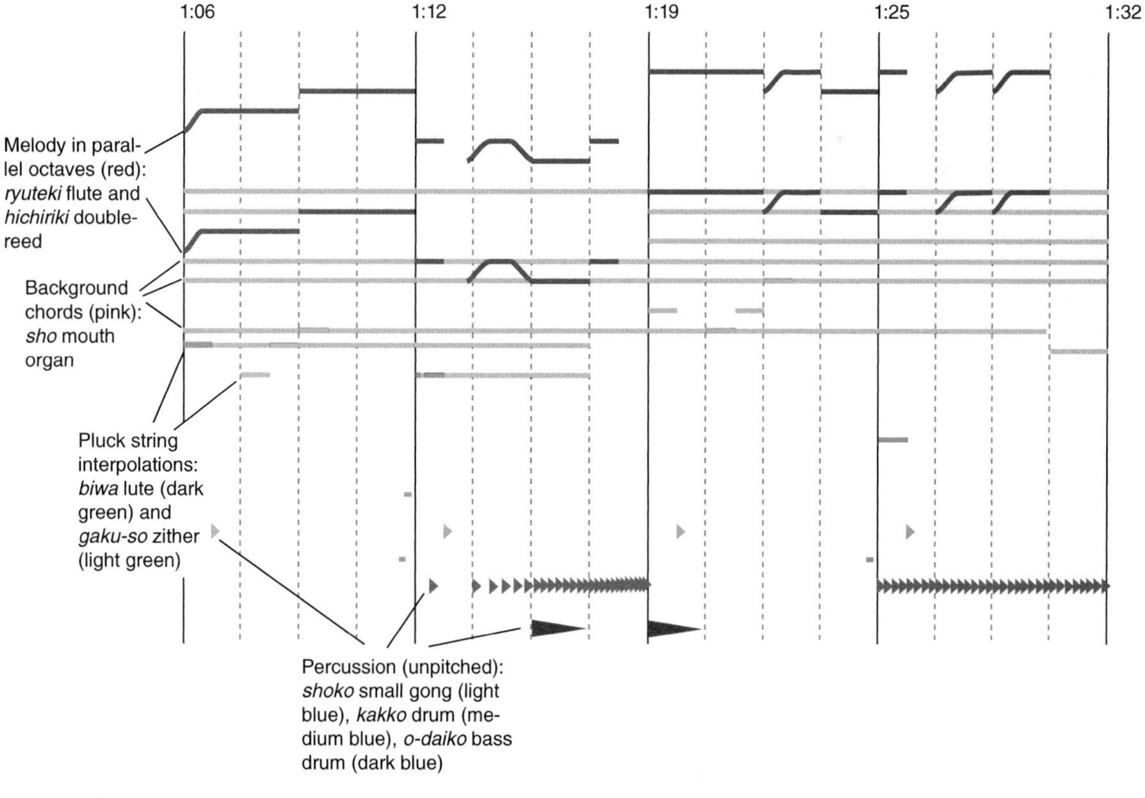

Melody in parallel octaves (red):
ryuteki flute and
hichiriki double-
reed

Background
chords (pink):
sho mouth
organ

Pluck string
interpolations:
biwa lute (dark
green) and
gaku-so zither
(light green)

Percussion (unpitched):
shoko small gong (light
blue), *kakko* drum (medium blue), *o-daiko* bass
drum (dark blue)

Listening Guide

A section

0:00	*Ryuteki* flute establishes the extremely slow tempo and carries the first melody, **A**.
0:07	*Kakko* (lead drum and conductor) and *shoko* (small metal gong) enter with sudden strikes. Despite an extremely slow and elastic tempo, the *kakko* conductor keeps the ensemble tightly integrated throughout the piece. The *shoko* continues striking just slightly after each of the strong beats.
0:09	*Kakko* accelerates the beat, still within the meter, as the *ryuteki* continues the melody.
0:12	The *tsuri-daiko* hanging bass drum strikes with a resonant thud halfway through the acceleration.
0:16	Just in advance of the next melodic phrase, the *sho* mouth organ enters with an enveloping chord that forms a background throughout the piece. The *sho* changes to certain standard chords, called *aitake*, throughout the piece, generally chosen so that the lowest tone corresponds to the main pitch of the melody at that point.

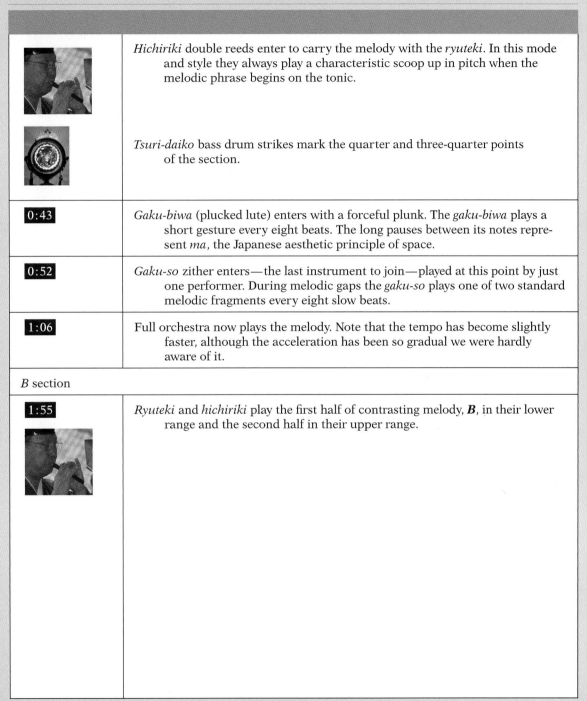	*Hichiriki* double reeds enter to carry the melody with the *ryuteki*. In this mode and style they always play a characteristic scoop up in pitch when the melodic phrase begins on the tonic.
	Tsuri-daiko bass drum strikes mark the quarter and three-quarter points of the section.
0:43	*Gaku-biwa* (plucked lute) enters with a forceful plunk. The *gaku-biwa* plays a short gesture every eight beats. The long pauses between its notes represent *ma*, the Japanese aesthetic principle of space.
0:52	*Gaku-so* zither enters—the last instrument to join—played at this point by just one performer. During melodic gaps the *gaku-so* plays one of two standard melodic fragments every eight slow beats.
1:06	Full orchestra now plays the melody. Note that the tempo has become slightly faster, although the acceleration has been so gradual we were hardly aware of it.

B section

1:55	*Ryuteki* and *hichiriki* play the first half of contrasting melody, **B**, in their lower range and the second half in their upper range.

(*continued*)

2:37	**B** melody repeats.
3:07	Percussion drop out of the texture as the **B** melody comes to a close. From this point to the end, the texture thins as other instruments gradually drop out.

C section

3:16	A new melody, **C**, enters and repeats. Unlike the previous melodies, **C** ends with a prolonged note, but not the tonic.

A section

4:26	**A** melody returns to again play twice. The tempo gradually increases (compare the durations of each section).

B section

5:32	**B** melody returns and again repeats.
5:52	*Sho* mouth organ drops out of the texture.
	Over the course of the final three minutes the instruments depart one by one. Their absence (keenly felt in the case of the *sho*) will carry as much impact as their sounds.

C section

6:35	**C** melody returns and again repeats.
	The last *ryuteki* flute drops out, leaving a single *hichiriki* playing the melody.

7:17	Last *hichiriki* drops out momentarily, leaving only the strings to play the **C** melody in fragments suggesting the whole.

A section

7:37	Solo *hichiriki* plays the **A** melody a final time.
9:06	*Hichiriki* drops out completely, and we hear only the ghostly whisper of the texture in the intermittent plucked strings that slow to the original tempo and end.

JAPANESE INSTRUMENTAL MUSIC

42

Music for the *Shamisen*

The **shamisen** is a fretless *long-necked lute* (Figure 42.1) similar to the Chinese *sanxian*, although it is thought to have been brought to mainland Japan via the island of Okinawa in 1562. Priest-musicians who had previously accompanied their songs with the *biwa* lute were the first to take up the *shamisen*. Thus *narrative songs*, **katarimono**, similar to those from the *biwa* tradition, make up a large portion of the *shamisen* repertory. *Shamisen* music plays an important part in *kabuki* theater music, but the most famous *shamisen* songs are the narratives that accompany **bunraku**, *puppet theater*. In *bunraku*, a master puppeteer and two assistants dressed in black, each manipulating a single large puppet, create complicated and stunningly graceful movements that make the puppets appear uncannily human. A single *shamisen* player and a separate narrator (Figure 42.2) usually accompany these plays. The *narrator*, **gidayu**, sings and speaks the narration and characters' dialogue with great force and melodrama.

The *shamisen* lute also accompanies *lyrical songs*, called **utaimono** or **jiuta**. As this music became more refined and entered the classical repertory in the eighteenth century, it became the basis for songs in **sankyoku**, *a chamber ensemble made up of* shamisen, koto, *and* shakuhachi (Figure 42.3). In keeping with the *jiuta* tradition, the *shamisen* player in these ensembles is also the singer.

Music for the *Shakuhachi*

The **shakuhachi** is a *vertical bamboo flute* (Figure 42.4). When originally introduced from China, the *shakuhachi* was associated with court music. In the Kamakura period, however, Buddhist monks of the Fuke sect, often displaced samurai, took up *shakuhachi* performance as an aid to meditation. Early monks blew repeating patterns of one or two pitches that occasionally grew into longer melodic fragments that monks, playing in unison, adopted as a *classical repertory for the* shakuhachi, known as **honkyoku**. The breathing cycles that are part of meditation establish a very slow, non-pulsatile rhythm that, rather than follow a fixed meter, arises out of these long phrases.

The *in* mode gives most *shakuhachi* music a melancholy character, and the breathy tone evokes the lonely wind. Although the tone is relatively soft, loud

FIGURE 42.1

The *shamisen* is a *fretless, long-necked lute* played with a very large plectrum, borrowed from the *biwa* lute, and has a somewhat louder tone than the *biwa*. The resonator of the *shamisen* is box-shaped and covered with cat skin. Its three strings, traditionally made of silk but today commonly nylon, are stretched over a long, thin fingerboard.

Courtesy of Gilbert Blount

FIGURE **42.2**
The *gidayu* (narrator) and *shamisen* player perform in *bunraku* puppet theater.

FIGURE **42.3**
In the *sankyoku* ensemble, the *koto* (left) plays the basic melody while the *shamisen* (center) and the *shakuhachi* (right) overlay more elaborate hetero-phonic variations. *Sankyoku* performances consist of suites of songs, sung by the *shamisen* player, and instrumental interludes. These interludes may feature re-sponsorial forms in which the focus shifts to each of the instruments in turn.

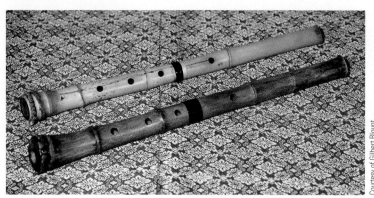

Courtesy of Gilbert Blount

FIGURE 42.4

The player of the **shakuhachi**, a *vertical bamboo flute*, blows over a notch carved into the side of one end. A small piece of ivory or buffalo horn is inserted in the notch to keep the edge sharp. The player plays a tone by tightly focusing an air stream over this notch, a very difficult technique. However, this rather unwieldy nature is the *shakuhachi*'s greatest strength, for it allows skilled players to attain a wide dynamic range and effects not possible on some other flutes—pitch bends, vibratos, microtones, tremolos (fast variations in loudness), and so on. Unlike its Chinese counterpart, the *xiao* (Figure 35.7), the *shakuhachi* is carved from the root of the bamboo tree, making it relatively thick and heavy.

bursts and expressive changes in dynamics are common. A single note may slowly grow louder from near silence, or it may begin with a startling chiff, the short puff of noise at the beginning of a tone. Overblowing can cause sudden high notes to precede the main note and shaking the head while playing can create vibrato.

Before the nineteenth century, *shakuhachi* instruction was offered only to Buddhist monks known as *komuso*. Later, two new schools of *shakuhachi* performance, *Kinko* and *Tozan*, began accepting lay students. Even today these organizations expect years of commitment and impose rigorous examinations on their students. *New compositions for the* shakuhachi, called **shinkyoku**, began to proliferate in the twentieth century. These new works often introduced new scales and non-traditional techniques. Western flute music especially influenced some of these pieces.

Music for the *Koto*

The *wagon*, an ancient zither, is apparently indigenous to Japan, but the far more widely used **koto** *zither* (Figure 42.5), related to the Chinese *zheng* and the Korean *kayagum*, was imported from China as part of the *gagaku* court orchestra. Although it has been a part of court music since medieval times, the *koto* became better known when it moved to the homes of the emerging middle class beginning in the seventeenth century. This movement was the result of the work of composer Yatsuhashi Kengyo (1614–85), who established the use of the *in* mode, created new playing techniques, and composed much of the early repertory for the *koto*. We will hear a *koto* composition by Yatsuhashi Kengyo as our audio selection.

The *koto* sometimes accompanies a woman singing a cycle of songs known as **kumiuta**. The meter of the original sixteenth-century *kumiuta* poems defined a constant phrase length, called a **dan**, that varied from sixty-four to one hundred-twenty beats. This form was carried over into purely instrumental compositions, creating slow but regular phrases that distinguish solo *koto* music from non-pulsatile *shakuhachi* music, for example. Each

Courtesy of Bill Shozan Schultz

FIGURE 42.5
The *koto* consists of thirteen silk or nylon strings stretched over a curved board resonator. Large bridges shaped like an inverted V that lift the strings above the resonator can be moved to tune the strings. The player plucks the strings with plectra attached to rings on the first three fingers of the right hand. The left hand bends pitches by pressing down on the string behind the bridge. The wide pitch bends affected by this technique are a distinctive ornament associated with the *koto*. (See the Chinese *zheng*, Figure 35.1)

GRAPHIC 42.1
The Variation of One
Four-beat Metrical Unit in
Rokudan no shirabe

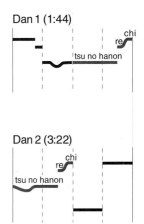

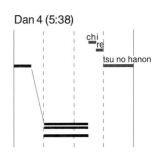

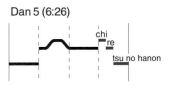

dan usually represents a variation of a basic melody, although unrelated interludes may be interpolated for the sake of variety.

A *Koto* Performance

Yatsuhashi Kengyo's *Rokudan no shirabe* is one of the most famous classical pieces for the *koto*. *Rokudan* means "six *dan*," and each *dan* is a variation of the first. Except for the four-beat introduction, each *dan* has exactly twenty-six metrical units of four beats, divided evenly into two halves.

You can see how the variation process works by comparing corresponding four-beat units in each *dan* variation. Using a characteristic motive—the notes *tsu no hanon*, *re*, and *chi*—Graphic 42.1 shows a particular four-beat segment as it appears in each *dan*. In the first *dan*, the motive occurs at the end of this four-beat unit, but in the second *dan* the motive moves to the beginning of the unit. In *dan* 4 and 5, the same motive is reversed. Furthermore, the increased speed of these *dan* requires that the player separately pluck *chi* and *re* rather than slide between them. Transformations of these sorts occur throughout the variations that make up a classical *koto* composition. The use of small motives holds this piece together and creates a unified performance in the midst of a serene and floating sound quality.

Listening Guide

0:00	First four beats on the *koto* announce central motive in simple, introductory form.
	This motive persistently reappears, sometimes in different octaves, in short form, elongated form, and so on.

First *dan*

0:07	Pungently dissonant repeated two-note chords also serve as a recurring landmark.
	Not all notes begin with a pluck. Listen to how the left hand presses down on the string behind the bridge to cause the pitch to slide to the next note. The player's left hand also creates some vibrato or slight bending of pitch on nearly every note.
1:31	Startling appearance of a pitch outside the scale, *hennon* characteristically withheld for just such striking occasions.

Second *dan*

2:04	Tempo slightly faster.
2:36	Example of an ornament called **waren**, *a quick strumming across the strings*.

Third *dan*

3:40	Another important ornament called **sa-rarin**, *a fluttering tremolo on a single string followed by a sweep down the strings*.

Fourth *dan*	
4:53	Tempo has increased noticeably. Variation and ornamentation somewhat more spare because of the faster tempo.

Fifth *dan*	
5:48	Tempo at least twice as fast as the beginning.

Sixth *dan*	
6:34	Final *dan* begins.
6:51	Listen for consistant sound of notes outside the scale through the phrase. Continued absence of the home scale creates a sense of tension.
7:09	Tempo suddenly begins to slow to original tempo, bringing a sense of serenity and completion.
7:22	A final *sa-rarin* reestablishes the scale and quietly closes the piece.

MUSIC OF THE JAPANESE THEATER

43

Noh Classical Theater

Noh is the classical theater of Japan (Figure 43.1). Like much Japanese fine art, it is highly refined, stylized, and reserved; to those unfamiliar with its conventions, it may seem inaccessible. Props and settings, reflecting the sparsity of the *ma* principle, are represented only symbolically, if at all. Similarly, the slow, weightless movements of the actors create spaces during which only the hollow sound of the *nohkan* flute pierces the silence. However, like the weightless mountains of Japanese landscape paintings, the experience of *noh* can surround the audience with a floating timelessness.

Despite this stylization, *noh*'s roots lie in folk dramas full of acrobatics, pantomime, and comic interludes that moved into the courts in the late fourteenth and early fifteenth centuries. During this period of political upheaval, *noh* served as an emblem of ruling-class status and sophistication as well as a reflection of its Buddhist and traditional values. In the last hundred years,

FIGURE **43.1**
The **hayashi**, the *musical ensemble that accompanies* noh *dramas*, includes (from left to right) a *taiko* cylindrical drum, the *o-tsuzumi* drum held in the lap, the small *ko-tsuzumi* drum held on the shoulder, and the *nohkan* transverse bamboo flute. The *taiko* is the same drum found in folk ensembles and *taiko* drumming groups. The *o-tsuzumi* and *ko-tsuzumi* are similar to but smaller than the double-headed cylindrical drums of *gagaku*.

the patronage of *noh* has shifted to include the middle class, and today *noh* is appreciated by educated connoisseurs.

Nearly everything about the *noh* play is standardized, from the musical ensemble to the structure of the play and the stage itself. Actors use stylized gestures that represent the expression of particular emotions to the audience familiar with these conventions. The actors often wear masks painted with graceful, understated elegance, that seem to come to life in the enveloping atmosphere of the play. *Noh* stories are usually drawn from mythology or ancient narratives, and since they are infused with the spirit of Zen, cause and effect and logical chronology are not as important as atmosphere and mood. Traditional *noh* performances were all-day events of five full *noh* plays with *comic interludes* known as *kyogen*. Today, it is common for a single *noh* play to be performed as an evening's entertainment.

Two or three principal actors perform in the *noh* drama, accompanied by a small male chorus and a small musical ensemble made up of a single flute and drums. The standardized stories and stylized speech and action are so well known to the expert performers that *noh* plays are not rehearsed. The musicians, too, know the order and placement of pieces that accompany the action of the play, and there is considerable give-and-take between the actors and the musicians. Most of the music in a *noh* drama is non-pulsatile, which frees the actors' expression as well as the audience's sense of time.

The *musical ensemble that accompanies noh* is called **hayashi**, and it is made up of four instruments: the *nohkan* bamboo flute and three small drums. A surprising variety of sounds can come from this spare ensemble. As the only melodic instrument aside from the singing voice, the *nohkan* leads the ensemble in all instrumental pieces, and provides expressive counterpoint to dialogue and songs. Most *nohkan* music consists of a large number of short, stereotyped melodies—motives appropriate to certain moods—that the performer varies and extemporaneously orders to fit the sections of the play.

Unlike other flutes, the *nohkan* has a smaller cylinder inserted between the mouthpiece and the fingerholes. Normally, when a flute player increases air pressure beyond a certain point, called *overblowing*, the instrument produces a tone an octave higher, but because of the *nohkan*'s unique construction, the tone produced is somewhat lower than an octave. This lack of emphasis on the octave tends to obscure the tonal sense, and it is not unusual for songs to start and end on different tonal centers. The resulting sense of suspended tonality is appropriate for the floating, dreamlike meditation of the *noh* theater.

The *ko-tsuzumi* is the smallest but most important drum in the *noh* ensemble. The ropes that are laced through the heads are held in the player's left hand and allow the player to control the drum's pitch by squeezing or loosening the ropes. The player also uses small pieces of paper attached to the inside of the back head to control the tone. Also important to these ensembles are the *shouts and exclamations from the drummers*, called **kakegoe**.

Noh drumming consists of certain standard patterns strung together and varied by each drummer. Different drummers may play different patterns at the same time, not necessarily synchronized, and this layered effect is one of the distinctive characteristics of *noh*. Nevertheless, the drummers are listening to one another. If anything, the freedom of the rhythm necessitates even closer attention than in more pulsatile music.

The singing style of *noh* is most closely related to *shomyo*, Buddhist chant. It is mostly free in rhythm, the pitch that the actor begins on is not necessarily important (unless he or she is singing with the chorus), and the vocal quality is rather tense. There are two types of singing: a kind of *free recitative in a heightened speech-song* called **kotoba** and *song melodies* called **fushi**.

Kabuki Classical Theater

By the late sixteenth century, *noh* theater had already become highly conventionalized and largely patronized by the samurai upper class. The emerging middle class turned to a variety of other entertainments, including *bunraku* puppet theater, folk dramas, acrobatics, and so on. According to tradition, in 1603 a famous female performer brought a Buddhist dance, along with other dances and pantomimes, into the secular setting of a *noh* theater. The performance was called **kabuki**, a word which then meant strange or out of balance but which has since come to be associated with this *genre of theater* (Figure 43.2).

FIGURE 43.2
In the *kabuki* drama *Musume Dojoji,* a woman atop a sacred bell reveals herself to be a demon. Behind her are the onstage *kabuki* musicians. In the front row are musicians of the *shitakata* ensemble including *o-tsuzumi* (shoulder drums, left) and *nohkan* (flutes, right). In the back row is the *debayashi* ensemble, which includes multiple *shamisen* players (right) and singer-narrators (left).

© Liba Taylor/CORBIS

Kabuki became wildly popular in the eighteenth and nineteenth centuries, and star actors were national celebrities. Over time, *kabuki* became conventionalized, but the genre has never been as rigid or as unchanging as *noh*. Today *kabuki* is a form of classical theater rather than a popular entertainment, although it continues to be supported by and popular among the middle and upper classes. While most *kabuki* plays come from a standard repertory, some troupes experiment with new plays and forms of staging.

Kabuki borrowed heavily from *noh*, *bunraku*, and other genres. The musical ensembles from these genres were incorporated wholesale, with no attempt to merge the groups. Thus the most distinctive musical aspect of *kabuki* is its use of not one but up to four different ensembles, each of which performs largely independently of the others. While the instrumentation and placement of these groups may vary depending on the play performed, a standard complement consists of four ensembles.

■ *Debayashi* The core of *kabuki* music, the *debayashi* ensemble was borrowed from the tradition of lyric songs accompanied by the *shamisen*. Made up of four to eight *shamisen* players and a chorus of male singers, the group sits on a platform onstage, usually in the center in the back, just in front of the backdrop.

■ *Shitakata* Sitting on a lower platform in front of the *debayashi*, the *shitakata* group uses the standard *noh* ensemble of *nohkan* (flute), *o-tsuzumi*, *ko-tsuzumi*, and *taiko* drums. *Debayashi singers* take the place of the *noh* chorus, and a second flute, the *takebue* or *shinobue*, occasionally joins the ensemble.

■ *Gidayu* This is the narrator-*shamisen* pair from *bunraku*, sometimes multiplied so that there are three or four of each. The *gidayu* narrates the play and comments on the action, much like a Greek chorus. The *gidayu* is usually placed either on a platform at one corner of the stage or behind a bamboo curtain to the side of the stage.

■ *Geza* Hidden from the audience, the *geza* is a group of musicians who provide stylized sound effects and music that set or accompany the scene. Clappers may accentuate footsteps, cymbals and gongs represent the sound of thunder, and so on. The instrumentation of the *geza* is not fixed but generally contains four or more musicians playing a *shamisen*, *nohkan*, and a large, diverse battery of percussion.

Kabuki scores are often drawn from existing pieces that are appropriate to a given situation and character. However, they may also be newly composed. It is not uncommon to have a different composer (or arranger) for the onstage and offstage ensembles. Many of the musical styles of *kabuki* have been adapted from the same sources as the instrumental groups. *Kabuki* also adapted some *noh* forms of movement, story structures and types, and so on. Nevertheless, *noh* and *kabuki* are clearly different.

Noh is a small theater form—there are just four instrumentalists and only a few actors—whereas *kabuki* is large in scale, employing a large number of musicians and actors and a large set. Movements and gestures in *noh* are subtle, a kind of code that audiences learn and understand. While gestures in *kabuki* can also be stylized, they are much more flamboyantly theatrical. Sets and props in *noh* are extremely simple and sparse, while sets in *kabuki* can be quite elaborate and may feature complicated changes executed in full view of the audience.

In its emphasis on musical diversity and grand spectacle, *kabuki* stands in strong contrast to the spare, contemplative atmosphere of *noh*, and yet both represent different sides of Japanese cultural ideals. While *noh* exemplifies the radiance of spiritual emptiness, the *kabuki* stories of great passion and violence exist inside a carefully controlled, strict discipline of dramatic form, acting, movement, and music.

 REFERENCES

Discography

Ensemble Nipponia. *Japan: Traditional Vocal and Instrumental Music*. New York: Elektra/Nonesuch 9-72072-2, 1976.

Kyoto Nohgaku Kai. *Japanese Noh Music*. New York: Lyrichord 7137, 1964.

Imperial Court Gagaku Ensemble. *Gagaku: Ancient Japanese Court and Dance Music*. Pismo Beach, CA: Legacy International CD 402, n.d.

Kodo: Heartbeat Drummers of Japan. Santa Barbara, CA: Sheffield Lab CD-KODO, 1985.

Miki, Minoru. *Selected Works*. Takuo Tanura cond. Pro Musica Nipponia. Tokyo: Camerata 30CM-55, 1982/1994.

Takemitsu, Toru. *Compositions of Toru Takemitsu*. Hiroyuki Iwaki cond. NHK Symphony. Tokyo: CBS Sony 58DC 282–58DC 283, 1984.

Various artists. *Japan: Semiclassical and Folk Music*. Paris: Auvidis/Unesco D-8016, 1974/1989.

Various artists. *Japanese Masterpieces for the Shakuhachi*. New York: Lyrichord 7176, 1980/1993.

Various artists. *Japon: Musique du Kabuki et du Jiuta-mai*. Paris: Auvidis B 6809, 1994.

Various artists. *Music of Japanese Festivals*. Tokyo: King Records KICH 2028, 1991.

Various artists. *Music of Okinawa*. Tokyo: King Records KICH 2025, 1991.

Bibliography

Harich-Schneider, Eta. *A History of Japanese Music*. London: Oxford University Press, 1973.

Isaku, Patia R. *Mountain Storm, Pine Breeze: Folk Song in Japan*. Tucson, AZ: University of Arizona Press, 1981.

Kishibe, Shigeo. *The Traditional Music of Japan*. Tokyo: Kokusai Bunka Shinkokai, 1969.

Malm, William P. *Japanese Music and Musical Instruments*. Tokyo and Rutland, VT: C. E. Tuttle Co., 1959.

———. *Six Hidden Views of Japanese Music*. Berkeley: University of California Press, 1986.

———. *Japanese Music and Musical Instruments*. Rutland, VT: Charles E. Tuttle, 1959.

Tanabe, Hisao. *Japanese Music*, 2nd ed. Tokyo: Kokusai Bunka Shinkokai, 1959.

— c. 200
Bronze-working imported from China. Some of the artifacts from this period include large bronze drums (actually idiophones) which may have developed into gongs.

— 5th C
Hinduism and Buddhism arrive in Java from India.

— 8th–9th C
Central Javanese kingdoms build great stone monuments that depict Indian musical instruments and a few indigenous instruments. There is some literary evidence of masked dances, possibly *wayang*.

— 14th–15th C
Height of the East Javanese Majapahit empire, whose influence possibly extends as far as the Philippines. Bronze gongs and similar instruments, possibly a result of these cultural connections, are found throughout Southeast Asia.

Indonesia

—— **15th C**
Islam is established in parts of Java, eventually bringing musical influences. However, the devotion to Hindu-based art forms, in particular the stories of the *wayang*, remains strong.

—— **16th C**
Majapahit empire falls. Some courts flee to Bali, which remains Hindu even as Islam is gradually accepted throughout Java and elsewhere in Indonesia.

—— **1602**
Dutch East Indies Companies chartered, beginning the period of Dutch colonization.

—— **18th C**
Central Javanese Kingdoms in Yogyakarta and Surakarta develop gamelan music and associated dance forms.

PART 8 ■ INDONESIA

INTRODUCTION TO THE REGION

44

FIRST LISTEN
CD 2:5
Ladrang Pangkur,
Gamelan Paguyuban
"Suko Raras"

It may seem unlikely that the most venerated and renowned art of the art-saturated Indonesian islands of Java and Bali is a *shadow puppet show*, but the ***wayang kulit*** (Figure 44.1) is not just an entertainment for children. Each play—narrated by a *single virtuoso puppeteer*, the ***dalang***, and accompanied by an *orchestra of mainly bronze instruments* known as the ***gamelan***—is an all-night epic that recounts the never-ending battles of the forces of light and dark, good and evil. Witnessing such a performance is like

---

— 1906
Dutch take control of Bali,
eliminating most courts
and their associated mu-
sic. New popular styles
emerge, notably the dy-
namic *kebyar* style, which
has remained the most
popular and important
genre in Bali.

— 1942–1945
Japanese occupation.

— 1948
Independence from
Dutch; Republic of In-
donesia founded.

glimpsing the ghostly echoes of the world of the gods and demons, of ancient kings and princes.

The puppets are flat and carved with lace-like features projected onto a large screen by the light of an oil lamp (traditionally) or an electric bulb (more commonly) so that their images flicker evanescently before the audience (Figure 44.2). Just as the intricately carved patterns of each puppet are supported by a buffalo horn center stick, so the ornate melodies of many gamelan instruments weave around a central core melody.

FIGURE **44.1**
From the audience's perspective, we see the shadow puppets of the *wayang kulit*. Behind the screen and light source, a single puppeteer manipulates the flat leather puppets. And behind the puppeteer sits the gamelan orchestra that accompanies the play.

William Alves

The stories of the *wayang kulit* typically come from the Hindu epics, the *Mahabharata* and the *Ramayana*, that recall this region's ancient Hindu kingdoms. Just as the equilibrium of heaven and earth, of good and evil, is fundamental to Hindu cosmology, so too is the performance space divided by a screen that creates two different realities. The same dualism is everywhere in the musical tradition as well—in the two different tuning systems, in the binary meters and forms, in the contrasting sections of loud and soft, fast and slow, vocal and instrumental.

It is not unusual for audience members to come and go during these nine-hour performances, eat snacks, and watch from both sides of the screen. Many come in anticipation of their favorite scenes, especially those that include the popular clown characters, whose improvised vernacular speech offers the *dalang* occasion for topical humor, even political jokes. What is important is not so much the specifics of the story with its gradual unfolding of heroic conflicts, but the mood and ritual-like atmosphere, the confirmation of the eternally revolving wheels of days, years, lives, and civilizations.

The Hindu cycles of life also form the foundation of the music as articulated by the periodic tolling of gongs in the gamelan. Today gamelan is one of the most famous music traditions in the world. The quiet complexities of the Javanese gamelan and the dynamic intricacies of the Balinese variety have entranced listeners for more than a century. In the chapters ahead we will look primarily at the rich traditions from cultures on the neighboring islands of Java and Bali, and in particular, at the composition and performance of gamelan music.

Geography Indonesia is a nation made up of a chain of over 13,000 islands mostly north of Australia and south of the Southeast Asian peninsula and

FIGURE 44.2
In this view of the *wayang* screen as seen from the *dalang*'s (puppeteer's) side, the *dalang* sits cross-legged in the center with his head just behind the lamp. The puppets are supported by sticks made of horn that are stuck in the banana tree log set horizontally below the screen. The puppets needed for the play are stored to the left (evil forces) and right (good forces) with the action taking place in the center.

William Alves

the Philippines. The capital is Jakarta, on the island of Java. Indonesia is now the world's fourth most populous country and Java is one of the most densely populated areas. The motto of the Republic of Indonesia, "Unity in Diversity," is a reflection of the enormous ethnic, linguistic, and musical variation that can be found among its peoples.

CHARACTERISTICS OF GAMELAN MUSIC

45

It would be hard to mistake the gamelan orchestras of Java and Bali for one another. The gently floating tones of the Javanese gamelan invite serene contemplation, "like flowing water," to quote a common metaphor, while the brilliant Balinese gamelan can be fast and dynamic. Nevertheless, beneath the surface, these neighboring islands share important elements in their history and culture that allow us to generalize about aesthetic features that they share.

■ **Orchestras Featuring Bronze Instruments** In these cultures that emphasize the importance of community, the orchestra rather than the solo performer represents the classical ideal. These large ensembles feature a number of drums, winds, and string instruments, but dominating the instrumentation are the famous bronze instruments, generally of two types: **metallophones** (*metal-keyed xylophones*) and tuned gongs, hanging vertically or suspended horizontally on taut cords.

■ **Compositions Guided by a Core Melody** A skeletal melody, the ***balungan*** in Java and ***pokok*** in Bali, directs the intricate parts of gamelan texture. Despite its very simple rhythm, the *balungan* is an artful combination of various contour types and melodic motives appropriate to the mode. For example, one tone of the five in the melody may be intentionally saved for an important point of change. The pattern of notes may be offset from the meter so that when it finally arrives on a strong beat, the event is marked with a satisfying gong stroke. By methods such as these, the *balungan* directs a constant flow of contrasts and resolutions.

■ **Polyphonic Texture** The *balungan* is only one of a rich fabric of melodies in gamelan music. Like the elaborate, lace-like carving of the *wayang kulit* puppet, various levels of faster melodies form filigrees that weave around the *balungan* core. These melodies are not guided by principles of harmony, but instead follow the *balungan*, periodically diverging and then returning to the *balungan* tones at important points.

■ **Colotomic Structure** The regular punctuation by gongs in gamelan music articulate the metrical cycle and create what musicologists call a colotomic structure. Depending on the form of a gamelan composition, a player tolls the largest gong every 8, 16, 32, 64 or more beats. The other gongs reflect this regularity on a smaller level, dividing the periods between the large gong strokes by 2, 4, 8, and so on. Thus these gongs build a cyclic hierarchical structure that serves as the foundation for the piece.

■ **Paired Families of Tuning Systems** Gamelan compositions are nominally in one of two tuning systems, *pelog* or *slendro*. ***Pelog*** *is a tuning system of seven pitches per octave with some adjacent intervals significantly larger than others.* ***Slendro*** *is a tuning system of five pitches per octave with the adjacent intervals close to the same size.* However, each gamelan's version of *pelog* and *slendro* is slightly different from that of every other gamelan, giving each set of instruments a unique sound.

■ **Stress at the End of Metrical Cycles** Most musical cultures number their beats from the start of a metrical unit so that beat one (the "downbeat") receives the most stress. However, beats in gamelan music are numbered so that the stress comes at the *end* of every metrical unit instead of the beginning. The fact that the Javanese hear the gong as the culmination of the cycle rather than its beginning has important consequences. Melodies often anticipate the tones of the *balungan*, for example.

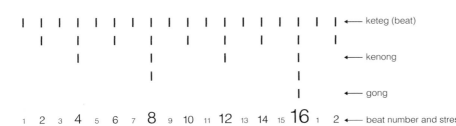

GRAPHIC **45.1**
The stress on beats in gamelan music

JAVA, ITS GAMELAN AND INSTRUMENTS

46

About half of the 130 million inhabitants of Indonesia live on the island of Java, historically the most politically and culturally influential island of the Indonesian archipelago. The most famous gamelan traditions come from Central Java, specifically the cities of Yogyakarta (also called Yogya) and Surakarta (also called Solo). Though separated by only sixty kilometers, they have had rival courts and traditions for the last 200 years (Figure 46.1).

Javanese Culture

Many Javanese follow a form of Islam that blends traditional Islam with belief in a spirit world and other remnants of Java's Hindu and pre-Hindu past. Hindu stories are still common in dramas and gamelan performances even if they have lost much of their religious, if not cultural, significance. Like many aspects of Javanese tradition, spirituality balances the light and dark sides. In such Javanese dramas as the *wayang kulit* shadow puppet play, the forces of good and evil are in constant contention. Such opposites exist even in a single character, and the best characters are those who keep these opposing forces in balance. Certain acts such as prostration, meditation, or good deeds strengthen one's personal spirit and influence one's daily life as well as religious status. Commissioning or taking part in a good musical performance may give a person spiritual strength. A sense of spirituality surrounds musical instruments and certain other inanimate objects, which are treated with respect.

The Javanese, especially the Central Javanese, highly prize **alus**, *a characteristic* sometimes translated as *refined*. This quality is reflected above all in the heroes of their dramas, especially the *wayang kulit*, who have balanced the spiritual forces within themselves and fulfilled their destinies. The counterbalancing side from *alus* is frequently given as **kasar**, usually translated as *coarse*. Even gamelans are sometimes classified by one of these qualities.

To the Javanese, *alus* includes indirectness in social intercourse. A Javanese asking a favor is not likely to ask directly, but instead expects the lis-

FIGURE 46.1
The Sultan's *kraton* (palace), seen above, is in Yogyakarta, Java. The sultan remains an important and respected cultural and political force in the region.

William Alves

tener to determine the unspoken meaning of the conversation and comply, thus preserving the pride of both asker and answerer. The qualities of indirectness and ambiguity pervade Javanese arts. The audience at the *wayang* see only the shadows of the puppets. Performers in a drama may present social commentary veiled by elaborate symbolism and historical references. Song lyrics may present a proverb hidden within the poem.

FIGURE **46.2** Displayed here is one of the royal gamelans at the court of Surakarta.

William Alves

The Javanese Gamelan

Javanese gamelan music is refined and often moderate and contemplative in temperament. A piece is likely to start with an instrument such as the *bonang* kettle-gongs or *rebab* fiddle playing in a seemingly offhand manner, as if just tuning up. However, this *short introduction*, the **buka**, actually leads the listener into the world of the gamelan and, more specifically, the mode and character of the piece to be played. Toward the end of the *buka*, the drummer, who functions as the conductor, enters to set the tempo. The end of the *buka* is marked by a stroke on the great gong, and everyone joins in.

Just as dramatic stories contrast the forces of light and darkness, gamelan performances feature sections in which the softer instruments bring their ornate melodies to the foreground and other sections in which the louder instruments dominate. The drummer subtly leads the ensemble through changes in tempo and character that suggest new perspectives on repeated melodies and the ways in which they together weave the sonic fabric.

A typical Javanese gamelan piece may last from three minutes to thirty, but about fifteen minutes is common. The drummer plays a loud cue to slow down and signals the approach of the ending. The great gong dramatically sounds its final note alone, followed by the rest of the gamelan.

Javanese Gamelan Instruments

The Javanese term gamelan is now used to describe ensembles throughout the archipelago, but especially the classical orchestras of mostly bronze instruments in Java and Bali. While the instrumentation of the gamelan may vary considerably depending on the region, function, and context, the most characteristic and obvious instruments are usually metallophones and gongs. Other instruments may include drums, wooden xylophones, zithers, fiddles, and bamboo flutes.

INSTRUMENTS OF A TYPICAL CENTRAL JAVANESE GAMELAN

FIGURE 46.3

The *saron* is a *thick-keyed metallophone with a box resonator* played with a single hard wooden or horn mallet in the right hand, while the left simultaneously damps the key previously hit. The *saron* are constructed in three different sizes, each size playing an octave apart. The *saron demung* is the lowest, the *saron barung* (shown here) an octave higher, and the *saron panerus* or *peking* an octave higher than that.

FIGURE 46.4

The *slentem* is the bass member of the *gendér* family. Unlike its higher-pitched relatives, it is played with a single large padded mallet.

FIGURE 46.5

The *gendér* (pronounced with a hard G) is a family of *thin-keyed metallophones with tube resonators*. Mallets with disc-shaped heads covered in felt strike the instrument with a soft, mellow tone. The *gendér barung* is the larger and lower-pitched of the two sizes of *gendér*; the *gendér panerus* is pitched an octave higher. A mallet is held in each hand and keys are damped with the palms or sides of the hands.

FIGURE 46.6

The *bonang* family comprises *horizontal bronze kettle-gong instruments*, of which there are two or three sets, each set tuned to a different octave: *bonang panembung* (lowest), *bonang barung* (middle), and *bonang panerus* (highest, shown above left). The gongs are laid across strings and set in a frame (shown below). Players hold a stick mallet in each hand, the mallets softened with cord wrapped around the end.

FIGURE 46.7

A *two-string vertical spike fiddle*, the **rebab** is played by the melodic leader of the orchestra. The *rebab*'s thin, singing tone leads the melodic instruments of the Javanese gamelan.

William Alves

FIGURE 46.8

The **gambang** is *a wooden xylophone with a box resonator*. Played in parallel octaves with two flexible mallets, their disc-shaped ends wrapped in felt, the *gambang* has a soft and delicate sound.

William Alves

FIGURE 46.9

The **celempung** (sometimes replaced by the smaller *siter*) is *a large zither plucked with the fingernails*. The ornate carving and feet of the instrument were influenced by European furniture of the colonial period.

William Alves

FIGURE 46.10

The **suling** is an *end-blown bamboo duct flute*.

William Alves

(continued)

INSTRUMENTS OF A TYPICAL CENTRAL JAVANESE GAMELAN

FIGURE 46.11

The **kenong**, *a set of large horizontal kettle-gongs*, seem similar to the *bonang* (Figure 46.6), but the *kenong* gongs have much taller, sloping faces and perform a different function.

FIGURE 46.12

The **kempul** are *small hanging gongs*.

FIGURE 46.13

The **gong ageng**, or simply gong, is *the largest vertical gong*, shown here next to the slightly smaller *gong suwukan*. These extremely low gongs dramatically end the metrical cycle of gamelan music.

FIGURE 46.14

In the Javanese gamelan, a single drummer usually plays two *double-headed drums*, **kendang**, set before him. The *ketipung* (left) is the smaller of the two and the *kendang gending* (below) is the larger. Other drums are sometimes used for dance or ritual pieces.

The most impressive instruments in the gamelan are the large, low-sounding, vertically hanging gongs. Gamelan gongs are carefully shaped to sound a definite pitch as well as a throbbing "wah-wah" effect. Unlike orchestras elsewhere in the world, which are usually defined by their personnel, gamelans are defined by a set of instruments, no matter who plays them. The instruments within one ensemble share a particular tuning system which is likely unique. For this reason, it is practically impossible to bring an instrument from one gamelan to another and play in tune.

While gongsmiths (instrument makers) build their instruments to play in either the *pelog* or *slendro* tuning system, Javanese gamelan instruments are often designed and built in pairs, so that there is one of each instrument for *pelog* and *slendro*. The instruments in one tuning system are set at right angles to their counterparts in the other tuning system so that the players can shift from one to the other by simply changing their sitting positions. Instruments from the two tuning systems are never played at the same time.

JAVANESE COMPOSITION

47

Although the *balungan*, the core melody played by the saron metallophones, often dominates the texture of Javanese gamelan compositions, musicians do not consider it the central melody of the piece. Instead they refer to a more ornate melody, the **lagu**, even though this melody is never explicitly heard—it exists only in the minds of the musicians. This underlying melody subtly guides the delicate filigree of the higher instruments and the lyrical countermelodies of the strings and singers into an elaborate polyphonic fabric. The *lagu*, like the shadow puppet, may be hidden from the audience, but we are always aware of its shadows from the ways the other instruments artfully suggest its presence.

The *Balungan*

The *balungan*, then, is a simplified version of the *lagu*, boiled down to its essential tones within a simple rhythm and limited range. The *balungan* is prominent not because it is the most important melody, but because it forms a middle ground between the slowly sounding gongs and the faster melodic instruments. When contemporary musicians want to notate or teach a composition, it is the *balungan* that they write down. A Javanese gamelan made up of experienced performers can perform a piece given only the *balungan*, the form, and some details of a style. The *saron* and *slentem* metallophones play the *balungan*, although the melody has to be restricted to their limited range. Skilled players can infer the rest of the instrumental parts in a manner appropriate to the style.

Melodic motives are very important to a *balungan*. They not only distinguish its identity, but also help establish the mode and character of the piece. These motives, which are familiar to the Javanese music lover, may signal a return to home territory or embarkation to a new section.

The *Kembangan*

Some writers have called the melodies with more notes per beat than the *balungan* "elaborating melodies," but the Javanese often refer to them as the **kembangan**, literally *the "flowering" of the music*. While guided by the same mode, contour, and other melodic forces that shape the *balungan*, they are hardly inessential decoration, but the heart of Javanese gamelan performance.

Often these elaborating instruments play variations on *certain known patterns*, called **cengkok**, that ultimately coincide with the *balungan* at the ends of phrases. A player chooses a particular *cengkok* based on the important tones in the *balungan*, the mode, the tempo, and so on. Some cadences, that is, phrase endings, have less finality and others sound more final and coincide with the sounding of the gongs. Thus the polyphony of a Javanese gamelan consists of many melodies, diverging and coming back together, the degree of agreement often depending on this elaborate hierarchical architecture.

The *rebab* player leads the melodic instruments, even though the drummer is the rhythmic conductor. The other elaborating instruments listen to the *rebab* for cues about when to move on to a new section or when to emphasize a certain register (range of pitches). The *rebab* plays a lyrical, almost singing line that often shadows the *balungan* and, more than any other instrument, brings to light the relationship between the simple *balungan* melody and the *lagu*.

Patet (Mode)

The guiding structure of melody in the *pelog* and *slendro* tuning systems is called **patet**, a term often translated as "mode" but that includes a hierarchy of stressed and unstressed tones and characteristic motives. These small fragments of melodies soon become familiar to one who has listened to the music for some time. These patterns are most prominent (and most studied) in the *balungan*, although they permeate all the melodies of the *gamelan*. Because all *slendro patet* share the same five nearly equidistant pitches, these motives may be the most identifiable features of the patet. *Pelog patet* use five-tone subsets of the seven-tone tuning system, so that all gamelan compositions are basically pentatonic. Each *patet* has certain emotional associations, which sometimes connect with their use in the *wayang kulit*. The three acts of the *wayang kulit*, each lasting nearly three hours, are themselves called *patet* because all the music of each act is restricted to a single mode.

Colotomic Structure

Colotomic structure refers to *the pattern of regular punctuation of the composition by certain gong strokes*; this structure is fixed and repeating for a particular type of compositional form. The large gong marks the slowest, or primary, punctuation. One gong note sounds every 8, 16, 32, 64, 128, or even 256 beats, depending on the colotomic pattern for that particular composition. A ***gongan*** is *the large phrase defined by the duration between successive gong notes*.

At the second level of punctuation, usually playing 2 or 4 times faster than the gong, is the *kenong*. The *kempul* plays at the same level of frequency but in between the *kenong* strokes. The first *kempul* beat within a cycle may be left *silent*, or ***wela***, in the Central Javanese style. The *ketuk* plays the next highest level of punctuation (in between the *kempul* and *kenong* beats), and the optional fastest level is played by the *kempyang*.

Because of the Javanese love of bilateral symmetry, reflecting the dualism of Hindu cosmology, almost all colotomic structures are based on powers of two. *Gongan* are usually 8, 16, 32, or 64 beats in length, and the other punctuations are based on successive halving of these large cycles. The sense is of an ever-turning cycle and cycles within cycles rather than an edifice of hierarchical progressions.

Thus the Javanese often classify forms not only by the number of beats between each gong type, but, more importantly, by their relative relationships. Since the *kempul*, when present, always plays in between the *kenong* notes, the number of *kenong* strokes per gong and the number of *ketuk* strokes per *kenong* define most Javanese forms.

For example, any form that has only two *kenong* strokes per gong is called a ***ketawang***. In Solonese terminology, the word *kerep* ("often") or *arep* ("sparse") in the name of the form indicates the number of *ketuk* strokes per *kenong* stroke, such as "*merong ketuk 4 kerep.*" These forms can be shown as a cycle, as in Graphic 47.1.

In these diagrams, each hash mark represents a beat, and time moves clockwise. The abbreviations are G for gong, N for *kenong*, P for *kempul*, and T for *ketuk*. Note that longer forms don't necessarily use the *kempul*, and the shorter forms may contain silence (*wela*) during the cycle's first beat when the *kempul* would otherwise play. Despite the differences between the forms, there are important similarities made clear by this representation—the *kenongs* always divide the cycle into four or two, for example, and that the *kempul/wela*, when present, divides the *kenong* phrase into two.

Ladrang—32 beats, a common form

Ketawang—16 beats with fewer *kenong* subdivisions

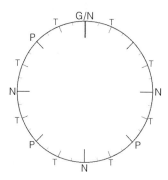

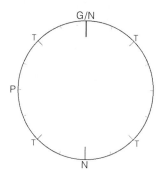

Merong Ketuk 2 Kerep or Candra—64 beats with 2 *ketuks* per *kenong*

Merong Ketuk 4 Kerep or Candra Dawah—64 beats with 4 *ketuks* per *kenong*

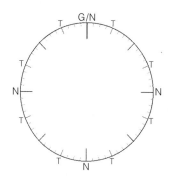

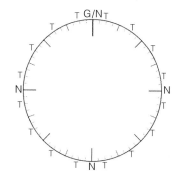

Irama and Stratification of Rhythm

Probably the most immediately striking aspect of the rhythmic structure of a Javanese performance is that, generally speaking, the higher an instrument's pitch, the more *notes it plays per beat*—that is, the higher its **rhythmic density**. The stratified rhythmic texture of Javanese gamelan music may include ten or more levels of rhythmic activity. The ratio of rhythmic density between each level of activity is two, or powers of two in a given colotomic form. For example, Table 47.1 shows the typical relationships for a *ladrang* (32-beat form). One of these levels is the beat and is usually, though not always, the rate at which the *saron demung, saron barung,* and *slentem* play the *balungan* notes.

The word ***irama*** refers to these *relationships between the rhythmic densities of various instruments to the beat.* Frequently a piece undergoes several changes in *irama*. To signal these changes, the drummer loudly plays a pattern that slows or speeds up the tempo. If the drummer slows the tempo, for example, when the tempo becomes so slow that it is half the original speed,

TABLE **47.1**

Irama I   The typical relationships between rhythmic densities (notes per beat) of instrument parts in a *ladrang* (32-beat form) in *irama* I in the Central Javanese gamelan. The *rebab*, voices, and *suling* are too free in their rhythm to fit easily into this table.

Level	Instruments	Typical rhythmic density
8	*bonang panerus, gendér panerus, gambang*	4 notes per beat
7	*bonang barung, gendér barung, peking*	2 notes per beat
6	*saron demung, saron barung, slentem*	1 note per beat
5	*bonang panembung, kempyang* (when present)	1 note per 2 beats
4	*ketuk*	1 note per 4 beats
3	*kenong, kempul*	1 note per 8 beats
2	(no instruments)	1 note per 16 beats
1	gong	1 note per 32 beats

TABLE **47.2**

Irama II   The relationships of instruments after shifting from Irama I (Table 47.1) to Irama II. Although the tempo of the beat is twice as slow in this configuration, the instruments of the first two rows in this table play twice as many notes per beat and therefore about the same number of notes per second as in *irama* I.

Level	Instruments	Typical rhythmic density
9	*bonang panerus, gendér panerus, gambang*	8 notes per beat
8	*bonang barung, gendér barung, peking*	4 notes per beat
7	(no instruments)	2 notes per beat
6	*saron demung, saron barung, slentem*	1 note per beat
5	*bonang panembung, kempyang* (when present)	1 note per 2 beats
4	*ketuk*	1 note per 4 beats
3	*kenong, kempul*	1 note per 8 beats
2	(no instruments)	1 note per 16 beats
1	gong	1 note per 32 beats

the fast melodic instruments (that is, the two *gendér*, the two *bonang*, the *gambang*, and the *peking*) shift up a level, and play twice as many notes per beat as they played previously. Because the tempo, or beats per second, has been halved, the number of notes per second of these instruments remains the same, but an important shift in relationships has occurred. Were the tempo of *Irama* I (Table 47.1) to change in this way, it would result in the relationships shown in Table 47.2.

In this example, the instruments playing faster than the *balungan* (one note per beat) have shifted from level 7 to level 8 or from level 8 to level 9, creating a new level. Changes to a faster beat (that is, *irama* shifting down) is effected the same way—the drummer loudly signals a new tempo and the musicians follow. When the speed has doubled, the higher-pitched instruments shift to half as many notes per beat.

A JAVANESE GAMELAN PERFORMANCE

48

Pangkur is a well-known classical piece in the Central Javanese repertoire, and versions of this piece exist in several *patet*. This example is in *patet manyura* in the *slendro* tuning system. *Pangkur* is in the form of a *ladrang*— that is, a 32-beat gong cycle divided into 4 by *kenong* strokes. Each of the phrases articulated by the *kenong* are divided again by the *kempul*, except for the first, in which the *kempul* is *wela* (silent).

Modern Javanese musicians notate *balungan* melodies using **kepatihan**, or cipher notation, in which numbers represent pitches. In the *slendro* tuning system the pitches are numbered 1, 2, 3, 5, and 6 with dots above or below to indicate octave displacements. The following graphic shows the *balungan* melody for *Pangkur* and clearly illustrates the way in which *patet manyura* stresses pitch 6, coming as it does at the most important point to coincide with the gong. For the colotomic notes, N stands for *kenong* (which actually sounds an octave higher), P for *kempul*, T for *ketuk* (shown without its pitch, which may vary among gamelans), and G for large gong (also shown without its pitch, which is very low). Note how the *kempul* and *kenong* together outline a simple melody that nevertheless retains the important movement that occurs on the stressed beats. The relative stress of the beats is shown by the font size of the beat numbers.

GRAPHIC **48.1**
Black rectangles mark *Pangkur's balungan* melody. Rectangles with letters indicate the colotomic notes.

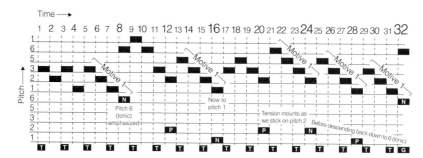

Certain motives also characterize *patet manyura*, especially the pattern 3–2–1–6 that ends the section. Javanese hear this motive as the equivalent of a continual step down, even though the pitch 6 is higher than pitch 1 when played by the *saron*. However, the musicians are listening not so much to the *saron* melody itself as to the *lagu*, the inner melody that the *saron* melody represents. In the *lagu*, unrestricted by the range of the *saron*, pitch 6 is in the lower octave, and therefore one step *down* from pitch 1. The melody of *Pangkur* repeatedly uses this stepping-down motive (motive 1) to establish different important tones, and thereby a journey to different tonal regions.

The *balungan* establishes this journey on many different levels. For example, if we look at every other note of the melody, that is, just those that land on the even-numbered or stressed beats, another melody is formed (in Yogyanese style the *bonang panembung* may play this melody) that retains the basic outline of the important *balungan* tones as well as interest on its own right. We can continue this process of distillation further by looking at just the *kenong* and *kempul* strokes, which makes clear the journey from pitch 6 and back again.

A well-composed *balungan* sounds good at a variety of levels in the context of the colotomic form and *patet*. This *kembangan*, or flowering, of the basic tones continues at levels of rhythmic activity even faster than the *balungan*. For example, the *bonang* in this piece plays a kind of elaboration known as **pipilan**, in which *a new melody is created mostly by alternating between pairs of* balungan *tones*, as shown in the next graphic. The gray rectangles represent the same balungan pitches in the lower octave to make clear the melody's relationship to the *bonang* part. Note that the *bonang* part creates a simple "flowering" or elaboration consisting of alternations between pairs of notes that follow the *balungan* pitches. The *bonang panerus* (the highest instrument of the family) plays the same patterns, but at twice the rhythmic density, thus alternating back and forth twice for every single alternation in this part.

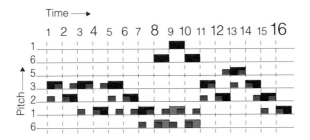

GRAPHIC **48.2**
In this section of Pangkur, red rectangles mark the *bonang barung* part. Black rectangles mark the original *balungan* notes.

At a level of greater rhythmic density, other instruments, including the *gendér barung*, *gendér panerus*, *gambang*, and *celempung*, weave more elaborate melodies around the *balungan*, coinciding at metrically important points, generally every four *balungan* notes. The section of the *gendér* part shown in Graphic 48.3 is a variation of a *cengkok* (a stock melodic outline)

CD 2:5. *Ladrang Pangkur*, Gamelan Paguyuban "Suko Raras." Djarwo Saminto, director

The *buka*—introduction

0:00	*Gendér barung* plays short solo *Kendang* drum enters, establishes the tempo and cues the orchestra's entrance

Part I—loud style, *Irama I*

0:06 	Great gong signals the end of the *buka* and the whole orchestra enters Orchestra plays first phrase (beats 1 to 8), ending with the descending motive 3 2 1 6 and *kenong* stroke. Establishes *patet manyura* by ending on pitch 6 and avoiding pitch 5.
0:11	Second phrase (beats 9 to 16), ends with the motive 5 3 2 1. This motive, a transposition of the characteristic *manyura* motive 3 2 1 6, now lands on pitch 1. Because of this new emphasis on pitch 1, the melody seems to take us to new territory.
0:16	Third phrase (beats 17 to 24) builds tension by emphasizing pitch 2. The third phrase introduces yet another transposition of the characteristic motive, this time to 6 5 3 2.
0:21	Drummer suddenly plays more loudly to indicate a change in texture for second gong cycle (*gongan*). Fourth and final phrase of the melody (beats 25 to 32) repeats the descending motive in successively lower transpositions. Now the 6 5 3 2 on which the previous phrase ended is followed by 5 3 2 1 and finally 3 2 1 6 that brings us back to the feeling of *patet manyura*. Gong indicates the end of the melody.

Part II—soft style, *Irama I*	
0:28	*Celempung* zither, *suling* flute, and *rebab* fiddle play intricate melodies elaborating on the *balungan; gambang* xylophone and *gendér* metallophones are also playing. Their intricate melodies shadow the *balungan*, weave around it, and always coming back.
4:03 **4:12** **4:24**	Drummer loudly signals a change in *irama* (rhythmic density). Tempo slows dramatically to about half the previous tempo. Faster instruments shift rhythmic density to play twice as many notes per *balungan* tone. While there are just as many notes per second, the fact that the melodic lines weaving around the *balungan* now have twice as far to go between each point of correspondence creates a new perspective, as if we are zooming in on the same melody. That shifting point of view is the essence of a change in *irama*, often used to give structure and variety to Javanese gamelan performances.
Part III—soft style, *Irama II*	
4:48	New gong cycle, slow melody
6:28	Sharp drum cue silences all but the *slentem, rebab*, and *suling*, suddenly opening up the texture for the gong to shine through.

(*continued*)

Part IV—alternating textures, *Irama II*	
6:32	*Slentem*, *rebab*, and *suling* (the very soft instruments) and the colotomic gongs create a lyrical perspective of the melody.
7:01	Other instruments return, but only briefly at the midpoint of the melody.
7:28	Drum cues return of full orchestra in time for gong.
Part V—new countermelody, *Irama II*	
8:15	Drum cue again opens up the texture to the *slentem, rebab*, and *suling*. *Saron* play a new countermelody, shadowed by the rebab. This new melody (composed, not improvised) still corresponds to the *balungan* tones at important points.
9:07	Rest of the orchestra reappears on a subtle drum cue in time for gong.
9:57	Drum cue opens texture once again. Solo *rebab* plays the countermelody; brief orchestral interruptions as before.
10:52	New *gongan* with the whole orchestra.
11:14	Drum signals a gradual increase in tempo at this mid-point in cycle.
Part VI—return of loud style, *Irama I*	
11:28	Gong sounds. Tempo has doubled, melodic instruments shift to the original *irama*, and the texture returns to the opening loud statement of the melody.
11:42	Drum signals the gradual slowing down of tempo to prepare for the ending.
11:58	Final tone of melody dramatically withheld until after the last gong has sounded.

known as *tumurun*, which the player has chosen because it is appropriate for a *patet manyura balungan* phrase that goes from pitch 1 to pitch 6, as in this example. Note how the melody corresponds with the *balungan* at beats four and eight. In between these beats, this supple melody diverges and returns to partial correspondence at beats 5 and 6.

What results is a rich polyphony of melodies that fit together like fractals, at different levels of activity. The players give the piece structure and maintain interest through changes in texture and *irama* (rhythmic density relative to the *balungan*).

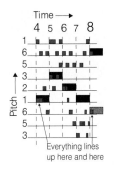

GRAPHIC 48.3
In this single phrase from *Pangkur*, red rectangles mark the *gendér barung* part and show its more complex "flowering" of the *balungan*, marked by black and gray rectangles.

 CD2, *Pangkur* examples: Track 6 *Gendér barung*, Track 7 *Rebab*, Track 8 *Gambang*, Track 9 *Kendang*, Track 10 *Bonang barung*

BALI, ITS GAMELAN AND INSTRUMENTS

49

Since the 1930s, when Western anthropologists, artists, and ethnomusicologists first explored its lush volcanic hillsides, the island of Bali has been justly famous in the West for its unique culture and embarrassment of riches in the arts. Today these hills echo with the sounds of motorcycles and tour buses, but arts and rituals are as much a part of daily life for the Balinese as they were in previous centuries. In Balinese communities, virtually everyone is an artist—a rice farmer may also be a poet, a housewife a dancer, a taxi driver a sculptor, or a construction worker a gamelan player. Professional musicians exist, of course, but are mainly associated with the modern music conservatories. Art is a natural part of community life for nearly everyone.

The complex web of social obligations to one's local community, or *banjar*, is a crucial part of life for the Balinese, and represents the Hindu virtue of *dharma*, fulfilling one's place in society and harmony with the world. Cooperation within one's community and society as a whole is deeply ingrained and reflected in aspects of social life from the distribution of irrigation water, which is controlled by certain priests, to the formation of neighborhood music and dance clubs that play for local rituals, competitions, spiritual fulfillment, or for enjoyment.

Unlike its neighbor Java, which converted to Islam hundreds of years ago, Bali remains a primarily Hindu region in which rituals form a nearly constant part of daily life. These ceremonies often require elaborately decorated offerings of fruit and flowers to the gods as well as an offering of music. Rituals, artistic performances, even concerts for tourists and the most mundane of everyday events can be spiritually charged and connected to the supernatural (Figure 49.1).

FIGURE **49.1**
An audience at a Balinese village watches dances during one of the frequent gamelan performances. Villages may commission a performance for an important ritual, such as the anniversary of the founding of a temple. In such a case the most important audience may be gods.

William Alves

Characteristics of the Balinese Gamelan

The Balinese gamelan, while outwardly similar to the Javanese version, plays a thrilling, dynamic music apt to create a flood of sensory impressions (Figure 49.2). All the gamelan parts interconnect, not through controlled individual elaborations, as in Java, but through memorization of set parts, sometimes composed communally, so that each of the parts cooperates precisely with the others.

One of the most famous and characteristic techniques of the Balinese gamelan is the creation of a melody through the combination of two or more extremely fast and rhythmically intricate interlocking parts. Interlocking means that when one of the two melodies is playing, the other may be resting, and vice versa, so that, heard together, they form a single unbroken line. As in other aspects of Balinese life, the split-second timing of such techniques requires absolute cooperation.

Another remarkable facet of Balinese performance, especially in the style called **kebyar**, is the ability of the entire orchestra to stop and start on a dime and to play seemingly non-metrical rhapsodic sections as if they were a single instrument. There is no esoteric secret behind such ability—just hours and hours of rehearsal.

Another distinctive characteristic of the Balinese gamelan is the fact that the instruments are *deliberately detuned* from one another, producing a jarring effect that the Balinese cultivate. The detuning is not haphazard but

FIGURE **49.2**
A Balinese gamelan
plays at a ceremony.

precisely calibrated to give a constant "wah-wah" effect, a kind of sparkle to the sound that one can hear especially as the sound decays.

The Balinese gamelan shares some of the characteristics of the Javanese gamelan: colotomic structure (the periodic punctuation by gongs), a tempo conducted by drummers, compositions made up of repeated sections, and of course the similar instruments—Table 49.1 compares the two varieties. Nevertheless, it is unlikely that one would mistake the loud and brilliant sound of the Balinese gamelan for the often sedate, meditative music of its neighbor. Both traditions have points of correspondence that converged, especially during the period of the great East Javanese kingdoms 500 years ago, but the directions they have taken reflect their different cultures.

The *Gamelan Gong Kebyar*

On humid summer nights on the streets of Bali's largest city and capital, Denpasar, one can hear the nearly constant echoes of gamelans even above the motorbikes and shouts from street food stalls. This is the time of the *Pesta Kesenian Bali*, or Bali Arts Festival, an enormous annual competition and showcase for everything from temple offerings to mask-making to fashion, and, of course, different types of gamelan.

Unlike the ensembles of Java, where the classical gamelan has become a more or less standardized set of instruments that plays for many different repertories, styles, dances, and dramas, Bali has many distinct types of

TABLE 49.1
A Comparison of Generalizations About Balinese and Central Javanese Characteristics in Gamelan Music

Balinese	Central Javanese
dynamic, extreme contrasts	generally sedate, "like flowing water"
fast interlocking rhythms	moderate, simple rhythms
bright, exciting	refined, gentle
distinct gamelan ensembles	standardized set of gamelan instruments
pairs of instruments clearly detuned to give a jarring effect and characteristic shimmering sound	octaves slightly detuned to give a very subtle life to the sound
slow core melody in background	slow *balungan* melody often dominates texture
instrumental compositions common	vocal music with gamelan common
dance often fast and exciting	dance often extremely graceful and stylized
sudden stops and starts in *kebyar* style	tempo mostly constant except for *irama* shifts and slowing down at end
little or no improvisation	improvised variations of *cengkok* patterns
highly precise	ambiguous
competitive	non-confrontational, indirect

gamelan, some common and others rare, each with its own repertory and often performance contexts. But the most popular type of gamelan by far is the **gamelan gong kebyar** (also called *kebyar* and *gong kebyar*), whose brilliant sounds seem to be nearly everywhere.

This large ensemble not only plays for the dance after which it was named, but also accompanies other dances, ceremonial and occasional music, and unaccompanied instrumental performances. The word **kebyar** literally means to flare up like the lighting of a match and that is an apt description for the explosive non-pulsatile introductions found in many *kebyar* pieces. The main body of a *kebyar* composition consists of a series of repeated sections in which core melodies serve as foundations for amazingly fast and virtuosic figurations. Unlike other traditional repertories, *kebyar* compositions are not necessarily associated with a dramatic form or dance which tells a story.

Competitions at the Bali Arts Festival are not small affairs for connoisseurs, but elaborate, exciting events attended by thousands of spectators from all over the island. The rivalry is fierce and the audience merciless. A wrong note may result in a chorus of boos, a dazzling passage in spontaneous applause and yells of encouragement.

The rise of such pan-Balinese festivals in the past century and especially the last thirty years or so brought some important changes to performance practice, and nowhere are these changes more evident than in *kebyar*. The style has become faster and more virtuosic, with greater precision. Performances are also often visually flashy—the **ugal** (lead metallophone player) may spin his mallet for example, and dull facial expressions can lead to deductions of points.

There are several different stories about the birth of *kebyar*, but most agree that it was a style that emerged around 1915, at the same time as the decline of the courts following the Dutch takeover of the island in 1906. *Kebyar*'s spectacular, dynamic style appealed to the common people who dominated the organization of gamelans in the absence of the courts, and the *kebyar* style quickly spread throughout the island. Many old court gamelans were recast into *kebyar* instruments, so that today the earlier gamelan types are relatively rare. While the more ancient instruments often include all seven pitches of the *pelog* scale, the instruments of the gong *kebyar* are usually tuned to a five-tone subset of *pelog* known as **selisir**.

The *Kebyar* Instruments

The *kebyar* orchestra contains two families of metallophones. Softer single-octave instruments play the slow-moving **pokok** or core melody, and bright two-octave instruments mainly play the very fast figuration. All of these metallophones typically have thin keys suspended over individual tube resonators. Players of the *pokok* metallophones use padded mallets, giving the section a soft, mellow tone that creates a resonant underpinning for the rest of the orchestra.

The metallophones that play fast figuration are collectively referred to as the **gangsa** and include (from low to high): **ugal** (also called *giying*), **pemade**, and **kantilan**. Each of the metallophone instruments, with the possible exception of the *ugal*, has a partner with which it is precisely detuned. There are usually four players on each of the *pemade* and *kantilan* so that each detuned pair can play interlocking parts with another pair. The **reyong** is a set of twelve kettle-gongs mounted horizontally in a frame. Unlike the similar Javanese *bonang*, four players share the single row of kettle-gongs, often playing virtuosic interlocking figuration. The *suling* is a vertical flute that plays an elaborate form of the melody in soft sections. Often several (two to four) play together heterophonically.

The *kendang* (drums) lead the orchestra. Usually played by two players, the *kendang* control the tempo and dynamic level and signal repeat or dance cues. Like the other paired instruments, the two drummers often create interlocking patterns of their own. **Ceng-ceng** are cymbals that reinforce the drum patterns. The colotomic underpinning is provided by a single player who plays up to three types of gongs, along with the important **kempli** player, who helps synchronize the fast parts by playing a metronomic beat on this single kettle-gong.

INSTRUMENTS OF A TYPICAL BALINESE *GAMELAN GONG KEBYAR*

William Alves

FIGURE 49.3
Shown here are the gongs and *pokok* metallophones of a Balinese gamelan. In the back row are two **jegogan**, the *lowest metallophones of this group*, which play every other or every fourth note of the *pokok*. In the middle row are a *gendér* (not part of this section) and two **calung** or *jublag metallophones that play the pokok an octave higher than the jegogan*. In the front row are the two **penyacah**, *optional metallophones tuned an octave higher than the jublag*.

Courtesy instrument collection of the Music Department of Pomona College

FIGURE 49.4
The **gangsa**, shown here, is the collective name for *the metallophones that play fast figurations elaborating the core melody*. Those in the back row are the **kantilan** (generally four in the ensemble) that are struck with a single wooden mallet in the right hand while the left hand damps the sound. The metallophone on the left is a **pemade** (generally four in an ensemble) that plays the same figuration as the *kantilan* but an octave lower. In the foreground is the **ugal**, or *giying* (generally one or two in the ensemble), *a low-octave metallophone that plays the main melody with elaborations* and leads the *gangsa* section. In the background are the **gong** (*the largest hanging gong*), the **kempur** (a medium-sized hanging gong), and *the high-pitched hanging gong* **kentong** or *kemong*, which often divides the cycle into two. In front of the *gangsa* is the **kempli** or *kajar, the single kettle-gong that keeps the beat.*

BALINESE COMPOSITION AND PERFORMANCE

50

The *Topeng* (Mask Dance) and *Kebyar*

In Bali, dances can be dynamic and exciting with rapid angular motions suddenly and effortlessly changing to slow, fluid movements. One traditional dance commonly in the repertoire of the *gamelan gong kebyar* is the mask dance or **topeng**, in which the solo dancer represents the character depicted in the mask (Figure 50.1).

The dance begins with a brief solo by the *ugal*, the large metallophone that leads the *gangsa* (melody elaboration) section. The drummer joins to set the tempo, and then the entire gamelan answers with an explosive chord and begins to play. At this time the dancer enters. The music for *topeng* dances

FIGURE **49.5**
The *reyong* is a *single set of twelve kettle-gongs mounted horizontally in a frame* and shared by four players.

William Alves

FIGURE **49.6**
The *ceng-ceng* cymbals (1 or 2 performers) reinforce drum patterns. The bottoms of these small cymbals are always mounted on the back of a carving of a turtle, representing the animal that holds up the world in Hindu mythology.

William Alves

consists of a series of ***tabuh***, or *short repeated melodies* (ostinatos), played in their most complete form by the *ugal*. The *penyacah*, if present, plays a simplified version of the same melody, one note per beat; the *jublag* plays every other note of the *penyacah* melody or one note every two beats; and the lowest *jegogan* plays every other note of the *penyacah* melody or every four beats. After the ostinato has been established, the players of the *reyong* kettle-gongs enter, playing fast interlocking figuration.

The musicians, like the dancer, seem quiescent but alert, softly playing this repeating pattern. Suddenly, the dancer makes a bold movement. This movement, called an ***angsel***, is a cue to the drummer, who in turn loudly cues the rest of the gamelan. At the drummer's signal, the gamelan moves out of the ostinato and plays a loud cadence (ending) phrase. This new phrase (itself called an *angsel*) may serve as a signal to move on to the next

FIGURE **50.1**
Topeng is the masked
dance-drama of Bali.

William Alves

section, depending on the subsequent cue from the drummer. Thus the drummer, in cooperation with the dancer, signals via audible cues what sections to play when and how many times. The *angsel* breaks form an important structural element not just in dances, but in many types of gamelan pieces, and may signal complicated variations, alternate melodies, or sectional changes.

Most Balinese dances are based on this system of repeating melodies interrupted by *angsel*. In dances such as those of the *topeng* genres, the exact placement of the *angsel* is left up to the dancer, but in ensemble temple dances, for example, the *angsels* come at set points in every performance. Gamelan pieces not based on dances may still rely on repeated melodies, but the melodies can at times be very long and elaborate, especially in slow ritual repertories.

Kecak

Around a flickering fire late at night, a group of bare-chested men sit in concentric circles to perform one of Bali's most famous forms of music called *cak* or **kecak** (pronounced "chak" and "kechak"). This music does not use instruments at all. Rather, the roles of the instruments are taken over by the shouts, chants, and songs of the men, so that they themselves become the gamelan. Invented in the 1930s as a form of dance drama often representing stories from the *Ramayana* epic, the origins of the music go much further back to a now rare ritual for communicating with dead ancestors.

The performance may include a narrator who sings and speaks the story in the manner of the *dalang* puppeteer in the *wayang* shadow puppet play, and sometimes dancers. Several men take on the roles of the colotomic instruments of the orchestra, including the *kempli* (imitated with the syllable "pung!"), the *kentong* (a small hanging gong imitated with the syllable "tong!"), and the large gong (whose low wavering sound is imitated with a rolled "sirrrr!").

Suddenly a shout goes up from the leader of the chorus and the men begin shouting the syllable "chak!" in different interlocking patterns, so that the result is electrifying polyrhythmic shouting that sounds something like "chakachakachakachaka . . ." The following graph illustrates these interlocking patterns. When sounded together, these rhythms evoke the terrifying monkey army of King Rama in the *Ramayana* story.

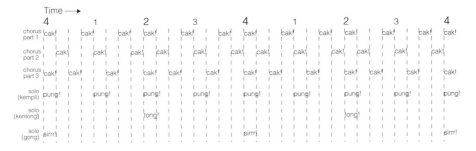

GRAPHIC **50.1**
The Interlocking
Rhythms of *Kecak*

Interlocking Patterns   Whereas the more rhythmically dense melodies of the Javanese gamelan create a dense polyphonic tapestry from the combination of all the individual instrument lines, Balinese figuration is characteristically based on the precise cooperation of rhythms and melodies that interlock like puzzle pieces. Cymbal players in processional gamelans, known as **belaganjur**, and other forms use the same rhythms as in *kecak* to create these exciting patterns.

When pitched instruments such as metallophones or kettle-gongs play such figuration, the interlocking patterns have to be carefully coordinated not only to each other, but to correspond to important pitches of the *pokok*, or core melody. This lightning-fast figuration thus creates one more level of melody in the *gamelan* texture. A composer carefully works out these precise interlocking melodies before the performance. There is no room for improvisation.

Kotekan   Possibly the most dazzling technique of the *kebyar* style is the type of figuration known as **kotekan**. In *kotekan*, the players of the *pemade* and *kantilan* metallophones or *reyong* divide into two parts, known as the *polos* and the *sangsih*, each of which consists of fast, complex syncopations, which when played together form a very fast composite melody, precisely interlocking the two parts. In Graphic 50.2, half the *pemade* metallophones play the notes represented by the light blue rectangles (the part called the *polos*),

Listening Guide

Kawitan section—introduction

0:00	*Ugal* metallophone plays a short melody.
	Drummer follows and sets the tempo.
0:03	Balance of orchestra enters and . . .
	Calung plays the *pokok* core melody.
	Jegogan plays a slower abstraction (every fourth note) of the *calung* melody.
	Gangsa (*ugal, pemade,* and *kantilan* metallophones) play a simple elaboration of the melody in unison.
	Ceng-ceng cymbals and *kendang* drums add noisy life to this introduction as . . .
	Barong (dancers) enters.
	The *calung* and *jegogan* players use padded beaters that give the piece a resonant foundation that nevertheless remains in the background.
0:21	*Ugal* and *suling* flutes (in heterophonic accompaniment) play an interlude.
0:26	*Gangsa* respond with *kotekan* (interlocking parts) to end the section.

Pengawak section—main body (a more expansive melody than in either first or last sections)

0:29	Transition again features *ugal* and *suling*.
0:41	*Kotekan* flurry follows.
0:47	*Gangsa* interrupt with three short notes created by hitting the bar while holding it with the other hand.
	Gangsa repeat the phrase and introduce a more expansive section.

0:55	*Gangsa* with *kotekan* accompany extended melody.
	Notice that *kotekan* figuration does not have to be loud; in fact, the preference is to play it lightly, cleanly, and softly. Every note is clearly heard, even though the melody is split between the two parts.
1:28	Melody repeats.

Pengecet section—fast ending

2:42	Colotomic structure suddenly contracts as dance picks up energy.
	Gong alternates with the *kentong* (a high-pitched gong) every two beats.
	Melodic instruments repeat a simple pattern while the drummer and dancers improvise an exciting interlude.
2:55	*Angsel—barong* dancer suddenly leaps and the drummer responds with three loud strokes—signal to the orchestra to move on to main body of *pengecet* section.
2:58	Orchestra plays the exciting body of the *pengecet* section.
	Ever faster *kotekan* play an electric finale.
3:16	Drummer loudly signals an *angsel* responding once again to signal from *barong* dancers.
	Although the dancers have some freedom in the placement of the *angsel*, it must always occur at the proper place in the colotomic structure and often, as in this case, in the melody.
	Gangsa instruments interrupt their otherwise continuous figuration.
4:01	Another *angsel*.
4:44	Final *angsel* signals a break.
4:49	Short repeated pattern (ostinato) until the *barong* dancers exit.
5:02	Drum signals a slowing tempo to anticipate the end of the piece.

CD 2:12 Balinese gamelan examples

while the other half play the notes represented by the pink rectangles (the *sangsih*). When they overlap, it is always on a unison pitch (colored purple here), and the two parts combine to make a single unbroken and very fast melody. This melody corresponds at important times to the notes of the core melody, or *pokok*, played by the softer *calung* and *jegogan* metallophones in different octaves. This particular subset of the seven-tone *pelog* tuning system uses only pitches 1, 2, 3, 5, and 6, and the irregularly spaced grid lines roughly represent the gapped intervals between the steps of this scale.

GRAPHIC 50.2
Kotekan

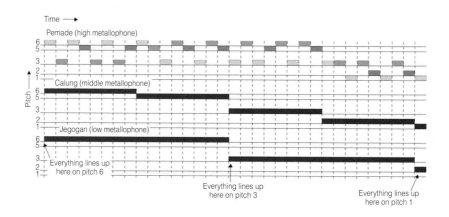

A Balinese Gamelan Performance

Gending Pengalang or *Bebarongan* is used to accompany the famous **barong** dance of Bali. The *barong* is a mythical dragon-like animal that is the holy protector of a village (Figure 50.2). In a dance-drama acted out for certain ceremonies (and, today, for tourists), two men dress up in an elaborate *barong* costume and dance together, generally accompanied by a *kebyar*-style orchestra.

In this drama, Rangda, an evil witch, challenges the *barong*. Sometimes the man who plays Rangda goes into a trance in which he is possessed by her spirit. Other men of the village also go into trances and try to attack Rangda with ceremonial daggers called *kris*. However, Rangda's magic is too strong, and she forces the *kris* back against her attackers. Under her spell, each of these men tries mightily to stab himself, but is protected by the *barong*, so that no matter how hard they push, the *kris* never draw blood. In the end the *barong* defeats Rangda and saves the village.

Like many Balinese pieces, *Gending Pengalang* is

FIGURE 50.2
Beneath the costume for the *barong*, the mythical dragon who protects Balinese villages, are two dancers; the one in front controls the jaws of the beast.

William Alves

in three large parts, which the Balinese sometimes refer to as the "head," "body," and "feet" of the composition. More formally, they are called the *kawitan*, *pengawak*, and *pengecet*.

51 LOU HARRISON AND THE AMERICAN GAMELAN

In 1955, the ethnomusicologist Mantle Hood brought a Javanese gamelan to the University of California, Los Angeles, with the then unusual idea that American students could best learn about Javanese musical culture by playing gamelan music under instruction from a Javanese master. Many colleges throughout the world, especially in the United States, have since followed this example, so that today many non-Indonesians play in hundreds of these ensembles outside of Indonesia, some becoming expert gamelan musicians in their own right.

Inspired by this tradition, in 1970 the American experimentalist composer Lou Harrison (1917–2003), along with instrument builder William Colvig, constructed an "American *gamelan*" out of aluminum tubes, bars, and plates. Growing up in the rich cultural stew around San Francisco's Chinatown and other minority communities, Harrison was influenced by traditional Asian music. While he absorbed many other influences as an experimentalist composer in the 1930s and 40s, Harrison developed a highly individual melodic style.

In the 1960s, Harrison traveled to Japan, Korea, and later to Indonesia to study their music firsthand. While he was very fond of the music of all of these cultures, it was the Javanese gamelan that most profoundly affected him. He immediately began composing for the ensemble he and Colvig built and was soon building others and studying with master Javanese composer and musician K. R. T. Wasitodiningrat. He composed dozens of works for gamelan, often in combination with Western instruments. Other composers followed his example, sometimes establishing gamelans to play only non-traditional American compositions.

Despite the surface similarities of Harrison's gamelan compositions to traditional Javanese music, to Javanese listeners his work is distinctive and unmistakably non-traditional. An example of Harrison's gamelan music is the deeply moving *Threnody for Carlos Chávez*. Carlos Chávez was a famous nationalistic Mexican composer and friend of Harrison's (see Chapter 59, page 295). A **threnody** is a lament, a piece that mourns the loss of someone. This is one of several of Harrison's works in which solo Western instruments and the gamelan meet in a symbolic cultural exchange, this time featuring a viola (a bowed chordophone of the violin family).

Harrison originally wrote the piece for *gamelan degung*, a kind of chamber gamelan from West Java, although it can also be played on Central Javanese instruments with extended ranges. The *saron* parts are divided into

Betty Freeman

FIGURE 51.1
Lou Harrison plays
a *suling* flute.

an upper and lower part. Harrison also asked for a **gentorag**, a *rare bell-tree instrument* found only in certain archaic ceremonial gamelans.

The feature of this piece that is most strikingly different from traditional gamelan music is the meter. Javanese music almost always uses a meter based on hierarchical divisions of two. In *Threnody*, however, all the divisions are by three, and the third unit of the group receives the stress. There are three notes (or equivalent rests) in the upper *saron* part for every one in the lower part. There are three notes in the lower part for every *kempul* stroke. There are three *kempul* strokes in each large phrase, and three phrases make up a *gongan* (section ending with the gong). In the three beats leading up to the middle *kempul* stroke in each phrase, there is a rattling of the *gentorag* and three notes in the *bonang*. Unlike traditional pieces in Central Java, there is no *kenong*.

The very first three notes (after the gong), 6–5–6, in the upper *saron* part set up a pattern that forms much of the fabric of the piece on different levels. This motive—a step down and returning to the original pitch—can also be found in the lower *saron* part. That part also begins with 6–5–6, but at a slower metric level. The next measure is the same, but transposed up a step. Only the last measure of the phrase is different, this time going down two steps and varying the melody of the upper part. Thus this first phrase can be represented as AA′B (A′ is a variation of A). This A A′B form also forms the basis for the sections that follow this one, as well as the way in which those sections fit into the large-scale scheme of the piece. Therefore, the basic patterns of the *saron* melodies and the colotomic parts adhere to Harrison's basic A A′B structure on many levels. This gives the work a profound unity that is very much in keeping with Javanese aesthetics.

Lou Harrison considered the gamelan as legitimate an ensemble as the Western symphony orchestra, and, just as there are Indonesian composers who write for the Western orchestra, he felt that there is nothing wrong with Western composers returning the compliment. Indeed, as the number of practicing gamelans in countries outside of Indonesia continues to grow, the number of composers writing pieces incorporating these beautiful instruments and musical practices has grown as well.

REFERENCES

Discography

Javanese Gamelan Music

Gamelan Pura Paku Alaman, Yogyakarta. *Javanese Court Gamelan*, rereleased as *Java: Court Gamelan*. New York/Los Angeles: Elektra/Nonesuch 9 72044-2, 1971/2003.

Pawiyatan Kraton Surakarta. *Court Music of Kraton Surakarta*. Tokyo: King Record Co. Ltd. KICC 5151, 1992.

Sarasehan Krawitan Surakarta. *Chamber Music of Central Java*. Tokyo: King Record Co. Ltd. KICC 5152, 1992.

Various artists. *Java: Palais Royal de Yogyakarta* (4 CDs). Paris: Ocora C 560067-70?, 1973/1995.

Balinese Gamelan Music

Gamelan Semar Pegulingan, Kamasan, Bali. *The Heavenly Orchestra of Bali*. New York: CMP Records CMP 3008, 1991.

Gamelan STSI. *Music of the Gamelan Gong Kebyar*. El Cerrito, CA: Vital Records 401, 1996.

Various artists. *Bali: Gamelan and Kecak*. New York/Los Angeles: Elektra/Nonesuch 9 79204-2, 1989.

Lou Harrison & the American Gamelan

Harrison, Lou. *Gamelan Music*. Ocean, NJ: MusicMasters 01612-67091-2, 1992.

Bibliography

Javanese Gamelan Music

Becker, Judith and Alan H. Feinstein, eds. *Karawitan: Source Readings in Javanese Gamelan and Vocal Music* (3 vols.). Ann Arbor, MI: Center for South and Southeast Asian Studies, University of Michigan, 1984–1988.

Hood, Mantle. *The Evolution of the Javanese Gamelan* (3 vols). Wilhelmshaven, Netherlands: Heinrichshofen, 1980.

Kunst, Jaap. *Music in Java: Its History, Its Theory and Its Technique*, 3rd ed. The Hague: Nijhoff, 1973.

Lindsay, Jennifer. *Javanese Gamelan: Traditional Orchestra of Indonesia*. Singapore/New York: Oxford University Press, 1992.

Sorrell, Neil. *A Guide to the Gamelan*. London, Boston: Faber and Faber, 1990.

Sumarsam. *Gamelan: Cultural Interaction and Musical Development in Central Java*. Chicago: University of Chicago Press, 1995.

Balinese Gamelan Music

McPhee, Colin. *Music in Bali*. New Haven, CT: Yale University Press, 1966.

Tenzer, Michael. *Balinese Music*. Berkeley: Periplus Editions, 1991.

Tenzer, Michael. *Gamelan Gong Kebyar: The Art of Twentieth-Century Balinese Music*. Chicago: University of Chicago Press, 2000.

c. 700–143 BCE

Classical Greek civilization, a crucial source of much European and Arabic music theory and philosophy. The singing of epic songs, traditional in this region, perhaps dates back to the time of the Homeric bards.

1st–5th C CE

Period of Roman Empire. In 395, the empire breaks up into Eastern (Byzantine) and Western halves, precipitating an important cultural, religious, and musical schism that helped distinguish Eastern from Western Europe.

5th–9th C

Middle Ages. Magyars arrive in Hungary from Central Asia and bring with them distinctive musical characteristics.

9th–10th C

First Russian state established amid Byzantine influence from modern Turkey. Precipitates Russian conversion to Eastern Christianity and adoption of Eastern liturgical chant distinct from the less elaborate Western ("Gregorian") chant. Other regions, including Poland, Hungary, Slovakia, and the Czech Republic, adopt Roman Catholicism.

PART 9

Eastern Europe

1240
Mongol invasion and establishment of Mongol Empire throughout Central Asia bring Asian influences.

14th–15th C
Turkish and Russian dominance. The Roma, known to the Europeans as "Gypsies," migrate from Asia to Europe and settle especially in southeastern and central Europe, but also in Italy, France, and Spain.

1345–1913
Ottoman Turks control much of Greece, the Balkans, Bulgaria, Romania, Hungary, and Albania, where they introduce Islamic musical and cultural influences that remain strong in many areas today.

18th C
Russia, a growing international power, seeks closer ties with the West and establishes Western European–style court music. Russia still relies on serfdom, and, as in many areas of Eastern Europe, the agricultural economy influences a rich heritage of folk song.

▶

PART 9 ■ EASTERN EUROPE

INTRODUCTION TO THE REGION

52

Although listeners familiar with Western European choral music will recognize some of the elements in the song *Dilmano, Dilbero*—a diatonic scale and harmonies—the brash singing style and unfamiliar meter exhibit a very different and in some ways ancient aesthetic. In 1904 the young Hungarian

---

1812–13
Defeat of Napoleon's invasion of Russia. Breakup of Hapsburg control over much of Europe leads to nationalist movements in Eastern Europe.

Late 19th C
Many Eastern European composers emphasize nationalism. These composers sometimes collected folk songs and sparked an interest in their countries' folk music heritage.

1906
Béla Bartók (1881–1945) and Zoltán Kodály (1882–1967) begin collecting and studying Eastern European folk songs.

1917
Soviet Revolution leads to state sponsorship of national music and folk music.

composer Béla Bartók had a similar listening experience that would change the path of his career. Vacationing in the resort town Gerlicepuszta (now Ratkó in Slovakia), he heard a young nursemaid (Lidi Dósa) sing a haunting, simple tune. It was Bartók's first glimpse of the authentic folk heritage of his country.

FIRST LISTEN
CD 2:14
Dilmano, Dilbero

It may seem strange that Bartók was unfamiliar with the musical traditions of his own country, but he was raised in an upper-middle-class, urban culture that rarely mixed with the peasantry. He knew only the sentimental parlor songs and the earthy, flamboyant dances of the urban dance bands popular in Hungary at that time. The overly expressive, somewhat exotic sound of these bands had inspired Hungarian Romantic composers such as Ferenc (Franz) Liszt, whose *Hungarian Rhapsodies* (1852 and 1880) captured the sentimental, often patronizing, view of the hearty peasant.

To Bartók, the sentimental "slop" (as he called it) of popular music did not represent the authentic voice of the Magyars (indigenous Hungarians). Hungary was then under the rule of the Austrians, as it had been under the Hapsburgs and Turks at various times since the Middle Ages, and Bartók was devoted to the nationalist cause then sweeping many areas of Eastern Europe. At the same time, however, modernist innovations in music were just beginning in Europe, and Bartók found himself torn trying to reconcile his own creative voice with nationalist elements in his music.

All that changed when he heard Dósa's song, a song completely unlike either the syrupy popular violin tunes or Western European folk songs. Bartók immediately wrote down the song and later wrote to his sister that this revelation had inspired him to "collect the finest examples of Hungarian folk music and raise them to the level of works of art."

Although the collection of folk songs was not a new idea—folk-song societies of Britain, for example, had inspired the nationalist composer Ralph Vaughan Williams—never before Béla Bartók and his friend Zoltán Kodály had this study been so comprehensive, systematic, and scientific (Figure 52.1). In adopting such a scholarly approach, Bartók went beyond styles

---

1932
Soviet Union begins policy of Socialist Realism in the arts and censors or withdraws support for music not explicitly in service of the state. Industrialization, collective farming, suppression of religious practices, and censorship bring great changes to folk and popular music.

1946–1989
Cold War. Soviet Union installs satellite communist states in Eastern Europe. Creates professional "folk" ensembles, controls and refines their expression.

1985
Gorbachev introduces policy of *glasnost* (openness), effectively ends strict government control over the media and the arts, and accelerates popularity of Western popular music styles.

1991
Breakup of Soviet Union and collapse of Eastern European communist governments bring new freedom in the arts and reinvigorate national heritages and folk music, sometimes now in new hybrid popular forms.

FIGURE **52.1**
Bartók recording folk
songs on a cylinder
recorder in 1907
in Daraz, now
Drazovce, Slovakia.

© CORBIS

which romanticized superficial aspects of peasant culture to discover the true nature of his cultural heritage.

Furthermore, Bartók did not stop his investigations with the Magyars, but followed lines of influence to the Slovaks, the Serbs, the Romanians, the Bulgarians, the Croatians, the Macedonians, the Turks, and even into North Africa. Bartók was a respected ethnomusicologist before he was known as one of the century's most famous composers.

Bartók heard in this peasant music a truly original voice of astonishing beauty, one that resonated with his own expression as a composer. Transcending the superficial quotation of peasant melodies, Bartók wove folk influences deeply into his compositions.

From the mind–bendingly complex meters and spicy dissonances of the Balkans to the epic singing traditions that likely date back to Homer, Eastern European folk music has a stark and unique beauty. As a crossroads of the many cultures of Asia, the Middle East, and Europe, Eastern Europe forged truly distinctive traditions in its diverse cultures.

Geography Eastern Europe here includes the Baltic states, Poland, the Czech Republic, Slovakia, Hungary, Romania, Bulgaria, Albania, the states of the former Yugoslavia, Greece, and the parts of the former Soviet Union that are ethnically Slavic, including Moldova, Belarus, and the Ukraine. This Part will concentrate on Hungary, Bulgaria, and Russia. Because of Russian expansion and settlements, Russian culture extends into vast parts of Central Asia. The Central Asian republics of the former Soviet Union have sizable ethnic Russian minorities, and thus two (or more) distinct musical traditions coexist in them.

CHARACTERISTICS OF EASTERN EUROPEAN FOLK MUSIC

53

Historically, the dominance of peasant culture in Eastern Europe coincides with the importance of folk song. The subjects and functions of these songs were closely tied to peasant life and included harvesting songs, other work songs, and songs for village occasions such as holidays and weddings. However, during the communist period, industrialization, collective farming, and censorship caused many of these songs (the ones Bartók collected, for example) to disappear, at least from their original context.

Still, the forms and spirit of these folk songs remain in many modern environments. Weddings, for example, are still very important events in these regions and may consist of several days of rituals and celebrations, each day having its own songs and dances. Today these songs and dances may be accompanied by amplified bands with a mixture of indigenous and popular instruments (Figure 53.1). Songs for other occasions, such as Christmas and other holidays, are also popular.

Here are some of the distinctive characteristics of the songs and other music of this region that help distinguish Eastern European folk music from that of Western Europe.

- **Non-pulsatile Songs** In many areas of Eastern Europe some genres of song have no fixed beat and often have expressive, florid ornamentation. Some of these elaborate and emotional song types show evidence of Middle Eastern influence.

- **Asymmetric Meters** Areas of the Balkans, especially Bulgaria, are known for their complex meters with beats that quickly change duration.

- **Repetitive Dance Rhythms** Many dances of these regions are known as much by their characteristic propulsive rhythms as their meter. In some areas, these *short rhythms repeat even as the melody notes change*, a technique known as **isorhythm**.

- **Bright Timbres** In many regions of Eastern Europe, singers, especially women, commonly cultivate rich and brassy timbres.

- **Epic Songs** An important tradition in this region, though less common today, these hours-long songs of heroic tales are sung by a single bard.

- **Socialist Realism** An aesthetic style during the Communist period in which the arts served the state, socialist realism enforced to greater or lesser degrees professional composition and so-called folk ensembles.

FIGURE **53.1**
The sort of Hungarian band that plays at weddings. In this case the band includes a violin, tenor saxophone, accordion, and, in the right foreground, a *cimbalom*, a trapezoidal hammered dulcimer with multiple courses (several strings per pitch) made of metal. The hammers are covered with cotton to soften the timbre.

© Michael S. Yamashita/CORBIS

Epic Songs

Homer, the legendary southeast European author of the *Iliad* and *Odyssey*, did not read or recite his famous epics, but like generations of bards before and after him, sang them. Such epic singing can still be found in Eastern Europe as well as Turkey, Central Asia, China, even Southeast Asia. Epic singing traditions also existed in Western Europe, notably in Ireland, but generally died out after the Middle Ages.

Specially trained in this art form, the singers are usually men, professionals or semi-professionals who have memorized poems often of several thousand lines. Some epic performances, split over successive nights, are several days long. The performer memorizes a certain number of stock melodies and applies them to fit the poetic meter and mood of the text. Improvised ornamentation is always important, and these variations give life to what would otherwise be literally repeating melodies.

The epic singers usually sing without accompaniment, or they accompany themselves on an instrument such as a fiddle or plucked string instrument. In only a few traditions do other musicians accompany the epic singer. In part, this is a practical decision, because it is very difficult for accompanying musicians to follow a singer in a partly improvised, perhaps non–pulsatile song. When the singer accompanies himself, he is able to imitate, anticipate, and play along with his improvisations in a way that would be difficult or impossible for a separate accompanist.

Today many epic traditions have died out or are endangered. The last singers of *Russian epics*, called **bilini** or **starini**, sang about wars against the Tartars during the late Middle Ages, epics that died out in the early twentieth century. The art is still lost, despite attempts during the Soviet period to reinvigorate the tradition with Socialist Realist stories.

In Finland, the epic tradition is drawn from the *Kalevala*, the story of the legendary Finn leader, Väinemöinen. The Kalevala songs are traditionally accompanied on the **kantele**, *a plucked zither*. Ukrainian songs from about the same period are called **dumy**. The songs of the Serbians recall their resistance to Turkish occupation during the thirteenth to seventeenth centuries, but there are also new compositions. Serbian epic singers, like the Croats, Montenegrins, Bulgarians, Romanians, and other people from the same region, accompany themselves on a pear-shaped fiddle.

Asymmetrical Meters

Some cultures use not only beats which can be divided into two (simple meter) and beats which can be divided into three (compound meter), but also *meters which mix the two kinds of beats*, called **asymmetrical meters**. Asymmetric meters are especially popular in Greece, Bulgaria, and some other Balkan regions. For example, a group of two pulses and another of three may alternate to create a larger metrical group of five, as shown in Graphic 53.1. Another possibility would be to group them as 3 + 2. In either case, the groups are of unequal sizes and hence asymmetrical. At a slow tempo, we could hear each pulse as a beat grouped into these 2 + 3 patterns.

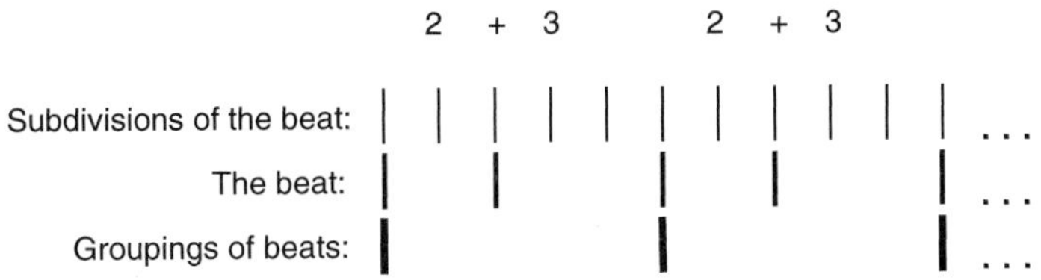

GRAPHIC **53.1**

In most cases, however, the pulses go by so fast (at times 320 per minute) that one hears the beat as occurring on the next metrical level. In those cases we say that *the beat changes length*. First it is three, then two subdivisions in length. These shifting beats often reflect particular dance steps, some of which take more or less time to complete.

Apparently, such asymmetrical meters were common in ancient Greece, where the language indicated accents in words by making the syllable twice as long, rather than giving it more stress, as in English. While the Greek language has changed, it is possible that the attraction to these meters has remained in the music.

Socialist Realism

A period of astonishing avant-garde activity in the Soviet Union of the 1920s came to an abrupt end when Stalin instituted the policy known as socialist realism. This doctrine, named by the writer Maxim Gorky, was in part a reaction to a perceived elitism and bourgeois self-absorption in the arts. Socialist realism held that all art should exist to serve the state, and through it, the people. In the early years of the Soviet Union, the state established professional so-called folk music groups, and many composers self-consciously created didactic and patriotic works.

In the 1930s, Stalin made socialist realism a part of his cult of personality, a path that was emulated in Maoist China. Avant-garde experiments were bitterly attacked, and some artists were imprisoned or even executed. The famous Russian composer Igor Stravinsky, who had used folk elements in his earlier works, left Russia forever in 1917; Dmitri Shostakovich and Sergei Prokofiev stayed in the Soviet Union and endured periodic censure from the government. Even folk musicians, whom the government could not always control as directly, were denied access to audiences and media. The disruption of traditional ways of life through collectivization, mass movements of workers to urban factories, and the homogenization of language and culture also caused the decline of many folk art traditions.

When the Eastern European states came into the Soviet orbit after World War II, they too instituted socialist realism to varying degrees. Some states, notably Poland, did not see modernism as necessarily inconsistent with socialism, although works glorifying the state and the people's cultural heritage were still encouraged. Since *perestroika* (restructuring) and the collapse of the Soviet state, socialist realism as a state policy exists in only a handful of countries, such as North Korea.

Professional Folk Ensembles

In their search for genuine artistic expression rooted in popular traditons and compatible with the interests of the state, some Communist governments formed ensembles of folk musicians who had sufficient training to play arrangements written by conservatory-trained composers. These works included such musical innovations as counterpoint and harmony that had been absent from peasant folk music prior to World War II.

In order to effect these innovations, musicians had to read conventional music notation. Notation enabled large orchestras of traditional instruments to play harmony, but the folk arts of improvisation and ornamentation disappeared or were greatly modified. Professional arrangers often created more refined structures and censored bawdy or political lyrics. Unlike traditional folk musicians, these professional groups enjoyed access to state record labels, radio, and television and were presented to the world as the authentic musical expression of the country. While the sources of the music remained for the most part folk songs and dances collected from the countryside, the refinements that professional groups introduced, as well as performance contexts so different from the traditions of the countryside, clearly distinguish these performances from other folk music.

In order to support these efforts, ethnomusicology in general enjoyed a good deal of state support in the Soviet Union and other communist states. Thanks to this support, collections and detailed studies of literally hundreds of thousands of folk songs now exist in Hungary, Russia, and other regions.

In 1973, the Russian musician Dmitri Pokrovsky formed a new group that applied these ethnomusicological studies to create a new sort of folk ensemble that recovered regional singing and improvisational styles. Because this approach threatened the authenticity of official folklore groups and because he revived religious and other censored lyrics, the Pokrovsky Ensemble found it difficult to perform and record its music. Nevertheless, Pokrovsky sparked a revival movement in folk music that accelerated after the social liberalization movement known as *glasnost* (openness) began in 1985.

HUNGARIAN FOLK MUSIC

54

Historical Background

The Magyars, the major ethnic group of Hungary, settled there between the fifth and ninth centuries. The Magyars are most closely related to the Finns and certain small ethnic groups in Russia, and the Magyar language and culture are quite distinct from those of the surrounding Slavic groups. As in many areas of Eastern Europe, for centuries the peasantry made up the largest portion of the population and created a musical heritage built on folk songs and dances.

Christianity came to Hungary in the tenth century and for centuries was the main patron of what art music there was. During the sixteenth century, when Hungary was under Ottoman Turkish rule, Turkish instruments and other musical influences entered Hungarian culture. Around the same time, the first Romani people had also settled in the region and brought their own distinctive musical culture. This ethnic group became known as "Gypsies" because of a mistaken notion that they originated in Egypt. Many Romani ethnic groups, each with distinct dialects and musical traditions, are scattered throughout Europe.

Romani instrumentalists became particularly sought after in the eighteenth century, when their music was often used as an attraction at military recruiting fairs. Thereafter Romani bands were associated with the word for *recruiting*, **verbunkos**, even in other contexts. These bands originally featured violins and bagpipes, but the bagpipes were soon replaced with the **cimbalom**, *the hammered zither* that probably came into Hungary from Turkey. The other *verbunkos* instruments were usually two violins (one playing the melody and the other a countermelody) and a string bass (Figure 54.1).

By the mid–nineteenth century, *verbunkos* bands had become famous throughout Europe as popular urban entertainment. Despite the fact that their repertory was unrelated to actual Romani folk music, the sound of the Gypsy violin remains famous even in present-day Budapest, the capital of Hungary. The popular tunes played by *verbunkos* bands often featured nondiatonic modes probably descended from Turkish influence, but sometimes known as Gypsy scales.

As Bartók, his colleague Zoltán Kodály, and other researchers showed, *verbunkos* music is not the music of the Magyar peasants. Indeed, with its distinctive scales, ornamentation, and frequent use of *rubato* (expressive changes or stretching of tempo), this music was very different from either the indigenous Magyar peasant music or the Romani folk music tradition. These qualities in turn influenced *nineteenth-century sentimental parlor songs* known as **magyarnota**. The *verbunkos* dances also influenced the development of the **csárdás**, a distinctive dance of contrasting fast and slow tempos in simple duple meter, now *the national dance of Hungary*.

FIGURE 54.1
This band led by Zsolt Boni plays outside a restaurant in Budapest; it includes two violins, a bass, and a *cimbalom*. This *cimbalom* (close-up image on the right), unlike the simpler form in Figure 53.1, uses string dampers controlled by a pedal mechanism like that used on a piano. Here, too, the ends of the mallets are covered in cotton to soften the tone.

The Characteristics of Hungarian Folk Song

By carefully studying and comparing music of neighboring regions and the Magyar's ethnic cousins in Russia, Bartók and Kodály were able to isolate at least two historical strata of folk song characteristics. The earliest folk songs show many Central Asian characteristics, including the **anhemitonic pentatonic scale**—*a scale of five pitches per octave with no semitones*—the type of scale used in China, Mongolia, and elsewhere in Central Asia. Later songs show European influence, including the use of diatonic scales.

What is most characteristic of these old songs, however, are their patterns of repetition and *transposition* (repetition at another pitch). Old Hungarian folk songs typically repeat a phrase transposed by the interval of a fifth. Hungarian folk songs also show distinctive rhythmic characteristics. Bartók named the most prominent rhythmic types ***parlando-rubato*** (an Italian term meaning *free speech rhythm*) and ***tempo giusto*** (an Italian term meaning *strict tempo*). Non-pulsatile, heavily ornamented *parlando-rubato* songs are common in many areas of Eastern Europe and often emphasize emotional expression and the meaning of the text, while *tempo giusto* songs emphasize repetitive dance rhythms. Sometimes songs of both types alternate or are paired for contrast.

Representative Hungarian Instruments

Hungarian musical instruments reflect the diverse influences of this crossroads nation. Related to the *santur* of the Middle East and probably introduced during the period of Turkish rule, the *cimbalom* hammered zither

(Figures 53.1 and 54.1) has become a highly cultivated instrument and often rivals the piano as a standard instrument in urban homes. The *citera* (Figure 54.2) is a *plucked zither with frets*. It is related to similar German and Scandinavian zithers as well as the mountain dulcimer from the United States. The Hungarian *furulya* (Figure 54.3) is a *shepherd's vertical duct flute*. Versions of this instrument reach up to a meter in length, and performers on this low flute sometimes murmur and hum while playing, creating a distinctive timbre.

FIGURE 54.2
The Hungarian *citera* is a plucked zither with frets. The melody is played on one or two strings while two other strings provide a drone.

Dance House Music

Under the Communist revival movement of the 1950s and 1960s, the Hungarian government established several professional folk music and dance groups. Dissatisfied with the refinements of these state-sponsored groups, in the 1970s two young folk dancers, Béla Halmos and Ferenc Sebö, like Bartók and Kodály before them, set out to collect folk music, primarily dances, from the countryside. Rather than present musicological museum pieces, however, Halmos and Sebö sought to incorporate the spirit of the music in a rousing new repertory played on amplified violins and bass in dance clubs. These clubs are known as *tanchaz* (dance houses), after the traditional village music hall.

During the 1970s and 80s, the growth in popularity of *tanchaz* music presented a challenge to the state-sponsored control of the arts and the definition of authenticity. *Tanchaz* musicians in neighboring Romania sometimes traveled secretly, without official permission, to ethnic Hungarian villages in Transylvania to collect folk music. Since the fall of communism, *tanchaz* has become state-supported, and musicians such as Márta

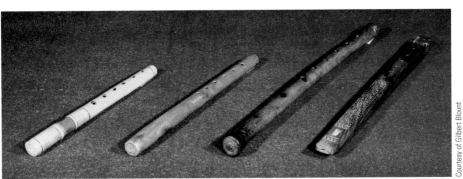

FIGURE 54.3
The *furulya* is a duct flute found in Hungary and surrounding countries. Pictured here are versions from different regions.

Listening Guide

CD 2:13. *Téglaporos a kalapom*. **Vocal, Mihály Váradi with István Balázs, Pál Balogh, Sándor Kardelás, and Ferenc Lakatos.**

0:00	Lead solo male singer, using the syllable "la," improvises a brief variation of the song tune to follow.
	This style of improvisation is called *pergetés* ("rolling"), and in this case is highly syncopated (metrical stress is shifted away from our expectations). The mode is diatonic, though not major or minor, and the tuning of certain tones is flexible.
0:06	Two more members join, one clapping, the other creating half-sung percussive sounds—*szájbögö*, or mouth bass—both providing a strong rhythmic framework for syncopated rolling melody.
	The vertical lines indicate the beats and the solid lines indicate the beginning of four-beat metrical units.
	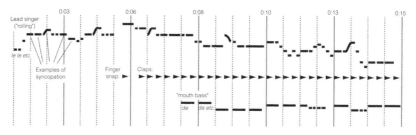
0:18	Lead singer launches main tune; humorous lyric describes the worker's life.
	Several exclamatory (but otherwise meaningless) syllables (shown in parentheses) enter the lyric merely for rhythmic effect.

T'glaporos a kalapom,   My hat is covered with brick dust,

Mer' a t'glagyárban kakom;   Since I live in the brick factory

(hej de) Onnét tudják,   (hey! de!) They know that I live
hogy ott lakom: there because

(mer') Téglaporos a kalapom.   (mer!) My hat is covered with
     brick dust.

[Translation by Rudolf Vig]

0:33	Lead singer uses neutral syllables for more elaborate rolling improvisation.
	More participants join, thickening the rhythmic accompaniment with more mouth bass and finger snaps.
0:48	Another verse from the lead singer, this time sending encouragement to dancers between rolled syllables.
	Mouth bass emphasizes the offbeat (the second of every beat division).
1:02	Next verse; singer doubles the rhythmic density of his syllables still within the main tune's framework.
1:16	Lead singer repeats lyric of first verse.
	Players add the sound of spoons on the tabletop.
1:30	Several verses follow. Singer inserts improvised syllables to encourage dancers.
	Mouth bass participants also shout their encouragement as the texture grows thicker and more exciting, and the tempo quickens.

© Béla Kása

© Béla Kása

FIGURE 54.4
Márta Sebestyén and the Hungarian music group Muzsikás play *tanchàz*, the now state-supported repertory that incorporates the spirit of folk dances on amplified violins and bass in dance clubs.

Sebestyén and Muzsikás are internationally famous (Figure 54.4). Today dance music may include gypsy bands and various electric instruments. As in other areas of Eastern Europe, wedding music bands are popular and may include clarinets, synthesizers, and drums.

Romani Folk Song

Although urban popular music bands defined Gypsy music in most people's minds, the Roma, or "Gypsy," ethnic minority has its own folk traditions unrelated to the popular songs of the *verbunkos* bands. Many Romani groups arrived in Hungary after the establishment of the verbunkos bands. While Romani folk music shares some of the diatonic modes found in Magyar folk music as well as their four-phrase form, the distinctively Magyar repetition at the interval of a fifth is rare.

Even more surprising is the absence of instrumental music, even for dances, among the Vlach and Romungre ethnic groups. To accompany dances, they sing a repertory of highly rhythmic songs that include fragmentary texts, vocables (nonsense syllables), and mouth sounds to create a kind of *vocal percussion* known as ***szájbögö*** (mouth bass). The dancers also use shouts, finger snaps, and claps to enliven the songs, as their Roma cousins in Spain do for the flamenco dance.

In addition to the dance songs, the Roma have a repertoire of *parlando-rubato* (unmeasured) songs that are typically slow and emotionally intense. The Romungres sometimes sing in improvised parallel thirds, and other groups at times improvise heterophony or simple polyphony.

A Performance of a Romani *Szájbögö*— Mouth Bass Song

This lively song is an example of a Romani *szájbögö* or mouth bass dance. The percussive accompaniment for these dances is created entirely by the impromptu rhythmic syllables, mouth sounds, and claps of the singers; there are no other instruments. Although many *szájbögö* dances are entirely without words, the lyrics of those that do are often light-hearted, humorous, nonsensical, and repetitive. Singers, dancers, and onlookers may offer shouts of encouragement or teasing.

BULGARIAN FOLK MUSIC

55

Historical Background

Bulgaria has several rich and distinctive folk music traditions that trace back to the mythological Greek musician Orpheus, who came from the region of Thrace. The
ethnic group known as the Bulgars came to this region in the seventh century and by the ninth century had adopted Christianity along with a form of
Byzantine chant. Despite the close association with Byzantine culture, Bulgarian Christianity has preserved a distinctive blend of Christian and pagan
customs and thought. Ostensible Christmas songs are thinly disguised harvest and fertility ritual songs, and Easter songs are tied to spring rituals such
as the turning of bundles of straw. Peasant women, not allowed to sing in
church, became the main carriers of the secular folk song tradition.

The Ottoman Turks ruled Bulgaria for almost 500 years, until 1878.
Turkish attempts at converting the Bulgarians to Islam were not generally
successful, and pagan elements were further entrenched in the religion of
the people. Only after Bulgarian independence did secular art music begin
to develop. In 1944 the country underwent a socialist revolution and became
part of the Soviet bloc. The government formed and supported professional
folk ensembles in preference to traditional folk music.

Filip Kutev (1903–1982) was a pioneering composer and choral director
who organized the Bulgarian State Radio and Television Female Vocal
Choir. He harmonized and arranged many folk songs while retaining many
of their distinctive characteristics. This choir was later recorded by the
American Nonesuch label and in the 1980s became very popular through
those recordings and subsequent tours. In 1992 Bulgaria became a multi-
party democracy, and, in the liberalization that followed, many types of music suppressed under Communism flourished, including Western popular
music. One of the most popular genres is the dance music played at weddings, which has now evolved from small folk dance ensembles to elaborate
amplified bands that now feature less traditional instruments such as the
clarinet and accordion.

Bulgarian Folk Songs

Folk songs can be divided according to function, and often each has its own
distinctive musical characteristics. Harvesting songs, for example, are generally sustained and non-pulsatile (*parlando-rubato*), with a narrow range
and an ornament called **provikvaniyo**—*a type of sudden yell upward at the
ends of phrases*. Many songs are associated with holidays and other seasonal
activities, although the actual subjects of the songs may be unrelated to the
season. Nevertheless, common themes, such as stories of resistance against
Turkish rule and songs of courtship and marriage, prevail. Pagan references

survive in songs begging for rain and in fertility rituals during the winter. Many of these songs and the annual traditions with which they were associated have changed or disappeared since the Communist era.

Some of the most elaborate folk rituals, as elsewhere in Eastern Europe, surround weddings. There are many types of wedding songs, one for each part of a ceremony that can last up to three days. Some of these songs are sung *antiphonally* (by alternating groups). Today weddings commonly feature bands playing amplified instruments, perhaps in combination with traditional instruments; accordions, clarinets, and electric guitars may join *gaida* bagpipes or a *kaval* flute.

Bulgarian folk music often has a narrow range; the *provikvaniyo* yell is an exception. Thus modes are most often made up of five or fewer pitches per octave. Diatonic modes dominate, but non–diatonic modes, some including microtones, can also be found, perhaps because of Turkish or Romani influence.

Folk polyphony is found in many regions of Bulgaria. Melodies with a drone are common to some areas, and singers occasionally use spicy parallel seconds. In the Pirin mountain region, heterophonic textures are common. Sometimes polyphony results when a slow and a fast song are sung simultaneously.

Bulgarian Rhythm

One of the most distinctive and well-known attributes of Bulgarian folk music is its use of complex asymmetrical meters. These meters are generally made up of beats of two different sizes, the longer beat half again as long as the short beat. When broken down to a common denominator, the long beats are represented as made up of three fast pulses and the short beats two.

As one might expect in a culture in which community and cooperation have been important in the rural areas, folk dances, such as line dances or *circle dances* (**horo**), tend to be lively and energetic communal activities. Some of these folk dance types are:

- ■ *Paidushko* round dance in 2 beats alternating 2 and 3 subdivisions, which we write as 2 + 3.
- ■ *Ruchenitsa* wedding round dance in 2 + 2 + 3.
- ■ *Daichovo* dance in 2 + 2 + 2 + 3.
- ■ *Grancharski horo* potters' dance in 2 + 3 + 2 + 2.
- ■ *Krivo horo* dance in 2 + 2 + 3 + 2 + 2.
- ■ *Khoro eleno mome* dance in 2 + 2 + 2 + 2 + 2 + 3.
- ■ *Buchimish* round dance in 2 + 2 + 2 + 2 + 3 + 2 + 2.

Since these beat subdivisions usually go by far too fast to be counted individually, it really makes more sense to feel the beat as a constantly shifting duration. The sequence of different beats may be related to the amount of time a particular dance step takes. Not all Bulgarian songs and dances are

FIGURE **55.1**
The *kaval* is a rim-blown flute found in Bulgaria and surrounding regions related to the *nay* of Turkey and the Middle East. This version is from Hungary.

Courtesy of Kovács László and Flótás

FIGURE **55.2**
The Bulgarian *gudulka* is a pear-shaped vertical bowed fiddle with three gut (sometimes metal) strings. Like Indian chordophones, this one has several sympathetic strings tied to the shorter pegs.

© Adam Woolfitt/CORBIS

in asymmetrical meters; regular meters and songs in free rhythm are also common.

Representative Bulgarian Instruments and Their Performance

The **kaval** (Figure 55.1) is *a rim-blown flute held at an angle in front of the player*. It is related to the Middle Eastern *nay* flute. The **gudulka** is a *pear-shaped vertical bowed fiddle with three strings* (Figure 55.2), occasionally having sympathetic strings as well. The **gaida** is a *bagpipe with a drone pipe and a melody pipe* (Figure 55.3). Well known for its distinctive virtuosic ornamentation, the *gaida* is a popular instrument for weddings and outdoor celebrations. The **tambura** is a *long-necked fretted lute with four strings or double courses*. Originally a melody instrument (unlike its Indian namesake) with drone strings, it now more commonly plays strummed chords. The **tupan** is *a large cylindrical bass drum*, slung across the body, and played with two sticks (Figure 6.26).

© Hideo Haga/HAGA/The Image Works

FIGURE **55.3**
A performer holds the *gaida* (bagpipe) at a festival in Bulgaria.

Listening Guide

0:00

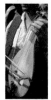

Instrumental ensemble introduces melody.

Gaida, gudulka, and *kaval* play the melody heterophonically, each with its own elaborate ornamentation. Note how the players automatically trill any extended note.

Gaida bagpipe and *gudulka* fiddle also play drone pitches.

Tambura lute vigorously strums accompanying chords and, with the *tupan* drum, emphasize the changing beat.

0:05

Choir enters with a fast 2+3+3 meter.

Filip Kutev carefully composed and notated the choral harmony. Despite occasional folk polyphony, such harmonies would not be found in traditional folk performances. While keeping the original folk melody clear, and harmonizing it within the narrow and low Bulgarian folk song range, Kutev emphasized the drone pitches of the accompanying instruments. This schematic of the first phrase shows how the melody aligns with the distinctive asymmetric meter.

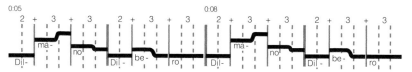

0:10

Meter changes strikingly in the second phrase of the melody.

In the lyric Dilbero (young man) has asked Dilmano (young woman) how to plant peppers.

The musical phrases and lyric repeat.

The asymmetrical meter shifts to add an extra beat of three subdivisions in the pattern 2+3+3+3 before returning to 2+3+3. This variation could indicate an extra dance step.

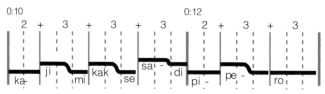

0:27	Dilbero continues: "To bloom and ripen"—in a contrasting musical phrase.
	Kaval flute returns with its thrilling ornamentation. It had rested during the first phrases to allow the singers the spotlight.
0:33	Meter returns to the changing pattern.
	Dilbero: "To gather, gather, gather/As much as you want." Lyric playfully emphasizes *"beresh"* (gather) on each of the long beats.
0:44	Instrumental ensemble repeats the introduction.
0:50	Dilmano answers: "Push here, poke there/Just like that, you plant peppers!"

Bulgarian instrumental playing styles are known for their especially florid ornamentation. On instruments such as the *gaida* and *kaval*, long notes are automatically decorated with trills or other ornaments, and players often interpolate short grace notes produced by flips of the players' fingers between main melody notes. Singers of non-pulsatile (*parlando-rubato*) folk songs often ornament those melodies in similar ways.

A Performance of a Bulgarian Folk Song

This short, lively tune, *Dilmano, Dilbero*, demonstrates a complex sequence of meters. Filip Kutev, the most famous arranger of traditional works for professional folk ensembles, arranged this song, originally from the Shopski region, for folk ensemble and women's choir. The text is humorous with its obscure double entendres between a flirting couple, but it also betrays an ancient connection between reproduction and agricultural fertility.

RUSSIAN FOLK MUSIC

56

Folk Songs and Genres

Although many folk songs disappeared during the Communist period, some genres, notably wedding songs, are still popular in rural areas. Folk wedding music includes a large number of subtypes including laments (**prichitaniya**), which are sung both at weddings and at funerals. Other traditional Russian folk song genres include work songs, short *work calls* (**pripevki**) similar to the *holler* of the United States, and calendar songs—that is, songs for a particular holiday or season (Figure 56.1).

Calendar songs, wedding songs, and laments share several features, despite the significant differences among regions in this large country. Scales often have only two to five pitches per octave and melodies may be limited in range. Semitones are common in these scales, unlike Central Asian pentatonic scales, and contribute to the particularly poignant character of laments. Melodies are frequently made up of combinations of simple repetitive motives.

Calendar songs also have distinctive

© Wolfgang Kaehler/CORBIS

FIGURE 56.1
This Russian folk band includes a *bayan* (button accordion, rear left), a *zhaleyka* (single-reed horn), and a *domra* (long-necked lute on the right).

rhythms that they share with many dance genres. Their rhythms are driving combinations of single pulses and divisions into two. These rhythmic motives often repeat many times, even while the notes of the melody change. This distinctive practice is called *isorhythm*. Occasionally polyrhythm results when a song accompanies a dance in a different meter; most dances include singing.

Russian folk songs are often sung by choruses, sometimes segregated by gender. Russian men's choruses in particular have become famous for their booming chest voices and extremely low ranges. Women singers often cultivate a rich, brassy tone quality. Responsorial singing is common in many repertories.

Heterophony and improvised polyphony is found in certain regions, particularly in lyric songs, such as those sung at traditional weddings. In South Russia, some singers improvise a higher part, often *following the original melody in parallel thirds or fourths*, a technique known as **vtora**.

Folk polyphony is even further developed in the neighboring country of Georgia where **table songs**, *sung traditionally around a table at a party or banquet*, include improvised polyphony of up to four parts. These parts are formed around a center melody by singing in parallel thirds and fourths, with ostinatos (repeating melodies) and bass drones. These Georgian and South Russian improvisations often lead to exuberant, surprising dissonances.

Russian Instruments The **balalaika** (Figure 56.2) is an instrument of the lute type with frets and a distinctive triangular sound body. Similar to the *balalaika*, the **domra** (Figure 56.1) is a lute with a round sound body, usually used to strum chords. A *plucked zither* described as having a wing shape, the **gusli** (Figure 56.3) is thought to have come originally from Byzantium in the Middle Ages and is indeed similar to the *kanun* of present-day Turkey. The **bayan** is a button accordion (Figure 56.1), a popular instrument since the nineteenth century, now found in many folk bands. The **zhaleyka** (Figure 56.1) is a *small single-reed shepherd's pipe*. In southern regions it appears in a version with double pipes, similar to the double-pipe, single-reed instruments found in the former Yugoslavia, Greece, and Egypt.

© Dave G. Houser/CORBIS

FIGURE 56.2

The *balalaika* is known for its distinctive triangular body. Here, a member of the folk music ensemble Kizh plays the bass member of the *balalaika* family. Originally a folk instrument, in the late nineteenth century it was made into a chromatic (that is, twelve pitches per octave) instrument in different sizes. In this form, groups of *balalaikas* formed popular entertainment bands and sometimes even large orchestras.

Courtesy of the Ossipov National Academic Folk Orchestra of Russia

FIGURE **56.3**
The *gusli* is a Russian zither that often has this distinctive "winged" shape.
In this form it is held upright and plucked in the player's lap. Like the Turkish
kanun, to which it is related, a series of small levers is sometimes used to change
the tunings of the metal strings.

Igor Stravinsky's *The Wedding*

Igor Stravinsky (1882–1971) is probably the most famous European art music composer of the twentieth century. Together with Bartók and others, he inaugurated the modernist style of music in the early twentieth century. While he was not an ethnomusicologist like Bartók, he was interested in the folklore and folk music of his country. These interests were encouraged by the great impresario Serge Diaghilev, who produced Stravinsky's first big successes.

Shortly before World War I, Stravinsky had begun to research folk songs and folk poetry relating to Russian weddings in order to celebrate his heritage. Traditional Russian peasant weddings of the time were elaborate affairs lasting several days, with music an integral part of many of the ceremonies and celebrations. Stravinsky's celebration of this heritage, *Svadebka* (*The Wedding*), depicted a traditional wedding as a *cantata*, a series of pieces for singers, chorus, and orchestra that tell a story but without opera's staging.

Stravinsky's work represents the songs, the toasts, the conversations, and the atmosphere of a peasant wedding in a kaleidoscopic montage, rather like the stream-of-consciousness technique of contemporary modernist writers. Using folk melodies, Stravinsky crafted new melodies that represented the essence of the folk melodic styles. For example, one type of song found throughout traditional wedding ceremonies is the **formula song**, so-called because it consists of short repeating rhythms and motives repeated over and over, sometimes with isorhythm and sometimes in asymmetric meters. Much of Stravinsky's *The Wedding* consists of these sorts of ostinatos.

Another genre associated with traditional weddings is the bride's expressive laments at her upcoming separation from her family. The bride's songs are sometimes supplemented by professional lament-singers hired by her family, resulting at times in polytonalities (more than one tonality at a time) and polyrhythms (different simultaneous meters) when they overlap—a technique that Stravinsky exploits as part of his modernist musical vocabulary. At the banquets that accompany these celebrations, each person involved in the wedding has a distinctive song that he or she sings as presents are exchanged. At the feast, ritual toasts are offered, and the bride's mother officially gives her away. The feast also includes a song teasing the father for giving away his daughter in exchange for vodka, and, finally, humorous songs of encouragement accompany the happy couple as they leave for the bedroom.

The Wedding was one of Stravinsky's last works dealing with Russian folklore and folk music. The results of the 1917 revolution turned the young liberal Stravinsky into an embittered reactionary in later life. The Soviet government promoted secular weddings, which, together with urbanization and collective farming, effectively ended many of the elaborate traditions Stravinsky lovingly portrayed.

 REFERENCES

Discography

Hungary

Bartók, Béla and Zoltán Kodály. *Bartók for Orchestra*. Adam Fischer cond. the Hungarian State Symphony Orchestra. Waystone Leys, Monmouth, UK: Nimbus Records NI 1771, 1992.

Various artists. *Gypsy Folksongs from Hungary*. Budapest: Hungaraton HCD 18028-29, 1995.

Various artists. *Tánchaz-Népzene: Hungarian Dance-House Folk Music*. Budapest: Hagyományok Háza HHCD0102, 2003.

Bulgaria

Bulgarskoto radio i televiziia, Zheni khor. *Le mystère des voix bulgares*. New York: Elektra/Nonesuch 9 79165-2, 1987.

Philip Koutev National Folk Ensemble. *Bulgarian Polyphony I*. Tokyo: JVC VICG 5001-2, 1990.

Various artists. *Village and Folk Music of Bulgaria*. New York: Elektra/Nonesuch 79195, 1965/1990.

Russia

Dmitri Pokrovsky Ensemble. *Wild Field*. New York: RealWorld 62316, 1993.

Pesen Zemli. *Russia: Polyphonic Wedding Songs*. Geneva: AIMP VDE 837.

Stravinsky, Igor. *Five Bridal Folk Songs, Les Noces, etc.* James Wood cond. New London Chamber Choir and ensemble, Oleg Shepel cond. Voronezh Chamber Choir. London: Hyperion CDA66410, 1991.

Other Regions

The Rustavi Choir. *Georgian Voices*. New York/Los Angeles: Elektra/Nonesuch 9 79224-2, 1989.

Various artists. *Village Music of Yugoslavia*. New York/Los Angeles: Elektra/Nonesuch 9 72042-2, 1971/1995.

Bibliography

Bartók, Béla. *Hungarian Folk Music*. London: Oxford University Press, H. Milford, 1931.

———. *Rumanian Folk Music*. The Hague: Martinus Nijhoff, 1967.

———. *Yugoslav Folk Music*. Albany, NY: State University of New York Press, 1978.

Czekanowska, Anna. *Polish Folk Music: Slavonic Heritage, Polish Tradition, Contemporary Trends*. Cambridge: Cambridge University Press, 1990.

Kodály, Zoltán. *Folk Music of Hungary*. New York: Da Capo Press, 1987.

Krustev, Venelin Georgiev. *Bulgarian Music*. Sofia: Sofia-Press, 1978.

Rice, Timothy. *May It Fill Your Soul: Experiencing Bulgarian Music*. Chicago: University of Chicago Press, 1994.

Sárosi, Bálint. *Gypsy Music*, trans. Fred Macnicol. Budapest: Corvina Press, 1978.

Warner, Elizabeth. *Russian Traditional Folk Song*. Hull: Hull University Press, 1990.

— c. 1150 BCE–1521 CE

A series of powerful and complex empires dominates central Mexico, including the Olmec, Zapotec, Toltec, and Aztec civilizations. Aztec rituals apparently included complex drumming patterns on the *teponatzli* (a wooden slit drum) and the *huehuetl* (a large footed drum). Other instruments included flutes, whistles, and trumpets. Mayan civilization dominates Central America and Incan civilization is located in the Andes.

— 1492

Christopher Columbus lands in Hispañola, opening the Americas up to European colonization. In 1521, Europeans take the capital of the Aztecs, which becomes Mexico City. By 1533, the Spanish defeat the Inca Empire.

— 1527

Spanish priests begin to teach European sacred music to indigenous people. Sixteenth-century forms include sacred songs and dramas called *autos*.

PART 10

Latin America

— 1538

First African slaves arrive in Brazil. Slave trade continues until the nineteenth century, bringing African influences to many regions, especially the Caribbean and along the Atlantic coasts of South America.

— 18th C

Touring theatrical groups perform popular songs and dances. Among those are Brazilian *lundus*, Mexican *sones*, and Andean *huaynos*.

— 19th C

Italian opera dominates theatrical music among the *criollos* or European descendents, although the Spanish *zarzuela* is also popular.

— 1816–1825

Most of Latin America gains independence from Spain and Portugal in the aftermath of the Napoleonic wars.

INTRODUCTION TO THE REGION

57

On a humid evening in Salvador, a large city on the coast of Brazil, in a simple building that serves as a *terreiro* (meeting place) for members of the Candomblé religion, three drummers and an iron bell player create an intricate polyrhythmic accompaniment to a call-and-response song led by the *terreiro's Pai de Santo* (father of saint). The participants, mostly Afro-Brazilians from the poor neighborhood that surrounds the *terreiro,* are on their feet, moving to the hypnotic, energetic beat (Figure 57.1). Although the music resembles that of Brazil's famous **carnaval** bands, this ritual is very serious and the music is spiritually charged. The song is a call to Oxossi (one

c. 1840–1920
Nationalistic musicians compose salon piano pieces and other works using the distinctive forms of folk songs and dances. This period is the height of popularity of European ballroom dances—polka (*polca*), waltz (*vals*), two-step

(*paso doble*), etc.—that become the basis for many popular forms, including Mexican *conjunto.*

1890s–1920s
Carnival festivals in Brazil begin dance competitions. The music of Brazilian *choros* folk bands eventually blends with African-influenced dances to create the samba.

1910s–1920s
The Argentinean *tango* becomes first Latin American dance to become widely popular in Europe and North America.

FIGURE **57.1**
An ensemble of three drummers plays a large repertory of polyrhythmic patterns to accompany rituals in the Candomblé religion.

© Stephanie Maze/CORBIS

of the Candomblé deities of African origin), a plea to come down and speak to those assembled. Suddenly, a woman in the crowd stops her dance, adopts an entirely different stance and manner, and everyone knows that Oxossi has descended.

The woman is in a trance; that is, Oxossi has taken control of her body and, speaking quietly to the *Pai de Santo*, answers questions and responds to requests for earthly interventions. Immediately, the drummers change their cadence to a song welcoming the spirit. In the view of Candomblé devotees, spirits inhabit many planes of existence beyond our own, and music is one way to reach beyond the realm of ordinary experience. These spirits may be indigenous, African, or even Catholic saints—in some traditions St. Sebastian is associated with Oxossi.

1930s
Adaptation of *mariachi* ensemble to suit urban needs, including the addition of trumpets. In this form, the ensemble is popularized through films and recordings.

1930s–1950s
Height of Latin big band popularity; many Latin dances introduced to North America in commercialized forms.

1960s–1980s
Sequences of military dictatorships in many Latin American countries, sometimes together with censors, parallel an explosion of youth culture and popular music: *MPB* in Brazil, *nueva canción* in Chile and Argentina, *chicha* in Andean countries, *salsa* in Puerto Rico and the United States.

About 5000 miles to the northwest is the Mexican city of San Luis Potosí. Here sacred dances also honor the same St. Sebastian, but with the very different sounds of the *huasteca*, an ensemble that features the sweet falsetto tones of a male singer accompanied by two guitars (in different sizes) and a lively violin. As penance for their sins, indigenous groups, perhaps inspired by medieval Spanish liturgical dances, may perform dances on the steps of the San Sebastián cathedral.

These two very different examples demonstrate not only the great diversity of Latin American music, but also the rich artistic hybrids that result from **syncretism**—*the fusion of cultures that takes place when different ethnic groups meet*. Anthropologists believe that at such times, similarities between the cultures are reinforced and their differences disappear or remain distinct. Thus musical traditions that had some common ground with those of the European invaders were preserved, albeit in hybrid forms. This combining of traditions is evident in the conflation of Catholic saints with African deities and in the mixture of African, European, and indigenous musical instruments, and also informs the cultural attitudes that continue to drive artistic creativity in this huge region.

Geography   Latin America describes South America and those parts of the Americas colonized by the Spanish and the Portuguese, including Mexico, Central America, and the Caribbean. Spanish is the principal language, but Native American languages are still spoken, Portuguese prevails in Brazil, and, especially in the Caribbean and Argentina, other European languages are spoken. A huge continent encompassing many ethnic groups, Latin America is unified by language and religion (Roman Catholic Christianity). Nevertheless, both indigenous and African cultures have made tremendous contributions to present-day culture.

58 CHARACTERISTICS OF TRADITIONAL LATIN AMERICAN MUSIC

Influences from European, African, and indigenous sources have shaped the characteristics of Latin American music. In areas where large-scale political structures existed at the time of the European invasion—principally the Aztec region of Central Mexico and the Inca empire in the Andes—indigenous culture and religion were especially influential, despite European attempts at suppression. African influence was especially focused in the Caribbean and other coastal regions. European musical characteristics are associated with the elite urban dwellers, known as *criollos*, and the *mestizos*, Latin Americans of mixed race. These terms have also come to refer to the different strata of music in these cultures, from the art music and theater of the *criollos* to the hybrid *mestizo* forms. The following are some of the distinctive characteristics forged from this rich synthesis:

■ **Use of Harmony** Folk and popular music throughout Latin America adopted European harmonic techniques and harmonic progressions, often heard in the guitar strumming.

■ **Parallel Thirds** Singers and instrumentalists thicken textures by adding a parallel melody two scale steps away that creates a consonant succession of intervals called thirds.

■ **Paired Phrases** Song texts are often written in *paired lines*, **coplas**, with pauses between lines. The first line of the pair ends with an unsettled feeling, which the second line resolves.

■ **Distinctive Dance Rhythms** Characteristic rhythms often derived from the **habañera** and **sesquialtera**, largely define Latin American dances.

■ **Rhythm Guitar** Vigorous harmonic strumming of the guitars, as well as percussion, emphasize dance rhythms.

Latin American Dance Rhythms

Latin American cultures are justly famous for their many dance forms, although the folk versions of some of these forms are quite different from their ballroom or popular namesakes. While most dances have strong national ties (the **samba** with Brazil, the **rumba** with Cuba, the **tango** with Argentina, and so on), some characteristics are common throughout Latin America (see Table 58.1).

In many cases it is possible to trace the origins of a dance back to a European model. Specific Iberian traits still found in some dances include foot stomping, finger snapping, and dancers contributing to the sound of the music in general. The contradance, a popular European dance of the eighteenth century, became, under Afro-Cuban influence in the nineteenth century, the *habañera*, made famous in the French opera *Carmen* by Georges Bizet.

The core rhythmic motive of the *habañera* (see graphic) became widely influential throughout Latin America and is still heard in this form in the Argentine tango, for example. Typically syncopated variations of this rhythm often correspond with rhythms of African origin, rhythms often found in such dances as the Cuban *danza*, the Brazilian *samba*, and the Dominican *merengué*. Other popular European dances, such as the waltz, the polka, the quadrille, and the two-step have also left important legacies, particularly in Mexico.

One of the most distinctive characteristics of many Latin American dances is the alternation between simple triple and compound duple meters—that is, between three groups of two and two groups

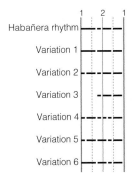

GRAPHIC 58.1
The basic *habañera* rhythm can be varied in many ways. Some of these syncopated variations correspond to rhythms characteristic of African music. Variation 1 is characteristic of many Latin American forms and is known as the *tresillo* rhythm in Cuba. Variation 2 is characteristic of the Dominican *merengué*.

TABLE **58.1**
Major Dance Forms of Latin America

Dance	Country of origin	Description
Bambuco	Colombia	a moderate *sesquialtera* courtship dance associated with the highlands of Colombia
Bossa Nova	Brazil	relaxed modern samba influenced by cool jazz
Cueca	Chile	fast *sesquialtera* couple dance
Cumbia	Colombia	African-influenced fast duple meter dance
Jarabe	Mexico	moderate *sesquialtera* dance
Joropo	Venezuela	fast *sesquialtera* couple dance
Malambo	Argentina	fast *sesquialtera* competition dance of *gauchos* (cowboys)
Merengue	Dominican Republic	fast African-influenced dance with a distinctive simple duple rhythm
Rumba	Cuba	highly syncopated simple duple rural dance, later known in a ballroom version
Samba	Brazil	a simple duple syncopated dance now known in many rural, urban, and ballroom types
Tango	Argentina	slow urban couple dance with pronounced downbeats

of three. In some forms the *two meters* may be *played simultaneously*, creating polyrhythm. This characteristic metrical type is called **sesquialtera** and is characteristic of the Colombian *bambuco*, the Cuban *cueca*, the Argentinean *gato* and *malambo*, and the Mexican *jarabe*.

Although the name and rhythm of the *sesquialtera* probably derives from Arabic influences in Spain, its place in many dances originates in African versions of the same polyrhythms. Many Latin American dances, including the Colombian *cumbia*, the Cuban rumba, and the Dominican *merengué*, clearly have their origins in or are influenced by African sources. The Brazilian samba is derived from earlier Afro-Brazilian dances such as the *batuque* and the *lundu*.

In the 1930s and 40s, films and recordings popularized Latin American dances in North America and elsewhere, and the big bands of the swing era refined the traditional rhythms to create ballroom forms often far different than their original models. Some of the forms often associated with jazz from the 1930s through the 1960s include the *mambo*, the *bossa nova*, the *conga*, and the *chachachá*.

Harmony

Probably the most distinctive characteristic of European-derived music is the use of harmony. The roots of European harmony lie in music theorists' classification of some musical intervals (two pitches at the same time) as consonant and others as dissonant. However, it wasn't until the beginnings of notation in the Middle Ages that composers worked out *ways to control simultaneous melodies* called **counterpoint** so that the movement from consonance to dissonance and back created movement from tension to resolution.

By the fifteenth century, these conventions resulted most often in certain standard chords—that is, collections of several simultaneous pitches—at points of resolution. By the eighteenth century, theorists codified these chords as a specific collection of pitches regardless of the octave or order in which they appeared.

For example, with a tonic of C and major mode—that is, in the key of C major, one such chord is the pitches C, E, and G, in any order or octave or with duplications. Three-note chords in this specific pattern are known as triads, and there are seven possible triads in a given key. Sometimes composers or performers add further pitches to the triads, but in most cases the triads remain the basis for European-style harmony.

In popular and folk music, the precise distribution of voices in counterpoint became less important than *the particular successions of chords*, known as **harmonic progressions** or chord progressions. In the so-called classical guitar tradition, the guitarist plays distinct simultaneous melodies, but many folk and popular guitarists strum the strings while the left hand fingers chords in standard positions.

Strumming chords has become a common technique in Latin American music and became the basis for guitar playing in much popular music in North America as well. While strumming does not easily permit the polyphonic textures of the classical guitar tradition, it does allow the guitarist to create strong rhythmic emphasis through the patterns and loudness of the strums. In blues and rock music, this role is called rhythm guitar, but the technique originated in Latin American folk and popular music.

Harmony has long been one of the central European elements in Latin American folk and popular music. Musicians even added harmony to monophonic indigenous melodies, provided the melodies used something close to a diatonic scale. Particular harmonic progressions characterize many popular dances and song forms as much as their rhythms or melodic characteristics. The use of harmony based on triads is also related to the characteristically Latin American practice of singing or playing in parallel thirds—that is, two simultaneous melodies that are the same but separated by the interval of a third. While probably related to folk practices from Europe, parallel thirds are also found in certain African regions.

Latin American Musical Instruments

Musicologists often categorize Latin American musical instruments through their origins—indigenous, African, or European—even though many of them represent hybrids or local variations of an existing model. Various types of vertical flutes, drums, and rattles are among the most widespread survivors of pre-Columbian (meaning before Columbus) indigenous instruments. The simple bow was the only chordophone on the continent before the Europeans, and European string instruments have made a large impact. Instruments of the violin family are now common, sometimes in folk versions made with improvised materials. Jesuit missionaries originally introduced the harp, which then became widespread in a form that often includes a distinctively large resonator.

The European chordophone that has had the greatest influence, however, is the guitar, which exists in almost uncountable forms throughout the region—with two to twelve strings, from very large bass instruments to tiny treble ones, played with vigorous strumming or by plucking single notes. European wind instruments, including trumpets, clarinets, accordions, and saxophones, are very common, as are European-style bands and classical orchestras.

African instruments are widespread in areas associated with the slave trade, especially the Caribbean and eastern South America. These instruments include many types of drums and idiophones as well as the musical bow. Refined versions of these instruments are now standard additions to orchestras and dance bands—the conga, bongos, claves, and timbales all come from Africa via Cuba—and the marimba is still played in its original form in Central America (Figure 58.1).

FIGURE **58.1**
Though originally from Africa, the marimba has become the center of a distinctive tradition of southern Mexico and Central America. Often multiple players play on a single instrument. It may be either chromatic (like a piano) or diatonic (white keys only), with or without tube resonators. The marimba also became associated with Latin dance bands and then North American jazz bands.

© Lindsay Hebberd/CORBIS

59 MUSIC IN MEXICO

At the time of the European invasion, the highlands of central Mexico were a part of the large and advanced Aztec empire. Many sources indicate that music was an integral part of the Aztec religious rituals. The Aztecs associated elaborate drumming patterns and perhaps flute melodies with particular rituals and days of the year, but all traces of Aztec religion (and hence religious music) that the Europeans could find they destroyed.

In a few short years, a cathedral was built and missionaries began to teach music to the Aztecs. These priests were astonished at the musical aptitude of the Aztecs, who readily adopted Spanish church and folk music. By 1540, one of the indigenous people had already written a mass in the European style. Even so, many elements of pre-Columbian music presumably survive and color some qualities of modern Mexican music. Syncretism can be found in many folk religious practices, including processionals and *folk religious dramas* called **autos**, in which music still plays an important part (Figure 59.1).

The *Son* and Other *Mestizo* Forms

The *mariachi* band has become the popular image of folk music in Mexico (Figure 59.2), but it is only one of a rich variety of distinct types of folk bands, each associated, like food and dress, with different regions within the country. Spanish writers noted this regionalization of Mexican *mestizo*

FIGURE 59.1
Every year around December 12, special groups of musicians and dancers called *concheros* (after the armadillo shells used in their lutes) lead processions to honor the Virgin of Guadalupe. Aspects of the rituals, such as the costumes, are derived from pre-Columbian Aztec models.

© Liba Taylor/CORBIS

FIGURE 59.2
Although the *mari-achi* ensemble has become a national symbol of Mexico, it was originally associated with the rancheros of the Jalisco region, and *mariachis* still wear traditional ranchero costumes.

music as early as the eighteenth century, especially through the form known as the **son**. While the *son* has come to refer to a wide variety of different song and dance types, all usually use the *sesquialtera* (juxtaposition of simple triple and compound duple meters), strumming guitars, and a fast stamping couple dance known as the *zapateado*.

The song lyrics are typically in pairs of lines, known as **coplas**. Each line usually corresponds to a musical phrase of regular length, with a pause between each line during which time the instruments (or shouts from the musicians) fill in. The first of a pair of phrases often ends (cadence) in an unsettled harmony and melodic tone, while the second resolves both the harmony and the idea expressed in the text. Many Mexican *sones*, as well as other forms, such as the northern *conjunto*, therefore have a kind of gentle back and forth motion between phrases and a regularity of phrases and harmony set atop vigorous rhythms and lively tempos.

Folk Bands in Mexico

Conjunto is a generic term for folk band in Mexico, although the term has become mostly associated with popular bands of northern Mexico and the Southwest United States. Other regions are known for their own types of bands, each with its own music, singing style, instrumentation, and traditional dress.

■ ***Chilena*** This type originated in Acapulco on the Pacific coast of Mexico, supposedly from Chilean sailors during the nineteenth-century gold rush, and it does show the influence of the South American *cueca*. The group usually includes a guitar, another small guitar called a *requinto*, and sometimes wind instruments and a string bass.

■ ***Huapango*** From the rural regions around Mexico City in central Mexico, this ensemble includes a *medium-sized guitar* known as a **jarana** and a *special large guitar*, the **huapanguera**. However, its most distinctive instrument is the violin, which plays fast running figures rather than the slow countermelodies of the mariachi.

■ *Mariachi* While this form originated in the ranches around Guadalajara, by the mid-twentieth century ensembles in their traditional charro costumes made their way to Mexico City street corners. There bands replaced the traditional harp with the more portable *large bass guitar* known as the **guitarrón** (Figure 59.3), and a pair of trumpets (more suitable for a noisy urban setting) replaced or supplemented the violins. In this form the mariachi band and its repertory of *ranchera* songs became famous through film and recordings, so that today it is a fixture throughout Mexico and in the United States. Its songs are typically love ballads, often sung in parallel thirds echoed by the trumpets and violins during instrumental breaks.

■ *Jarocho* This band from the Veracruz region (Figure 59.4) is known for its fast lively dances and songs such as the famous *La Bamba*.

© Sandy Felsenthal /CORBIS

FIGURE **59.3**
With its very large resonator, the **guita-rrón** is the distinctive bass instrument of the mariachi ensemble and is much more suited to strolling bands than the large harps and double basses used in other types of bands. It is played by plucking with the fingers, not strumming.

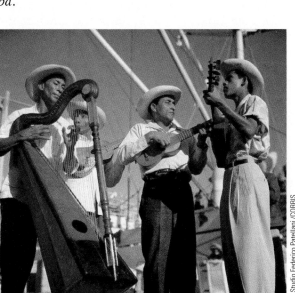

© Studio Federico Patellani /CORBIS

FIGURE **59.4**
A *jarocho* ensemble plays near the docks of Veracruz. The **arpa** (left) is a *diatonic harp with a very large wooden resonator*. This distinctive form of the harp is important throughout Latin America, especially in South American countries such as Paraguay, where it is the "national instrument." Sizes may vary from small versions that rest on the player's lap to very large harps carried by two people. It is often played in very rhythmic and even polyrhythmic plucking and sometimes the resonator may be hit as well. Because these harps do not use the system of pedals for chromatic tuning that was added to the European concert harp, traditional harp music is limited to one diatonic key without retuning. The **jarana** (second from left) is a *medium-sized strummed guitar*. The **requinto** (second from right) is a *very small guitar with four or five strings*. It is played melodically in *sones jarocho*, although small guitars in other traditions may be strummed.

A Performance of a *Son Jarocho*

The Mexican state of Veracruz stretches from tropical Gulf coast beaches to fertile volcanic mountainsides. For many years, amateur musicians dressed in traditional white shirts and hats periodically gathered for *large celebrations* called *fandangos*, at the center of which was a raised wooden platform to amplify the **zapateados**—*stamping, boot-tapping dances* that would go on perhaps until dawn. The *fandango* today is more likely to be a festival of invited musical groups, and the musicians are more likely to be professionals who play at restaurants and weddings. Even so, the exciting, rustic spirit of the music and dances of the *fandango* remain a vital part of Veracruz culture.

While often overshadowed by the ever-popular *mariachi* style, the traditional music of the Veracruz *fandango* is the *son jarocho*. The core *jarocho* ensemble is made up of three instruments: the **jarana**, *a five-course guitar slightly smaller than the Spanish guitar*; the **requinto**, *a small guitar*; and the **arpa**, *a diatonically tuned harp*. Other instruments may be added, especially a guitar, but the ensemble usually lacks the characteristic trumpets of the mariachi and the violin of the *huasteca* ensemble of neighboring regions.

Although the *son jarocho* usually lacks percussion instruments, the rhythmic and percussive use of the instruments of the ensemble more than makes up for it. The *jarana* and guitar players create these rhythms by alternating *patterns of up and down strums* called **maniqueos** or **rasqueado**. *Rasqueado* also refers to one of the most distinctive of these strokes in which the fingers unfold over the strings as the wrist moves down, creating a long emphasized strum that can be heard in this excerpt just as the guitar and *jarana* enter. This technique is also a characteristic of Spanish flamenco guitar and other styles in Latin America.

Like the more famous *jarocho* song *La Bamba*, *Siquisiri* (the name has no translation) is a traditional song, although the date of its origin is uncertain. Because of its greeting text, it is often the first song in a performance. However, only part of the text is fixed, and traditionally the lead singer improvises some of the lines. The lead singer is usually the guitarist or other instrumentalist and the remaining instrumentalists form the chorus. The texts of *sones jarochos*, like many Latin American songs, are based on Spanish poetic forms called *coplas*, or lines in pairs. The text of *Siquisiri* is in the form of a *sextilla*, in which the verses have six lines, although lines may be repeated, as in this case.

Conjunto

European ballroom dances were very popular in nineteenth-century Latin America, and hundreds appeared in salon arrangements for piano, including waltzes, two-steps, and, most importantly in Mexico, the polka. Many of these dance forms became especially popular in this region among the working-class people in newly settled northern Mexico and Texas.

At the same time, the diatonic button accordion was introduced in the north and, along with the *bajo sexto* guitar (Figure 59.5), became the foundation for dance bands that became very popular on both sides of the border. Many of these forms were made into songs, such as the revolutionary period *canciones revolucionarias*. By the 1920s these dance forms and songs had moved from the salon to the popular bands of the region, now known as *conjunto norteña*, or simply *conjunto*.

In the 1930s, with the arrival of commercial recording companies in the Southwest United States, *conjunto* (Figure 59.6) became very popular within Mexican immigrant communities. The instrumentation was now more or less standardized as accordion, guitar, string bass, and singer. Of these instruments, the accordion is the most distinctive sound of the ensemble, and it became a leading melody instrument when modern keyed varieties replaced the old button types.

While sharing the same kinds of harmonic patterns and song types with other bands, such as the mariachi, this ensemble also introduced innovations such as electric instruments and influences from North American rock. Today, *conjunto* is one of the most popular types of Mexican music, not only in Mexico, but especially in the Southwest United States.

FIGURE **59.5**
The *bajo sexto* (left) is a *bass guitar with six double courses tuned an octave lower than a traditional Spanish guitar.*

FIGURE **59.6**
A *conjunto* festival in Austin, Texas, spotlighting the accordion most characteristic of the ensemble.

Art Music in Mexico

Mexico has one of the richest legacies of art music from the colonial period in Latin America. Important cathedrals and music schools were established at Mexico City, Puebla, Morelia, and elsewhere. Secular theater developed in the eighteenth century with the production of Spanish *zarzuelas*, a *type of operetta*. As elsewhere in Latin America, native-born composers of the nineteenth century wrote mainly salon piano music. The importance of this music lay mostly in the growing interest in nationalism, under the influence of nationalistic trends in Europe. The first important nationalistic composer in Mexico was Manuel Ponce (1882–1948), who wrote piano suites and symphonic tone poems meant to evoke Mexican dances and folk tunes.

After the Mexican revolution, a revival of interest in indigenous culture influenced many artists, including the muralist school of Mexican painters, such as Diego Rivera and José Clemente Orozco. This so-called Aztec renaissance found its foremost musical expression in the compositions of Carlos

Listening Guide

CD 2:15. *Siquisirí*, Los Pregoneros del Puerto (José Gutiérrez, Gonzalo Mata, Oliverio Lara, Valente Reyes). Translations by Daniel Sheehy.

0:00 	Although performances of *Siquisirí* may vary among groups, it normally begins with a harp solo. The main harp melody consists of various arpeggios (sequential sounding of notes in a chord) outlining a harmony that alternates between two basic chords. The notes are grouped at times into twos and other times into threes. This pervasive alternation and overlapping of two meters, known as *sesquialtera*, helps define the distinctively propulsive rhythm of many *son jarocho* songs and dances.
0:07 	At this point the other instruments enter—in this recording the *requinto*, the *jarana*, and a six-course Spanish guitar. The players powerfully strum the *jarana* and guitar, alternating between the same two chords as in the introduction while emphasizing a *sesquialtera* rhythm. Meanwhile, the *requinto* and the right hand of the harpist play quick melodies and the left hand of the harpist plays the bass line.
0:25 The opening verso of *Siquisirí*.	After the instrumental introduction, the lead singer begins the song with the *verso*, a fixed text which here bids a good evening to the listeners (the text can be modified depending on the time of day and the audience). 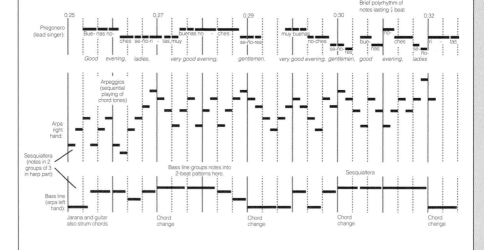

Especially helpful for Listening Guide was Daniel Sheehy's *The* Son Jarocho: *History, Style, and Repertory of a Changing Mexican Musical Tradition*. PhD diss. UCLA, 1979.

0:32	The chorus (the rest of the instrumentalists) sings the remaining lines of the fixed *verso*:

A todas las florecitas — All the little flowers

de rostros cautivadores — With the captivating faces

van las trovas más bonitas — We dedicate this beautiful verse

de estos pobres cantadores. — From these poor singers. |
| **0:39** | In the next contrasting verse, called the *estribillo*, the lead singer improvises verses for the occasion, usually standard lines introducing himself and the band, expressing appreciation for being there, or perhaps humorous teasing of members of the audience. Again, the six-line form of the *sextilla* is broken up, this time by interpolated lines in which the chorus answer each line or two with stock responses.

(Chorus: *Ay! Que sí, que sí, que no* — Ay! And yes, and yes, and no)

Leader: *Que traigo un pulido deseo . . .* — I have a nice wish . . .

(Chorus: *Ay! Que sí, que sí, que no* — Ay! And yes, and yes, and no)

Leader: *de decirte la verdad . . .* — to tell you the truth . . .

(Chorus: *Ahora sí, mañana no* — Now yes, tomorrow no)

Leader: *porque cuando yo te veo . . .* — because when I see you . . .

(Chorus: *Con la grande sí, con la chica no* — With the big one, yes, with the girl, no)

Leader: *volteas la cara pa' atrás.* — you turn your head away.

¡Si lo haces porque soy feo — If you do it because I am ugly,

reclámale a mi mamá! — complain to my mother! |
| **0:56** | This instrumental break is derived from the introduction, but now played by all the instruments. Throughout the *versos* and *estribillos*, the instruments continue their basic patterns, alternating between chords while emphasizing the *sesquialtera* rhythms. |
| **1:20** | The lead singer repeats the first two lines of the second *verso*, followed by the chorus singing last four lines. |

(*continued*)

1:33	The second *estribillo*. The translation below leaves out the responses from the chorus, which are the same as above:

Que ni la tan en su apogeo	Not the moon at its apogee
ni el sol tan capacitado	nor the sun is able
satisfacen los deseos	to fulfill one's desires . . .
como él que llega a Alvarado	like he who arrives in Alvarado,
y el arpa suena el trineo	and the harp sounds the high melody,
del "Siquisirí" afamado.	of the famed "Siquisirí."

1:50	The instruments suddenly drop out except for the harp, which now plays a rhythmically intricate solo.
2:30	The harp continues, but now it is the requinto player's turn for a solo. Unlike many small guitars in Latin America, the *requinto* of the *jarocho* ensemble is nearly always a melodic and not a strummed instrument.
2:48	The rest of the band joins in as the *requinto* and harp interlock their *sesquialtera* melodies.
3:05	A final *estribillo* ends the piece.

Que no hay muchacha que sea fea	There is no girl who is ugly
cuando viste de jarocha	when she dresses like a *jarocha*
y más cuando zapatea	and more so when she dances the *zapateado*
con tu gracia de morocha	with your grace of a dark woman
la tarima se cimbrea	the dance platform sways
y ésta es mi tierra jarocha. ¡Ay, ay!	and this is my *jarocho* land. Ay ay!

Chávez (1899–1978). In his famous *Sinfonia India* [*Indian Symphony*], Chávez used indigenous (Indian) folk songs and percussion instruments to evoke his ancient Mexican heritage. Chávez was also instrumental in the support of the national conservatory of music in Mexico City and served as conductor of the Orquesta Sinfónica de Mexico for many years.

Silvestre Revueltas (1899–1940), a contemporary and friend of Chávez, also wrote pieces representing Mexico's pre-Columbian past, but he is best known for his brash and dynamic representations of contemporary mariachis and other folk groups. In some of these he evokes the lively competitions of mariachi groups playing at the same time on the streets of Mexico City. These simultaneous sounds produce dissonant clashes, polyrhythms, and polytonalities (use of two or more keys at the same time).

MUSIC IN BRAZIL

60

Every year around February, the streets of Brazilian cities give way to an invasion of tourists, sidewalk food and beer stalls, seas of neighborhood dancers following trucks blasting out dance music like electric pied pipers, and the thunderous sounds of the most famous of Brazil's many musical traditions—the *carnaval*. In the days preceding Lenten abstinence, months of rehearsal come to a close for the **samba schools**, which parade through the streets, competing for the recognition of judges, street revelers, and millions who watch the spectacle on television. Each "school" consists of hundreds of elaborately costumed dancers on top of and beside lavish floats and a hundred or more percussionists who make up the *bateria*, or *samba band*. While the samba is most famous in this modern mass media form, its roots reach deep into the African and *mestizo* heritage of this country's vibrant musical heritage.

The Afro-Brazilian Heritage

Brazil is the largest country in Latin America and the only one to have been colonized primarily by the Portuguese rather than the Spanish, although there is a large indigenous population, and African slaves were first introduced in 1538. On plantations sometimes far from the influence of the church authorities and the European *criollos* of the urban areas, many of these slaves retained African languages and cultural elements of African ethnic groups such as the Yoruba (from present-day Nigeria), Ewe (Ghana), and

FIGURE 60.1
Of the folk festivals of Brazil, the most widespread is the *Bumba meu boi*, which involves the magical resurrection of a bull who saves the life of a slave. Many different varieties of music accompany folk dramas such as this, depending on the region.

Fon (Benin). As one can guess from the onomatopoeic name of one of their earliest characteristic dances, the **batuque**, the slaves also brought percussive ensembles, including drums, from Africa. As in West Africa, participants formed a circle and pairs took turns dancing in the middle, often including the touching of navels, a practice (which scandalized church authorities) known as *"semba,"* probably the origin of the word *"samba."*

Missionaries brought to these plantations the Iberian traditions of religious processions, dances, and didactic religious dramas. African people also appropriated these forms, sometimes to represent veiled satires of their masters or express an African identity (Figure 60.1). Like samba processions, these dramas are communal and to an extent participatory. The music may therefore involve many different types of instruments, although drums are usually prominent.

Another symbol of resistance to slavery is a **capoiera**, a stylized martial art dance. The musical instrument most associated with *capoiera* is the **berimbau**, a *musical bow tapped with a stick and equipped with a half-gourd resonator* placed against the chest (Figure 60.2). The player can effect slight changes in pitch by varying the tension or holding a coin as a bridge against the string, but the *berimbau* is mainly a rhythmic instrument, not a melodic or harmonic one. A tall drum called an **atabaque**, along with a tambourine

FIGURE 60.2
Three *berimbau* players (sitting against the back wall) accompany *capoiera*. Part dance, part game, part martial art, *capoiera* may have arisen as a way to train fighters for the resistance to slavery.

and **agogo** (double iron bell) may also join in the accompaniment. *Capoiera* remains very popular today, not only in Brazil, but also in *capoiera* clubs in the United States, Europe, and elsewhere.

After the emancipation of the slaves in 1888, many African-Americans emigrated to urban areas, especially those on the northern and eastern coasts, such as in the state of Bahia. In addition to bringing their music and instruments, they also brought their spiritual practices, which became distinct religions such as Candomblé and Umbanda. Music in these religions plays the crucial role of calling and welcoming various deities who take over the bodies of participants. Typically, an *agogo* and a set of three conical or barrel-shaped drums called, from smallest to largest, **le**, **rumpi**, and **rum**, accompany a complex repertory of songs, each unique to a particular spirit, with intense polyrhythms clearly related to the African and *batuque* precursors of the style (Figure 60.3).

FIGURE 60.3
The *rum* or largest drum of the *atabaques* ensemble accompanies folk dances and religious rituals, such as this ceremony of the Umbanda religion.

The Samba

Of the several popular Afro-Brazilian dances such as the *batuque*, the **lundu** was the one that filtered into urban salons as early as the eighteenth century. Still, the division between the music of the urban elite and the poor slum dwellers remained strong. The hillside slums, or *favelas*, were known for their *bands of street musicians*, called **choros**, who played versions of popular dances like the *lundu*, the polka, or the **maxixe**, a *highly syncopated Brazilian dance from the early twentieth century*. Such dances probably all fed into the vibrant parades that began accompanying pre-Lenten festivities in Rio de Janeiro around the turn of the twentieth century and became the famous samba (Figure 60.4).

FIGURE 60.4
The **repenique** (left) is a *medium-sized* deep *cylindrical drum*. The virtuoso leader of the samba band plays this drum with one stick and one free hand, producing a variety of tones. The **cuica** (middle) is a *friction drum*—a small stick is attached to the inside of a drum head, and the player rubs his fingers down the stick. The stick's vibration is resonated by the drum head, producing a quick, sliding tone. A skilled player can make this instrument sound like human speech or laughter. The **caixa** (right) is a *cylindrical drum with snares*—small wires that rattle against the head. While there are different sizes, *caixas* are usually shallower than the *repenique* and have a less defined pitch. Although these drums are commercially produced today, with modern tuning screws, plastic drum heads, and metal bodies, homemade versions are also common in villages.

FIGURE **60.5**
Blocos afro, such as this group from Bahia, are community percussion groups that have developed music inspired by African roots.

© Jeremy Horner/CORBIS

By the 1920s and 30s, neighborhood samba groups first formalized themselves as "schools" that local governments recognized, organized into competitions, and even used for political purposes. The samba became internationally famous, largely through the recordings and film performances of singer Carmen Miranda. The samba of professional big bands, often accompanying songs known as *samba cancão*, produced a more relaxed and refined version of the dance than the percussive *samba de morro* or "dark" samba of the poor African-American neighborhoods.

Although the samba bands of today's *carnaval* are professionally produced and highly rehearsed, they are still largely made up of amateur percussion ensembles from working-class neighborhoods. Since the end of the military dictatorship in 1985, parades have even included themes of social protest. In the 1970s and 80s, musical clubs known as ***blocos afro*** championed a reintroduction of self-consciously African elements into their bands as a way to reestablish African traditions and an ethnic identity (Figure 60.5). Apart from the *carnaval*, the rhythms of the samba continue to form a dominant influence throughout Brazilian popular music.

MPB—*Música Popular Brasileira*

In 1959, Antônio Carlos Jobim and João Gilberto produced an album called *Chega de Saudade*, which referred to a new sound, called "*bossa nova*" in the liner notes, meaning "new skill or knack." Unlike the commercial big-band sambas, these intimate songs featured sophisticated harmonies and rhythms and emphasized the poetry of the lyrics. In place of the large percussion section of samba jazz was a smooth and refined rhythm driven by intricate syncopations on a single guitar, called *violão gago* (stammering guitar).

While the *bossa nova* also became a familiar ballroom dance, its original form was very influential for the next generation of Brazilian popular songwriters, whose music became known in general as ***música popular brasileira*** or **MPB**. The composers Caetano Veloso and Gilberto Gil brought electric instruments and rock influence into the mix, and others, such as Milton Nascimento and Jorge Ben, introduced African elements. After the 1964 military coup, their cheerful sounds, irresistible rhythms, and oblique lyrics often masked dark social and political protests. In response, the government censored many songs, imprisoned some songwriters, and forced others into exile.

Still, MPB remained widely popular through the end of the military dictatorship in 1985. As newer composers introduce further innovations, the echo of the samba rhythm usually remains, as does the often poignant juxtaposition of samba's festivity and optimism with references to continuing social problems.

Art Music in Brazil

As in most of Latin America, professional music directors at the large Catholic cathedrals wrote the first art music in Brazil. One of the best of these composers was José Mauricio Nuñes Garcia (1767–1830), a mixed-race composer who worked under the patronage of the first emperor of Brazil, Dom João and wrote many masses in the style of Mozart or Haydn. By the middle of the nineteenth century, the theater replaced the church as the primary patron of art music. Pianos became popular instruments in the salons of the urban *criollo* class, and a vibrant music publishing industry followed. Some professional pianist-composers began to arrange traditional genres such as the lyrical ***modhina***. While the refined result may not have had a great deal of resemblance to the original folk form, these experiments were the first steps in the direction of nationalism and a distinctive cultural heritage.

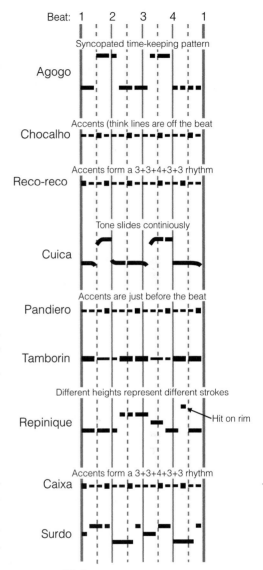

GRAPHIC 60.1
A representation of an example ostinato of a *samba bateria*. Some instruments, in particular the *repinique*, may play variations, but all stay within this basic pattern for the duration of this section. Though the instruments do not have definite pitch, some of them can vary the pitch through different strokes, shown here as variations in the heights of the lines for each instrument. The *agogo* (double bell), *chocalho* (rattle of small cymbals), and *reco-reco* (metal spring scraper) form the idiophone section. The *pandiero* (tambourine), *tamborin* (frame drum), *caixa* (snare drum), and *surdo* (bass drum) form the drum section that follows the *repinique*.

The most famous of Brazil's composers was Heitor Villa-Lobos (1887–1959). Although he was the son of amateur classical musicians and learned cello and clarinet at an early age, he was just as at home with the folk and popular musicians of his day. At eighteen, instead of studying European classical music at the conservatory in Rio de Janeiro, he traveled around Brazil, collecting folk songs and performing as an itinerant musician.

His largely intuitive style is full of life and energy, but he was aware of the contemporary modernist movement in the arts in Europe. His dissonant, "primitivist" adaptations of folk and popular styles made him a controversial figure when he went to Paris in the 1920s. Upon his return, he became a pedagogue, lobbying the Brazilian government for reforms and funding of music education throughout the country.

Villa-Lobos's two most famous series of pieces are his sixteen *Choros* and his nine *Bachianas Brasilieras*. As suggested by the title, the *Choros* are an homage to the vitality of the roving popular street bands that Villa-Lobos participated in as a young man. The *Bachianas Brasilieras* are a seemingly unlikely marriage of the unity and classicism of the works of the great eighteenth-century composer Johann Sebastian Bach and the vibrancy of the folk and popular music of Brazil. The *Bachianas Brasilieras* include movements evocative of *modhinas*, *choros*, and Brazilian dances, but often using eighteenth-century European forms. This style, called **neoclassicism**, was also popular in Europe and the United States during the same period.

MUSIC IN ANDEAN COUNTRIES

61

Every February, the impressive sounds of bands of fifty or more panpipe (*siku*) players echo down the streets of the Peruvian city of Puno on the shores of Lake Titicaca, as they, together with dance troupes and pilgrims, celebrate the festival of the *Virgen de la Candeleria* (Figure 61.4 on page 302). While ostensibly a feast of the Roman Catholic Christian church, this lively celebration has elements that reach far back into the pre-Columbian past of this Andean region. Early European writers noted monthly festivals tied to agricultural cycles among the Incas, and while Christian feast days absorbed these events, villages and cities throughout the Andes still host thousands of syncretic festivals every year.

The Aymara-speaking people of this region associate Mary, the mother of Jesus, with Pachamama, the Incan earth goddess whose benevolence allows crops to grow in the cold, dry air at this great altitude (some 3800 meters or 12,500 feet). While priests celebrate mass in the churches and cathedrals, in other parts of the city celebrants make offerings of wine and seeds wrapped in coca leaves, accompanied by special ritual melodies, to ensure a bountiful harvest from Pachamama/the Virgin for the coming year.

Other festivals and musical instruments are associated with Pachatata, the father god of the mountains.

The performances of the *siku* bands also represent a male/female duality. Because the technique of blowing puffs of air over the tops of the tubes of panpipes makes smooth or fast melodies difficult, *siku* bands create melodies through alternation playing. By splitting up the notes between two groups of players (the "male" and "female," although they are usually all men), the players can also avoid getting dizzy constantly blowing over the pipes in the thin mountain air. Large *siku* bands in this area have several different sizes of *sikus*, playing in parallel octaves or other intervals. The choreography these bands accompany (little of this music exists without dance) represents this dualism through couple dances or dances of parallel lines. Wild improvising dancers dressed as devils or wild men likewise contrast with the holy rituals going on inside of the churches.

Aside from the people who speak Aymara around Lake Titicaca, most of the indigenous people of the Andes mountains ranging from Ecuador to Chile speak Quechua, the modern version of the language of the Incas. Even so, and despite many similarities, their music is highly regionalized. Some villages emphasize the music of the **kena** notch flute and **bomba** drum (Figure 61.2), while in others Spanish instruments such as the harp and violin predominate. The **charango** (Figure 61.3) is a small guitar popular in many regions.

The most popular dance form throughout the Andes is the **huayno**, *a lively duple meter dance* with a characteristic long-short-short rhythm, often played on a *bomba* (Figure 61.4). Above this constant foundation is a highly syncopated, often lilting melody. Traditionally couples with scarves dance the

Courtesy Danlee Mitchell

FIGURE **61.1**
Panpipes, known as *siku* (Aymara language), *antara* (Quechua), or *zampoña* (Spanish), are common throughout the Andes and high Amazon regions. They consist of stopped narrow tubes of bamboo of varying lengths tied together in one or two rows. The player directs an air stream over the edge of these stopped pipes the way one plays a soda bottle. *Siku* come in many different sizes, from tiny soprano versions to very large bass ones such as this. Players often create melodies through alternation playing, although in some regions, bands of *siku* play together in parallel intervals.

(2) Courtesy of Carlos Quinche

FIGURE **61.2**
An Andean musician plays the **kena** (notch flute) on the left, and the **bombo** (bass drum) on the right.

FIGURE 61.3

The **charango** (shown here in performance and displaying the back shell) is a small guitar-like lute with five double courses of nylon or metal. Traditionally the resonator is made from an armadillo shell. Today the endangered armadillo is protected in many regions, so that *cha-rangos* are often made from wood. It may be strummed or played melodically.

FIGURE 61.4
Aymara people from Bolivia play *sikus* and *bombo* drums for the *Dia del Campesino* or Farmer's Day festival. The **bomba** is a cylindrical double-headed drum of various sizes, played with a padded mallet.

huayno, sometimes with *zapateado* (foot stamping), especially during the fast final section, known as the *fuga* (meaning escape or running).

Until the mid-twentieth century, the music of the Andean countries was largely segregated like the people, isolating the indigenous peoples of the mountains and their culture from the urban *criollos* of the coastal regions who cultivated music and instruments more directly related to European models. Following liberalizing reforms and economic changes that brought many mountain dwellers to the cities, new musical styles were forged, and the music of the *campesinos* (mountain peasants) became the basis for a pan-Andean popular music sound.

Because of the ethnic mixtures they represented, these forms were known as mestizo music. Mestizo bands combined *charangos* and guitars, harps and mandolins, *sikus* and synthesizers, and added harmonies to Andean melodies. One of the most popular of these hybrid sounds is **chicha**, *a style combining the Colombian* cumbia, *Cuban percussion, and North American rock with the local* huayno. The styles developed by descendents of African slaves in some coastal areas represent yet another distinctive hybrid, an important element of which is the percussiveness of the **cajón**, an open wooden box that a drummer sits on and plays with his or her hands.

This dense swirl of cultural influences—indigenous, European, and African—coalesces into unique expressions in different regions and villages, often each with its own type of ensemble. Even with European harmonies and instruments, the echos of the area's ancient past resonate within the music of the festivals and street corners, here as elsewhere among the rich traditions of Latin America.

 REFERENCES

Discography

Music of Mexico

Chávez, Carlos. *The Complete Symphonies*. Eduardo Mata cond. London Symphony Orchestra. Englewood Cliffs, NJ: Vox Box CDX5061, 1992.

Gutiérrez, José, Felipe Ochoa, and Marcos Ochoa. *La Bamba: Sones Jarochos from Veracruz*. Washington DC: Smithsonian-Folkways SF 40505, 2003.

Pregoneros del Puerto, Los. *Music of Veracruz*. Cambridge, MA: Rounder Records 5048, 1990.

Revueltas, Silvestre. *Hommage à Silvestre Revueltas*. Fernando Lozano cond. Orchestre Philharmonique. Paris: Forlane UCD 16614, 1990.

Various artists. *Anthology of Mexican Sones*, 3 vol. Mexico: Corason CO-101-103, 1993.

Various artists. *Conjunto! Texas-Mexican Border Music*, 6 vol. Cambridge, MA: Rounder Records 6034, 1988–94.

Music of Brazil

Various artists. *Beleza Tropical: Brazil Classics 1*. Fly/Sire Records 25805-1, 1989.

Various artists. *Brazil Roots Samba*. Cambridge, MA: Rounder Records RDR-5045, 1989.

Villa-Lobos, Heitor. *Bachianas Brasilieras No. 5-2-1, etc*. Lazare Gozman cond. the Leningrad Chamber. Paris: Le Chant du Monde/Melodia 278 644, 1978.

Music of the Andes

Inti-Illimani. *Andadas*. Danbury, CT: Green Linnet Records GLCD 4009, 1993.

Various artists. *Mountain Music of Peru*, 2 vol. Washington DC: Smithsonian-Folkways SF 40020/40406, 1994.

Other Latin American Music

Various artists. *Caribbean Island Music*. New York: Elektra/Nonesuch 9 72047-2, 1972/1998.

Various artists. *Cuba: Afroamérica. Afro-Cuban Songs and Rhythms*. Geneva: AIMP LIII/VDE 959, 1997.

Bibliography

Appleby, David P. *The Music of Brazil*. Austin: University of Texas Press, 1983.

Béhague, Gerard. *Music in Latin America: An Introduction*. Englewood Cliffs, NJ: Prentice-Hall, 1979.

Clark, Walter Aaron, ed. *From Tejano to Tango: Latin American Popular Music*. New York: Routledge, 2002.

Geijerstam, Claes af. *Popular Music in Mexico*. Albuquerque: University of New Mexico Press, 1976.

Otter, Elisabeth den. *Music and Dance of Indians and Mestizos in an Andean Valley of Peru*. Delft: Eburon, 1985.

Schechter, John M., ed. *Music in Latin American Culture: Regional Traditions*. New York: Schirmer Books, 1999.

Schreiner, Claus. *Música Brasileira: A History of Popular Music and the People of Brazil*, trans. Mark Weinstein. New York: Marion Boyars, 1993.

Stevenson, Robert M. *Music in Mexico, A Historical Survey*. New York: Crowell, 1952.

CREDITS

These pages constitute an extension of the copyright page. We have made every effort to trace the ownership of all copyrighted material and to secure permission from copyright holders. In the event of any question arising as to the use of any material, we will be pleased to make the necessary corrections in future printings. Thanks are due to the following authors, publishers, and agents for permission to use the material indicated.

Shankar Foundation, Photo by Vincent Limongelli **132**:
William Alves **133**: (27.5) William Alves **133**: (27.6)
© Arvind Garg/CORBIS **133**: (27.7) © Macduff Everton/
CORBIS **133**: (27.8) © E. O. Hoppé/CORBIS **134**: top,
Courtesy of Gilbert Blount **134**: bottom, Courtesy of
Gilbert Blount **145**: British Library [nhil 021 0001546,
Add.Or.28] **146**: (0:00 & O:10 bottom) William Alves
146: (0:00) William Alves **146**: (0:10, 0:22 top, 0:35)
William Alves **147**: (0:55, 2:56 bottom) William Alves
147: (2:56 top) Courtesy of Gilbert Blount **148**: (2:03,
3:17, 5:30 top) William Alves **148**: (5:30 bottom) Cour-
tesy of Gilbert Blount **150**: © Kapoor Baldev/CORBIS
Sygma **154**: (O:15) William Alves **155**: (all) Courtesy of
Gilbert Blount **156**: © Chris Lisle/CORBIS **158**: Courtesy of Terry Riley via Elision Fields and Tom Welsh

Part 6. **163**: © Asian Art & Archaeology, Inc./CORBIS
170: top, Courtesy Minnesota Chinese Music Ensemble
170: bottom, Courtesy Minnesota Chinese Music Ensemble **170**: top center, Courtesy of Danlee Mitchell **170**:
bottom center, Courtesy of Danlee Mitchell **171**: top,
Courtesy Minnesota Chinese Music Ensemble **171**: bottom center, Courtesy Minnesota Chinese Music Ensemble **171**: top center, Courtesy of Gilbert Blount **171**: bottom, © Michael S. Yamashita/CORBIS **172**: top,
Courtesy of Danlee Mitchell **172**: bottom, © Asian Art &
Archaeology, Inc./CORBIS **174**: Courtesy of Minnesota
Chinese Music Ensemble **176**: top, Courtesy of Min-
nesota Chinese Music Ensemble **178**: © Roger-Viollet/
Topham/The Image Works **182**: © Dean Conger/CORBIS
183: © Dean Conger/CORBIS **184**: (0:00 right) Courtesy
of Minnesota Chinese Music Ensemble **184**: (0:00)
Courtesy of Danlee Mitchell **184**: (0:08) Courtesy of
Minnesota Chinese Music Ensemble **185**: (2:37) Cour-
tesy of Minnesota Chinese Music Ensemble **186**: (3:25)
Courtesy of Danlee Mitchell **186**: (3:47) Courtesy of
Minnesota Chinese Music Ensemble

Part 7. **191**: Courtesy of Bill Shozan Schultz
195: © Michael S. Yamashita/CORBIS **197**: top center,
Courtesy of Bill Shozan Schultz **197**: bottom center,
Courtesy of Gilbert Blount **197**: bottom, Courtesy of
Gilbert Blount **197**: top, © Kenneth Hamm/Photo Japan
198: top, Courtesy of Gilbert Blount **198**: bottom, © Mit-
suru Kanamori / HAGA /The Image Works **200**: (0:07
bottom) Courtesy of Gilbert Blount **200**: (0:07 top; 0:09)
Courtesy of Gilbert Blount **200**: (0:12) Courtesy of
Gilbert Blount **201**: (0:16 bottom) Courtesy of Gilbert
Blount **201**: (0:16, 1:55) © Kenneth Hamm/Photo
Japan **202**: (6:35) © Kenneth Hamm/Photo Japan **203**:
(7:17,7:37,9.6) © Kenneth Hamm/Photo Japan **204**:
Courtesy of Gilbert Blount **205**: bottom, Courtesy of
Bill Shozan Schultz **205**: top, © Michael S. Yamashita
/CORBIS **206**: Courtesy of Gilbert Blount **207** Courtesy
of Bill Shozan Schultz **208**: top, Courtesy of Bill Shozan

Schultz **210**: © Toshiro Morita / HAGA /The Image
Works **212**: © Liba Taylor/CORBIS

Part 8. **219**: William Alves **220**: William Alves **222**:
William Alves **223**: William Alves **224**: top, William Alves
224: bottom center, William Alves **224**: top center,
William Alves **224**: bottom, William Alves **224**: bottom,
William Alves **225**: top, William Alves **225**: bottom,
William Alves **225**: top center, William Alves **225**: bot-
tom center, William Alves **226**: top center, Courtesy of
Danlee Mitchell **226**: top, William Alves **226**: bottom
center, William Alves **226**: bottom, William Alves **234**:
(0:00 bottom) William Alves **234**: (0:00 top) William
Alves **234**: (0:06) William Alves **234**: (0:21) William
Alves **235**: (0:28 top) William Alves **235**: (0:28,6:28)
William Alves **235**: (6:28 bottom) William Alves **236**:
(6:32 bottom, 8:15 bottom) William Alves **236**: (6:32,
8:15,9:57) William Alves **238**: William Alves **239**:
William Alves **242**: top, William Alves **242**: bottom,
William Alves **243**: top, William Alves **243**: bottom,
William Alves **244**: William Alves **246**: (0:03 bottom)
William Alves **246**: (0:03 center, 0:26, 0:47) William
Alves **246**: top, (0:03 top) William Alves **247**: (3:16)
William Alves **248**: William Alves **250**: Photo by Betty
Freeman

Part 9. **256**: © Archivo Iconografico, S.A./CORBIS
257: © Michael S. Yamashita/CORBIS **262**: left, © Barry
Lewis/CORBIS **262**: right, © Barry Lewis/CORBIS **263**:
bottom, Courtesy of Gilbert Blount **263**: top, © Barry
Lewis/CORBIS **266**: © Béla Kása **269**: top left, Courtesy
of Kovacs Laszlo and Flotas **269**: top right, © Adam
Woolfitt/CORBIS **269**: bottom, © Hideo Haga /HAGA/
The Image Works **270**: bottom, (0:00) © Adam Woolfitt/
CORBIS **270**: top, (0:00) © Hideo Haga /HAGA/ The
Image Works **272**: © Wolfgang Kaehler/CORBIS **273**:
© Dave G. Houser/CORBIS **274**: Photo courtesy of the
Ossipov National Academic Folk Orchestra of Russia

Part 10. **281**: © Stephanie Maze/CORBIS **286**:
© Lindsay Hebberd/CORBIS **287**: © Liba Taylor/COR-
BIS **288**: © Neil Beer/CORBIS **289**: top right, © Sandy
Felsenthal/CORBIS **289**: bottom, © Studio Federico
Patellani/CORBIS **291**: bottom, © Bob Daemmrich/The
Image Works **291**: top, © Kit Kittle/CORBIS **292**: left,
(all) © Studio Federico Patellani/CORBIS **294**: left, (all)
© Studio Federico Patellani/CORBIS **296**: top, © Collart,
Herve/CORBIS Sygma **296**: bottom, © Stephanie
Maze/CORBIS **297**: bottom, © Genevieve Naylor/
CORBIS **297**: top, © Ricardo Azoury/CORBIS **298**: © Je-
remy Horner/CORBIS **301**: bottom, Courtesy of Carlos
Quinche **301**: top, Courtesy of Danlee Mitchell **302**:
top left, Courtesy of Danlee Mitchell **302**: top right,
Courtesy of Gilbert Blount **302**: bottom, © Nik Wheeler/
CORBIS

INDEX

accelerando (*increase in tempo*), 20

accent (*loud or sharp attack*), 23

accordion (*portable keyboard reed instrument with bellows*), 102, 267–268, 286, 291

Achaemenid dynasty, 76

Ade, Sunny, 71, 73

adhan (*Islamic call to prayer*), 81, 82

aerophone (*wind instrument*), defined, 30, 35–38. *See also individual instruments*

Afghanistan, 81, 109, 123

Africa, 5, 6, 7, 44–74, 281; arts participation, 49, 51, 57; dance, 49, 57–58, 60–63, 71–72; family relationships in, 46–48, 59; forms 17, 57–69; geography, 44; history, 44–46; influence in Latin America, 282–284; instruments, 33–35, 39–41, 43, 47, 51–56, 58–59, 64–66; language and music, 47–48, 50, 60–62, 64; and Middle East, 45, 51, 53, 55, 57; nationalism, 46, 71; popular music, 46, 48, 70–72; structure, 60–63, 66–69; textures, 27–28; and Western music, 2–4, 65, 68, 70–72

Afrika Shrine, 70

Afro-Beat (*Nigerian popular music style*), 70

Agha al-kamani, Khi'dr, 93

agogo (*Brazilian double metal bell*), 58, 297, 299

air column (*aerophone vibrating space*), 35

aitake (*sho chord transitions*), 200

akadinda (*bow harp from Uganda*), 56

Akan (*West African ethnic group*), 73. *See also* Ashanti

alap (*non-pulsatile melodic introduction in Indian classical music*), 136, 145, 149, 151–152

alapana. *See* alap

Albania, 253, 256

Alexander of Macedon, 76

Alhambra, 96

al-jil (*Middle Eastern popular music style*), 93

alternation playing (*interlocking performance of melody*), 54, 301

alus (*Javanese virtue of refinement*), 222

America. *See* Latin America, North America, United States

American gamelan, 249–251

Andes, 278, 300–304; dance, 301, 303; European influence, 303; indigenous influence, 300–301, 303; instruments, 301–302; popular music, 303; religious music, 300–301, 303

anga (*beat grouping in South Indian meter*), 142

angle harp (*category of chordophone*), 34–35, 55

angsel (*break phrase or cue in Balinese music*), 243, 247

Anloga, Ghana, 47

antara (*Andean panpipes*). *See* siku

antara (*second half of Indian form*), 145, 147

antiphonal form (*alternation between groups*), 87, 100, 268

anupallavi (*contrasting section in South Indian vocal form*), 151, 152, 154–155

apala (*West African drum*), 71

apartheid, 46

Arabic culture, 76–78, 84–86, 87–96, 103, 104, 252, 284; and Africa 45; and Central Asia, 106; and Latin America, 284

arep (*relative density of ketuk in Javanese forms*), 229

Argentina, 280, 282–284

arghul (*Middle Eastern single reed instrument*), 86

Armenia, 76, 78, 79, 84, 85

arohana/avarohana (*ascending/descending scale in India*), 138–139, 141, 153

arpa (*Latin American harp*), 289–290, 292–294

arpeggio (*sequential sounding of chord notes*), 292

art music, defined, 5–6

Aryan language group, 124

asavri (*North Indian that scale*), 139

Ashanti (*West African ethnic group*), 40. *See also* Akan

Ashkenazi Jews, 101–102

Assyria, 76

asymmetrical meter (*meter not divisible into equal parts*), 258–259, 268–269, 271, 274

atabaque (*Afro-Brazilian drum*), 296–297

atoke (*iron idiophone from Ghana*), 58, 60

atonality (*music which has no sense of tonic*), 10

Atsia, 46, 60–63

atsimewu (*large drum from Ghana*), 59, 61–62

Austin, Texas, United States, 291

Australia, 219

Austria, 255

auto (*Latin American religious folk dramas*), 278, 287

avarta (*tala cycle in North Indian meter*), 142–144

avritti (*tala cycle in South Indian meter*), 142

axatse (*bead rattle from Ghana*), 58, 60–62

Ayinde, Sikiru (*West African popular musician*), 73

Aymara, (*Andean ethnic group/language*), 300–302

Azerbaijan, 38, 76

Aztec civilization, 278, 282, 287, 291

B

Babylon, 76

Bach, Johann Sebastian, 300

Bachianas Brasilieras (Heitor Villa Lobos), 300

Baghdad, Iraq, 78, 87

baglama (*Turkish long-neck lute*), 84

bagpipes (*reed instrument with bag air reservoir*), 261

Bahia, Brazil, 297–298

Bahrain, 89

Bai Juyi, 169

bajo sexto (*Mexican bass guitar*), 291

bala. *See* balafon

Balachander, 159

balafon (*West African xylophone*), 53, 65

balalaika (*Russian lute with triangular resonator*), 273